SPORTS STARS

SPORTS STARS
VOLUME 1

A - K

Michael A. Paré

An Imprint of Gale Research

SPORTS STARS

Michael A. Paré

Staff

Kathleen L. Witman, *U·X·L Assistant Developmental Editor*
Carol DeKane Nagel, *U·X·L Developmental Editor*
Thomas L. Romig, *U·X·L Publisher*

Keith Reed, *Permissions Associate (Pictures)*
Margaret A. Chamberlain, *Permissions Supervisor (Pictures)*

Shanna P. Heilveil, *Production Assistant*
Evi Seoud, *Assistant Production Manager*
Mary Beth Trimper, *Production Director*

Mark Howell, *Page and Cover Designer*
Cynthia Baldwin, *Art Director*

The Graphix Group, *Typesetting*

Paré, Michael A.
    Sports stars / Michael A. Paré.
        p.   cm.
    Includes bibliographical references and index.
    ISBN 0-8103-9859-1 (set : alk. paper) : $38.00 —ISBN
0-8103-9860-5 (v. 1 : alk. paper). — ISBN 0-8103-9861-3 (v. 2 : alk. paper)
    1. Athletes—Biography—Juvenile literature.   [1. Athletes.]
I. Title.
GV697.A1P32   1994
796' .092' 2—dc20   94-21835
[B]   CIP
                                                                                      AC

Cover photographs (from left to bottom right): Jim Abbott, Kristi Yamaguchi, and Shaquille O'Neal, all AP/Wide World Photos.

♾™ This book is printed on acid-free paper that meets the minimum requirements of American National Standard for Information Sciences—Permanence Paper for Printed Library Materials, ANSI Z39.48-1984.

Printed in the United States of America

10 9 8 7 6 5 4 3 2

Contents

Biographical Listings
VOLUME 1: A-K

Biographical Listings

VOLUME 2: L-Z

Athletes by Sport

BASKETBALL

BICYCLE RACING

BOXING

FIGURE SKATING

FOOTBALL

TENNIS

TRACK AND FIELD

Reader's Guide

The many outstanding athletes participating in amateur and professional sports today cannot all be profiled in one two-volume work. Those whose stories are told in *Sports Stars* meet one or more of the following criteria. The individuals are:

- Currently active in or recently retired from amateur or professional sports

- Considered top performers in their fields. Most athletes profiled in *Sports Stars* will be well known to the reader

- Role models who have overcome physical obstacles or societal constraints to reach the top of their professions.

Format

The 80 entries in *Sports Stars* are arranged alphabetically in two volumes. Each biography begins with a section titled "Growing Up," focusing on the athlete's early life and motivations, followed by a section called "Superstar," highlighting the career of each profiled athlete. Each entry also contains a "Scoreboard" box that lists the athlete's top awards and other statistics for quick reference, sidebar boxes with information of high interest to the reader, and one or more photographs. Readers can write to their favorite athlete by referring to the "Where to Write" section at the end of most entries.

Additional Features

Sports Stars includes a list of athletes by sport and a comprehensive subject index to allow easy access to people and events mentioned throughout the two volumes. Cross references are made in the entries, directing readers to other athletes in the set who are connected in some way to the person whose life is being described. Sources are provided for each entry, as well as a list for further reading by sport.

Acknowledgments

The editor would like to thank the U•X•L staff for their patient guidance in the completion of this work. Most of all, the editor would like to express his gratitude to his wife, Ellen, without whose hard work and support *Sports Stars* could never have become a reality.

Comments and Suggestions

We welcome your comments on this work as well as your suggestions for individuals to be featured in future editions of *Sports Stars*. Please write: Editor, *Sports Stars*, U•X•L, 835 Penobscot Bldg., Detroit, Michigan 48226-4094; call toll-free: 1-800-877-4253; or fax: 313-961-6348.

Photo Credits

Permission to reproduce photographs appearing in *Sports Stars* was received from the following sources:

AP/Wide World Photos: pp. 3, 11, 18, 26, 28, 32, 39, 45, 52, 61, 63, 74, 77, 80, 85, 91, 98, 105, 111, 123, 130, 135, 150, 156, 158, 164, 186, 193, 199, 201, 215, 220, 226, 228, 234, 240, 249, 258, 264, 271, 277, 280, 320, 334, 343, 355, 369, 390, 397, 407, 413, 416, 421, 429, 435, 442, 448, 449, 456, 462, 471, 477, 489, 497, 503, 505, 510, 518, 524, 529, 537, 551, 558, 564, 571, 578, 584; UPI/Bettmann: pp. 35, 117, 210, 340, 469, 490; Reuters/ Bettmann: pp. 67, 94, 143, 172, 207, 233, 256, 327, 348, 378, 384, 386, 392, 483, 509, 516, 544, 553; Reuters/Bettmann Newsphotos: p. 71; UPI/Bettmann Newsphotos: p. 177; Allsport: p. 363.

JIM ABBOTT

1967—

With his 95-mile-an-hour fastball, Jim Abbott is one of the best pitchers in the American League. In 1988 he won the championship game that captured the gold medal for the U.S. Olympic baseball team against Japan, and in 1989, without spending a day in the minor leagues, he won 12 games for the California Angels in his rookie year. In five seasons, Abbott has won 58 games, despite having only one hand. A hero to many physically challenged children and adults, Abbott has shown that it is possible to overcome problems and become a success.

"Courage is so much more than playing baseball with one hand."—Jim Abbott

GROWING UP

James Anthony Abbott was born September 19, 1967, in Flint, Michigan, with a right arm that ended half way between the elbow and wrist. His father, Mike, is a salesman, and his mother, Kathy, is a lawyer. When Abbott was five, his parents fitted him with an artificial limb that had clamping metal hooks he could use as fingers. Though he tried to adjust, Abbott found the device uncomfortable and by the age of six had stopped wearing it. To this day he does not use an artificial limb.

SCOREBOARD

WON GOLD MEDAL GAME FOR U.S. OLYMPIC BASEBALL TEAM IN 1988.

JOINED CALIFORNIA ANGELS IN 1989 AND NEVER HAD TO PITCH IN MINOR LEAGUES.

WON 18 GAMES FOR ANGELS IN 1991.

PITCHED A NO-HITTER FOR NEW YORK YANKEES IN 1993.

A ROLE-MODEL FOR MILLIONS OF PHYSICALLY CHALLENGED CHILDREN AND ADULTS.

ONE OF THE BEST PITCHERS IN THE AMERICAN LEAGUE.

THE "ABBOTT SWITCH." His parents encouraged Abbott to play sports, hoping that he would play soccer, a game in which use of the hands is not allowed. But the boy loved baseball. So his dad taught him a move that helped make him an effective fielder: While throwing the ball with his left hand, Abbott balances his glove on his right wrist, just above the point where that arm ends. On his follow-through he slips his hand into the glove and is ready to field the ball. After fielding a batted ball, he tucks the glove under his right arm, the ball rolls down his left arm to his hand, and he makes the throw.

Though it sounds hard—and slow— this move is made so quickly and smoothly that it is barely detectable. To perfect the move, Abbott spent many hours throwing a ball against a brick wall and working on the switch to catch it. "Jim has always been well adjusted, self-motivated—academically and in sports," his mother told *Sports Illustrated*. "After a while what he did we took for granted." When he was young his hero was **Nolan Ryan** (see entry), the hard-throwing future Hall of Famer who holds the major league record for strikeouts. His favorite baseball team was the Detroit Tigers and he liked to collect baseball cards.

GOOD LEFT ARM. As a kid, Abbott never felt different because he didn't have a right hand. "I just learned to play," Abbott told the *Orange County Register.* "I didn't have to overcome anything. I don't remember ever waking up and saying to myself, 'Today, I'm going to go out and play baseball with only one hand.' I just went out to play baseball. My hand is more of an issue now than it was when I was six or seven years old." He also said: "I don't think people should make so much of it. I was blessed with a good left arm and a not so good right one." Abbott says some kids teased him, but no one was ever really mean.

Abbott got his start as a pitcher in a Little League game when he was 11, after the regular pitcher got sick. He threw a no-hitter in that game. The press, who soon learned of the young one-handed hurler, was full of stories about teams testing Abbott's fielding ability, only to be stopped cold by the "Abbott switch." When Abbott was a high school freshman, the coach of an opposing team ordered his first eight hitters to try to get on base by bunting. The first one made it; then Abbott threw out the next seven.

THREE-SPORT STAR. At Flint Central High School, Abbott demonstrated his all-around athletic ability. He led the intramural basketball league in scoring. He quarterbacked the varsity football team to a 10-2 record and the state football semifinals, and averaged 37.5 yards as a punter. In one playoff game, Abbott threw for four touchdowns. And, of course, he was a star on the baseball team. In his senior year, Abbott threw four no-hitters, struck out an average of two batters per inning, and gave up fewer than two hits per game; he also batted .427, with a team-high seven home runs. In addition to pitching, he played left field, first base, and an inning at shortstop. His coach, Bob Holec, said: "He's a tremendous competitor, but not because of his handicap. Jimmy doesn't think he has a handicap."

BEATS CUBA. After he graduated from high school, the Toronto Blue Jays drafted Abbott in the 36th round and offered him a $50,000 salary to play in their minor-league farm system. Instead, Abbott decided to attend the University of Michigan. In 1987 as a sophomore at Michigan, Abbott won 11 games, lost only three, and posted a 2.08 earned run average (ERA). Following that season he was chosen to play for Team USA in the Pan-American Games. The team coach, Ron Fraser, had doubts about Abbott's ability, but soon learned there was nothing to worry about. Abbott had an 8-1 record in the tourna-

Jim Abbott

ment with a 1.70 ERA, and became the first American pitcher in 25 years to defeat the powerful Cuban national team. (After the game, Cuban leader Fidel Castro came out of the stands to congratulate Abbott.) The Americans won the silver medal.

OLYMPIC HERO. In honor of his achievements in 1987, Abbott won the Golden Spikes Award as best amateur baseball player in the country and became the first baseball player ever to win the Sullivan Award, given to the best amateur athlete in the United States. Abbott pitched the U.S. team past Canada, ensuring a spot for the Americans in the 1988 Summer Olympics in Seoul, South Korea. National pride was on the line for the U.S. team. The Americans had been defeated by Japan at the 1984 Olympics in Los Angeles, California—a shocking, almost unbelievable upset. The United States would face Japan once again for the gold medal, and Abbott would be the starting pitcher. Abbott pitched the full nine innings and made a spectacular fielding play in the bottom of the eighth to end a Japanese rally. The Americans came away with a 5-3 victory and Abbott, the hero of the day, was swarmed by his celebrating teammates.

SUPERSTAR

ANGELS'S PICK. Abbott pitched at Michigan for three seasons, earning a record of 26-8 and an ERA of 3.03. In June 1988 the California Angels drafted Abbott in the first round. Despite his success in college and in the Olympics, some people were still unconvinced that Abbott could be a major league pitcher. Entering the 1989 season, few thought Abbott would secure a position with the major league team. And if the Angels did use him in the majors, critics said, it would only be to attract fans who would want to see the one-armed pitcher. This kind of talk made Abbott angry because he did not want to be seen as a physically challenged player but as a good major league pitcher. He knew that wouldn't be easy, but he was determined to try to make it happen.

Angels's manager Doug Rader recognized very early that Abbott had a great left arm. In spring training Abbott consistently threw the ball 93 miles per hour and showed great poise under heavy media pressure. During spring training Abbott sometimes received up to 100 letters a day from physically challenged children and adults who looked to him as a hero and role model. He also received many requests for interviews because of his unique ability. Though Rader worried about rushing Abbott to the majors, he realized he had few pitchers who were more talented. When the Angels left training camp, Abbott was a member of the team, becoming one of the few major league pitchers who never played a game in the minors.

ROOKIE YEAR. In 1989 Abbott, like any rookie pitcher, had both good and bad streaks. After six starts, Abbott's record stood at 2-3 and his ERA was an unimpressive 4.50. The pressure was incredible. Not only was Abbott pitching for his team but for millions of physically challenged fans all over the country, many of whom had made special arrangements to come out and see him pitch. Abbott eventually turned his season around. He went 10-9 the rest of the way, lowered his ERA to 3.92, and pitched two shutouts. His final record was 12-12, but in his 12 losses the Angels scored only 23 runs. Abbott's performance helped the Angels stay in the pennant race and finish with a 91-71 record.

At the end of the 1989 season, Abbott came in fifth in the voting for American League Rookie of the Year. "It was a tough year," he told the *Orange County Register.* "It was a long year. But it was a great year. It was an awfully big challenge and I sincerely hope I gave it my best effort. I didn't expect to conquer the world, but I gave it my best. That's how you live with yourself over the winter."

BEST SEASONS. Abbott stayed in southern California during the off-season to work with the Angels's pitching coaches. He had a great fast ball, but needed to develop a curve ball. This was one area where having only one hand hurt Abbott,

PETE GRAY

In 1945 the St. Louis Browns signed an outfielder named Pete Gray. At the time most of the regular major league players were in the U.S. armed forces fighting World War II, so many other players who wouldn't normally have had the opportunity got a chance to play major league baseball. Gray, who batted .218 with no home runs and 13 runs batted in, would have been forgotten by now except for the fact that he had only one arm.

because he could not keep the ball in his glove and prevent batters from knowing what pitch he was going to throw. In 1990 he had an off season, going 10-14 with a 4.51 ERA, but came back strong in 1991, improving his record to 18-11 and lowering his ERA to 2.89 (fourth in the American League). Abbott finished third in the voting for the American League Cy Young Award, given annually to the league's best pitcher. Despite having a great pitching staff, the Angels finished in last place.

1992 was a frustrating season for Abbott. He finished the year with a 7-15 record, but his 2.77 ERA was fifth best in the league. The problem was that California scored fewer runs than any other team and Abbott had to almost shut out the other team in order to win. When the season ended the Angels traded Abbott to the New York Yankees for three players. Many who are traded to New York, the largest city in the United States, have problems adjusting to media pressure. Abbott was no exception, and it showed in his record for 1993—11-14 with a 4.37 ERA. On September 4, 1993, however, Abbott entered the record books when he pitched a 4-0 no-hitter against the Cleveland Indians. Though he was disappointed with his first season as a Yankee, Abbott continues to work to improve. In the future he hopes to walk fewer batters and develop a better curve ball.

OFF THE FIELD. Even though Abbott has become a successful major league baseball player with only one arm, he does not want to be thought of as physically challenged. He spends a great deal of time working with physically challenged children, reminding them that nothing is impossible with the right attitude. Abbott is active in many organizations, helping to raise money for people affected by a variety of challenges. Although he would like to spend more time helping others, his job as a major league baseball pitcher takes up most of his time.

Abbott has refused to feel sorry for himself, and, in fact, feels lucky that he's been able to make his dream come true.

"Courage is so much more than playing baseball with one hand," he told the *Sporting News*. "That's not courage. Courage is fighting a war; being a parent of a child who is very sick; being a child and being sick, facing death. That's much more courageous than earning a lot of money to play baseball."

WHERE TO WRITE

C/O NEW YORK YANKEES,

YANKEE STADIUM, BRONX, NY 10451.

ANDRE AGASSI

1970—

> *"As a person, I'm simple and low-key, but by the same token I wouldn't give up the fame I have."—Andre Agassi*

Andre Agassi is perhaps the most popular tennis player in the United States. His television ads for Nike sportswear and Cannon cameras have been very successful and fans love his style, both on and off the court. For many years Agassi was unable to win one of the most important events in tennis, the Grand Slam tournaments—the Australian Open, French Open, Wimbledon, and U.S. Open. Experts claimed that unless Agassi won one of these tournaments he didn't deserve his fame. But he silenced his critics in 1992 by winning Wimbledon—the most important tournament in the world. A born-again Christian, Agassi insists that "image" isn't everything.

GROWING UP

Andre Agassi was born April 29, 1970, in Las Vegas, Nevada, the youngest of four children. His father, Emmanuel ["Mike"] Agassi, an Iranian immigrant who represented his native country as an Olympic boxer in 1948 and 1952, was determined that one of his children should grow up to be a tennis great. The family moved to Las Vegas where the weather was excellent for year-round tennis. According to *Newsweek,* his dad hung a ball and racquet over Andre's crib and showed him basic tennis moves using a ping-pong paddle and a balloon.

LIKE ANY TOWN. Las Vegas is best known for its gambling casinos and bright lights. Agassi, even though his dad worked at a casino, feels this image of Las Vegas is false. He never felt that growing up in Las Vegas was any different than growing up in "Sioux City, or some other place in Iowa or anywhere else." As a youth, Agassi spent more time going to fast-food restaurants than to casinos. "That's all there is to it," he told *Tennis*. "It's nothing too exciting."

Agassi's skill at tennis soon attracted attention. He could serve the ball by the time he was two, when his dad built a court in the family's backyard. At a 1974 tennis tournament held in Las Vegas, there were more people watching the four-year-old Agassi than the established stars. Tennis great Jimmy Connors helped Agassi celebrate his birthday by hitting balls with him for fifteen minutes. His dream at the time was to win Wimbledon, the most famous tournament in tennis.

MOVES TO ACADEMY. When he was 13, Agassi left his regular school and went to live at the famous Nick Bollettieri [tennis] Academy in Brandenton, Florida. "My father saw this story on Nick on [the television show] *60 Minutes* where it showed him making these little kids cry and everything, and thought that was the place for me," he jokingly told the *New York Times Magazine*. At the Academy, Agassi attended classes and afterward played tennis for five hours each day. The Academy was famous for training great tennis players, including **Jim Courier** and **Monica Seles** (see entries).

Agassi was only an average player at the Academy, and the pressure of trying to live up to his father's dream made things very difficult, "I missed out on all the normal things, like proms and football games and graduation," Agassi told *Tennis*. He began to have problems with fellow students and coaches, and experimented with beer and marijuana. Instead of kicking Agassi out of the Academy, Bollettieri helped him use his energy more constructively.

TURNS PRO. Agassi had a successful amateur (unpaid) career, winning five United States Tennis Association (USTA) national junior titles. After signing a contract with Nike, he decided to turn professional at the age of 16 and, after a long slump, thought about quitting tennis. But after talking it over with the minister who had accompanied the tour, Agassi decided to stick it out. His faith in God provided him with, "peace of mind and the understanding that it's not a big deal if you get beat," he told *Sports Illustrated.*

BIG YEAR. Agassi won his first tournament in 1987 and moved up in the rankings from number 41 to 24. He had a great year in 1988, winning six tournaments (four in a row), earning a 63-11 record, and reaching the highest ranking of his career—number three. He reached the semifinals of both the French Open and the U.S. Open, had a 23-match winning streak, and won three matches for the United States against Argentina in the international Davis Cup tournament. He passed the $1 million mark in career prize money in 1988, making him the second-youngest player to accomplish this feat at 18 years, 8 months (German player Boris Becker was the youngest). He was named the Association of Tennis Professionals' "Most Improved Player of the Year."

FAN FAVORITE. In addition to his success on the court, Agassi drew attention with his flashy clothes, his long hair, and the way he played the game. "To see [Agassi] is to think of MTV," said *Sports Illustrated.* "The kid ... has a teenage hipster's style and swagger. He has a killer smile. He looks like he might arrive for matches by skateboard. He has big brown eyes that drive the girls wild." Tennis players are often known to be low-key, but not Agassi. He was a fan favorite, blowing kisses to the crowd after good shots, or throwing his shorts into the stands, and hitting tennis balls to the fans.

OVERRATED? When he won only one tournament in 1989 and again lost in the semifinals of the U.S. Open, many critics began to doubt Agassi's skill, calling him spoiled and overrated. Some players were jealous of the money Agassi made as spokesperson for Nike and Donnay tennis raquets, especially since he hadn't won any big tournaments. Agassi also created a controversy by refusing to participate at Wimbledon from 1988 to 1990 because he didn't like playing on grass and because tournament officials would not let him wear his brightly colored clothes. (At Wimbledon, players are allowed to wear only white clothes.)

"All the attention and the controversy I inspired threw me for a loop," Agassi told *Tennis.* "For the whole year of 1989, I got away from being who I was because I became too concerned with what others were thinking of me. I second-guessed myself so much that after a while I didn't really know who I was, and I've got to be honest about this: I wouldn't wish that feeling on my worst enemy."

Andre Agassi

In 1990 Agassi won four tournaments and lost in the French Open finals to Andres Gomez, 6-3, 2-6, 6-4, 6-4, the first time he had ever been in the finals of one of the Grand Slam tournaments. He followed this success by reaching the finals of the 1990 U.S. Open. Unfortunately his opponent was **Pete Sampras** (see entry), who was on an incredible hot streak. Using a serve that often traveled faster than 100-miles-an-hour, Sampras defeated Agassi 6-4, 6-3, 6-2. Agassi ended the year on an up note, helping the United States team defeat Australia and win the world tennis championship in the Davis Cup tournament. He finished the year by winning the first-ever Association of Tennis Professionals World Tour Championship, a tournament made up of the best players in the world.

"CHOKING?" In 1991 Agassi won only two tournaments and was again runner-up at the French Open, this time to his for-

IMAGE ISN'T EVERYTHING

Agassi became famous in Cannon camera adds for his line, "Image is everything," meaning that how a person looked or acted was more important than what the person was really like. He was criticized for supporting this idea, but says he doesn't really believe what he says in the ads. "I'm amazed at how the 'image is everything' label got pinned on me," Agassi told *Tennis*. "To me, it wasn't ever anything to think about. It was a commercial, somebody's storyboard. I played a part that a company paid me to play. If you believe what somebody says in a commercial, then you'd walk out of every movie you ever saw thinking it was a true story."

mer Academy roommate Courier, 3-6, 6-4, 2-6, 6-1, 6-4. The loss was especially tough on Agassi because he only had to win one of the last two sets for the title. Many accused Agassi of "choking" in big matches and not playing well when the pressure was on. "I thought I had that [choking] licked when I played Jim [Courier] in '91," Agassi told *Tennis*. "And I did—for a while. I went out there to win and then when we had that rain delay [after the first set] I got scared that I was going to lose. It's as simple as that." Agassi finished 1991 ranked number 10 in the world, but in January 1992 he fell out of the top 10. Many thought his career might be over at age 22.

SUPERSTAR

BIG WIN. Because he hadn't won a Grand Slam tournament, and because he lost in three finals, it was hard for Agassi to prove his critics wrong. Entering the Wimbledon tournament in 1992, he was not considered a contender and ranked only 17th in the world. He'd played the tournament for the first time in 1991 and claimed that he couldn't play well on the grass surface at Wimbledon. Hoping to overcome this problem, Agassi worked out with the legendary John McEnroe, who had achieved great success at Wimbledon. "We hit it off well," McEnroe said. "He's young ... he's very, very smart. He asks good questions."

With a powerful forehand and his ability to return even the hardest serves, Agassi began to surprise the experts. He defeated former Wimbledon winners Becker and McEnroe and earned his way into the championship match, where he faced hard-serving Goran Ivanisevic of Croatia. In an exciting match, Agassi defeated Ivanisevic, 6-7, 6-4, 6-4, 1-6, 6-4. When he won, Agassi fell to his knees and screamed with joy.

Always nervous about losing a big match, Agassi showed great courage in winning his first Grand Slam tournament. After losing a tough first set, he refused to quit. "I've realized my dream of winning a Grand Slam tournament," Agassi said. "To do it here [at Wimbledon] is more than I could ever ask for. If my career was over tomorrow, I got a lot more than I deserved, than I could ever ask for."

NO REPEAT. In 1993 Agassi skipped the Australian Open because of bronchitis, a disease that affected his breathing. He then hurt his wrist, forcing him to miss the French Open and limiting the tournaments in which he could play. Agassi was able to return to Wimbledon in 1993, to defend his title. Out of shape and bothered by his wrist injury, Agassi said he was unable to do pushups or shoot free throws in basketball. So he surprised many experts when he won his first four matches. "I've never been one to go on a lot of practice," he told *Sports Illustrated*. "If anyone can go on no practice, it's me." Agassi won four matches before being defeated by Sampras in the quarterfinals in five tough sets.

Agassi made headlines when actress Barbra Streisand showed up at his match against Sampras. The year before, Streisand had become a big fan of Agassi during the Wimbledon tournament. "I don't have a problem talking about Barbra," he told *Sports Illustrated*. "I've discussed the topic with her. As long as everything has a good feeling, it's O.K. People want to speculate on a love affair and a romance, and they wish it to be true."

Late in 1993 Agassi's long-time coach and friend, Nick Bollettieri, announced that he was leaving Agassi, a move that surprised and hurt the tennis player. At the U.S. Open, Agassi lost in the first round to Thomas Enqvist of Sweden, and it was clear his wrist was still bothering him. He missed the 1994

THE MAN IN THE MIRROR

"Every morning when I wake up," Agassi told *Tennis,* "the first thing I do is look in the mirror and ask, 'What is it that I want to do, and what is it that I need to work on today?' I do that because every night when you close your eyes to go to sleep, there are those few seconds when all the crud in the world, all the phoniness is behind you, and then you have to be honest with yourself. You have to assume personal responsibility for your life because, in the end, nobody else can see you in a mirror. You can only see yourself."

Australian Open because of the injury and it was unclear whether surgery would be required to repair the problem.

OFF THE COURT. Agassi spends much of his free time at home in Las Vegas. A born-again Christian, he reads the Bible almost daily and feels like he is on a mission. "I am blessed with a talent and I have an obligation to the Lord to make the most of it," he once told an interviewer. Despite his Nike ads for "Rock 'n Roll" tennis, Agassi likes Michael Bolton and "oldies" music. He finished his high school education through correspondence courses soon after he turned professional.

Throughout his career Agassi has tried to ignore people's criticism. As he told *Tennis:* "Why do I have to explain it [his life]? Really, why can't I just be who I am? As a person, I'm simple and low-key, but by the same token I wouldn't give up the fame I have. I'll be the first to admit that I enjoy it."

WHERE TO WRITE

C/O U.S. TENNIS ASSOCIATION,

1212 AVENUE OF THE AMERICAS, NEW YORK, NY 10036.

TROY AIKMAN

1966—

To be a professional quarterback it helps to be able to move, especially when big defensive players want to tackle you. Moving is one thing at which Troy Aikman is an expert. When he was 12, his family moved from California to Oklahoma, and after two seasons at the University of Oklahoma he transferred to the University of California at Los Angeles (UCLA). Now that he has led the Dallas Cowboys to two straight Super Bowl championships and established himself as one of the best quarterbacks in the National Football League (NFL), it seems unlikely that Aikman will have to move off the field for a long time.

"You wouldn't make the throws he makes unless you had unbelievable confidence."— Cowboys offensive coach Norv Turner

GROWING UP

Troy Kenneth Aikman was born November 21, 1966, in West Covina, California. He grew up in Cerritos, California, a suburb of Los Angeles, and was the youngest of the Ken and Charlyn Aikman's three children. As a boy Aikman had problems with his feet and had to wear casts up to his knees until he was 14 months old. When he was twelve his dad, an oilfield worker, moved the family to a farm outside of Henryetta, Oklahoma, where they raised cattle, pigs, and chickens. "I hated it," Aikman told *Sports Illustrated.* "I just couldn't understand why we moved there. My friends were in California, and I was already doing well in sports there." Like most kids, however, Aikman quickly made new friends and learned to like his new home.

FIGHTING HEN. Aikman always knew he would be a star and began to practice his autograph when he was nine years old. In California, baseball was his favorite sport, and he could throw the ball 92 miles per hour. In Oklahoma, however, football was the main sport and Aikman was the quarterback for the Henryetta High Fighting Hens, a team that had rarely won. In Aikman's junior year the Hens started out 0-8, but when they won their last two games the town celebrated because they qualified for the state playoffs for the first time in 30 years. (They lost in the first round.) In his senior season the Fighting Hens went 6-4 and Aikman was named to the all-state team.

SOONER BOUND. Following his senior year, the two major Oklahoma colleges, Oklahoma State University and the University of Oklahoma, offered him scholarships to play for their schools. Aikman was leaning toward Oklahoma State (whose coach at the time was his future coach with the Cowboys, Jimmy Johnson) because the team had a history of running the ball with very little passing. Oklahoma coach Barry Switzer (who was named as the new head coach of the Dallas Cowboys in March 1994) convinced him that he would have the opportunity to throw the ball, so Aikman decided to go there.

When Aikman arrived at Oklahoma in 1984 however, he found that Switzer didn't really plan to change his offense and, as he told *Sports Illustrated:* "He changed ... [the offense] a little bit, but the only real difference when I played was that we threw the ball 12 times a game instead of seven." Rushed into the lineup because of an injury to the Sooners's starting quarterback, Aikman started the first game against Kansas University. He wasn't very successful, going two for 14 for eight yards and throwing three interceptions, one of which was returned for a touchdown. Oklahoma was 5-0-1 at the time, but they lost the game to Kansas 28-11.

"My troubles at Oklahoma started with that game," Aikman admitted to *Sports Illustrated*. "The Kansas game shattered my confidence. It was very hard to come back my sophomore year and hear people saying I was going to be benched if I didn't have a great game." Aikman started and won the first three games of his sophomore year (1985), but broke his ankle in the Sooners's fourth game against the University of Miami. He was replaced by Jamelle Holieway, and although the Sooners lost to Miami, they won the rest of their games and the national championship.

MOVING ON. With Holieway now the starter, Aikman knew he would have to transfer if he wanted to play. "If I had stayed," Aikman told *Sports Illustrated,* "there was a good chance I'd be riding the bench my last two years and that would definitely have hurt my development as a quarterback." Coach Switzer, happy to avoid a quarterback controversy, helped Aikman find a new school, and called Terry Donahue, the coach at UCLA. "I really knew nothing about Troy Aikman ... [but] when I saw him move around, I finally started to get excited," Donahue told *Sports Illustrated*. "That's when I began to feel we had gotten something special."

BRUIN BOMBER. Although he had grown up in the Golden State, Aikman felt uncomfortable in the glamorous surroundings of southern California. "With the bright lights and the cars, it was so much different than what I was used to in Oklahoma," he told *Sports Illustrated*. His teammates treated him like a cowboy because he came from Oklahoma, chewed

Troy Aikman

tobacco, and liked country music. "They portray me as a hick just because I enjoy some of the things people in Oklahoma like," Aikman said to *Sports Illustrated*. "I think people expect me to come out wearing my boots and spurs."

After sitting out a season because of his transfer, Aikman won the starting quarterback job at UCLA in 1987. He threw for 2,527 yards and 17 touchdown passes in the 1987 season and finished the season as the second ranked passer in the country. The Bruins went 10-2 and won the Aloha Bowl. In Aikman's senior season the Bruins finished 10-2 again and won the Cotton Bowl. In his career at UCLA Aikman completed 64.8 percent of his passes for 5,298 yards and 41 touchdowns. He was named All-American and finished his career as the third-ranked passer in National Collegiate Athletic Association (NCAA) history.

TOP PICK. As the nation's top college quarterback, Aikman was a highly prized prospect in the 1989 NFL draft. Dallas had first pick in the draft, and made no secret of who they wanted. "Troy Aikman helps restore the Cowboy image," Cowboys owner Jerry Jones told *Sports Illustrated*. "He's got that winning aura [look]." Aikman signed an $11 million contract with the Cowboys, and Jones thought he was worth every penny. Aikman was happy to be going to Dallas, a city very close in distance and life-style to Oklahoma. "The environment, the atmosphere, those kinds of things mean a lot to me," Aikman told *Sport*. "I like where I come from. I wanted more of that."

FRESH START. Aikman joined the Cowboys as a new era was beginning. The team, one of the most successful of all-time, had fallen on hard times, going 3-13 the year before Aikman arrived. Arkansas businessman Jerry Jones purchased the team and fired coach Tom Landry, the only coach the team had ever had, and replaced him with his old friend and college roommate Jimmy Johnson, who had won a national collegiate championship at the University of Miami. During his first year with Dallas, Aikman was in competition for the starting quarterback position with another rookie, Steve Walsh, who had won 23 of 24 games for coach Johnson at Miami. Both Aikman and Walsh found it hard adjusting to the differences between college and professional football and spent hours studying the Cowboys's playbook.

ROOKIE BEATING. Aikman won the starting job, but for the 1989 Cowboys that wasn't a very safe position. The team finished 1-15 and Aikman took a pounding from opposing defenses, first breaking his finger and then being knocked out cold after throwing a go-ahead touchdown pass in a game against the Phoenix Cardinals. "I didn't even know that we had completed the pass," Aikman told *Sport*. "There were a lot of people scared. They thought I was either dead or paralyzed; I just didn't move for 10 minutes. When I finally came around, Coach Johnson was leaning over me, and he said, 'Nice pass.'" The play ended Aikman's season, one in which he threw only nine touchdowns, had 18 interceptions, and was 0-11 as the Cowboys's starting quarterback. "That was probably as low as I got," Aikman told *Sport*. "I knew it couldn't get worse."

It was hard for Aikman to lose his first year, as he told *Sport*: "I couldn't imagine the Dallas Cowboys ever being as bad as we've been." The Cowboys worked to improve the team, trading running back Herschel Walker, the team's only real offensive star, to the Minnesota Vikings for several players and draft picks. The trade turned out to be an excellent move. The players the Cowboys received moved right into their lineup and the team used the draft picks to acquire many outstanding players. Soon the Cowboys looked like one of the best young teams in the NFL, and Aikman was their leader. "All Troy needed was direction and a feeling for something that would work," Cowboys offensive coach Norv Turner told the *Sporting News*. "He's never had an ounce of doubt in his body about his own ability. You wouldn't make the throws he makes unless you had unbelievable confidence."

In 1990 things began to look up for Aikman and the Cowboys. Walsh was traded to the New Orleans Saints, **Emmitt Smith** (see entry) was drafted to play running back, and Aikman was now the unchallenged starter. The Cowboys were 7-7 when Aikman suffered another injury, separating his shoulder in a game against the Philadelphia Eagles. The Cowboys lost their last two games and finished 7-9, barely missing the playoffs. Nineteen ninety-one was a breakthrough year for Aikman and the Cowboys. Aikman was named to the Pro Bowl (all-star) game after completing 65.3 percent of his passes for 2754 yards. Dallas finished 11-5 and made the playoffs, but in Game 12 of the regular season Aikman injured his knee and missed four regular season games. He also missed the playoffs, a 17-13 victory over the Chicago Bears and a 38-6 loss to the Detroit Lions.

SUPERSTAR

COWBOY CRUSH. The Cowboys were not to be denied in 1992. Aikman had his best season ever, completing 64 percent of his passes for 3,445 yards and 23 touchdowns. Dallas finished the season 13-3, won the NFC East division title, and entered the playoffs on a roll. They crushed the Philadelphia Eagles, 34-10, in the first round of the playoffs and beat the San Francisco 49ers, 30-20, in the NFC Championship game. For the first time, Aikman would play in the Super Bowl.

MVP. Aikman's performance in the Super Bowl against the Buffalo Bills was one of the best of all time. Showing a steady hand under great pressure, Aikman led the Cowboys to a 52-17 thrashing of the Bills, who lost their third straight Super Bowl game. Aikman won the game's Most Valuable Player award after completing 22 of 30 passes for 273 yards and four touchdowns. (He gave the car he won to his sister.) During the playoffs Aikman threw 89 passes without an interception, breaking a record held by **Joe Montana** (see entry), and had eight touchdown passes. "A weight has been lifted off my shoulders," Aikman told the *Sporting News* after the game. "But now that I've won one, I don't want to be greedy, but I'd like to win two."

REPEAT. The Cowboys found themselves in big trouble at the start of the 1993 season, losing their first two games mainly because Emmitt Smith refused to play unless he was paid more money. Smith returned for the team's third game and the season turned around. The Cowboys finished 12-4 and once again won the NFC East division. Aikman had another solid year, completing an NFL best 69 percent of his passes for 3,100 yards. He also signed a new $50 million contract, making him one of the highest-paid players in football.

In the playoffs the Cowboys proved for the second straight year that they were the best team in the NFL. In the first round of the playoffs, against the Green Bay Packers, Aikman completed 28 of 37 passes for 302 yards and three touchdowns in a 27-17 win. Aikman was injured in the NFC Championship game against the San Francisco 49ers, but his sub, Bernie Kosar, threw a touchdown pass that sealed a 38-21 victory.

The win set up the first ever Super Bowl rematch, as Dallas once again faced the AFC champion Buffalo Bills. The game was closer than the previous year, but the final result was the same, with Dallas winning, 30-13. Aikman threw for 207 yards, but most of his day was spent handing off to Smith, who gained 132 yards and was the game's MVP.

In a move that surprised many, Cowboys owner Jerry Jones announced in March 1994 that he was replacing head coach Jimmy Johnson with former Oklahoma coach Barry Switzer, who had been Aikman's coach at Oklahoma. Most of the time, coaches are replaced when their team performs poorly; this was not the case with Johnson, who had coached the Cowboys to back-to-back Super Bowl victories. At a press conference announcing the move, Jones and Johnson—former college roommates—said that personal differences and personality conflicts between them were the reasons Johnson was leaving the team. The effect this will have on the Cowboys, who were very loyal to Johnson, remains to be seen.

OFF THE FIELD. A bachelor, Aikman lives in Dallas in a home decorated in a Western style. When relaxing, Aikman likes to listen to country music. He is the spokesperson for several products and earns a good deal of money outside of football. He remains a hero in Henryetta, where they've named a street after him (Aikman Avenue) and where he has contributed money to build a health and fitness center for the local school. He sponsors a scholarship program at his old high school as well as UCLA and has set up a foundation to raise money for children's charities in the Dallas area. For the last two years Aikman has been a finalist for the NFL Man of the Year award, honoring players for their contributions to the community. Even after winning two Super Bowls, Aikman tries to keep his success in perspective. "I understand my place in the world and where football fits," he told *Sports Illustrated.* "I'm very content with who I am and what I am. I'm not trying to be something people want me to be."

WHERE TO WRITE

C/O DALLAS COWBOYS, COWBOYS CENTER,

ONE COWBOYS PKWY, IRVING, TX 75063.

ROBERTO ALOMAR

1968—

During baseball games players and coaches will often tell the batter to "hit it where you live," which means to hit the ball out of the park all the way to their home. Roberto Alomar, the all-star second baseman of the Toronto Blue Jays, hits them where he lives all season long, because he lives in the hotel at the Toronto Skydome, the team's home field. A great hitter and an excellent fielder, Alomar has developed into an exceptional all-around player for the two-time World Series champion Blue Jays. The best player in a baseball family, Alomar has found a home in the Skydome, both on and off the field.

GROWING UP

Roberto Alomar was born in Salinas, Puerto Rico, on February 5, 1968. He was one of three children of Sandy, a major league baseball player, and Maria Alomar. Because their father was away eight months of the year playing baseball, the children were raised by their mother. Alomar's dad played in the major leagues for 15 seasons for eight different teams. "My mom always gave us confidence to do what we wanted to do," Alomar told *Sports Illustrated,* "but she never wanted me to

"I want to play. What else is there?"—Roberto Alomar

be a baseball player." Alomar's mom sent her children to Catholic school, was a strict disciplinarian, and made sure that Alomar studied hard. "I love baseball, but I know how hard it is to be good," she recalled in *Sports Illustrated,* "so I wanted him to prepare for another life."

BASEBALL BROTHERS. Both Alomar sons played baseball in Puerto Rico. Sandy, Jr., two years older than his brother, liked driving dirt bikes and studied martial arts, but didn't always want to play baseball. "Sandy didn't like baseball that much, and I always did," Roberto explained to *Sports Illustrated.* "He always wanted to be a pilot or something." "I wasn't the best guy—not in the little leagues, not in any league I played in," Sandy, Jr., told *Sport.* "I did what I was supposed to do to help us win. But I worked harder than the other guys."

Since he was a child, Roberto's dream was to be like his father—a major leaguer. "That's all I ever dreamed of—playing baseball in the big leagues like my dad," he confided to *Sport.* Alomar began playing organized baseball when he was seven years old, and was always the best player. Because of his natural talent, his coaches worried that he wouldn't work hard because the game came so easily to him.

SIGNS WITH PADRES. Baseball scouts were already interested in Alomar by the time he was 15 years old. He could have signed for more money with the Toronto Blue Jays, but chose the San Diego Padres. Alomar claims that his brother's signing with the Padres didn't affect his decision. "I knew I had a quicker chance of making it to the big leagues with the Padres," he told *Sport.* To make it a complete family affair, the Padres hired Sandy, Sr., to coach his sons in their first minor league season at Charleston, South Carolina, in the South Atlantic (Sally) League.

Sandy, Jr., struggled in his first two minor league seasons, batting only .207 and .215. Roberto, on the other hand, was an instant star. He batted .295 in his first season (1985) in Charleston, and won the California League batting title the next year with a .346 average with the Reno, Nevada, team. In 1987 the brothers were once again teammates with the Wichita, Kansas, team of the Texas League. Roberto batted .316 and stole 43 bases. Their team reached the league championship game, winning in the tenth inning on a hit by Roberto.

MAJOR LEAGUER. Alomar, now 20, felt he had played well enough during San Diego's spring training in 1988 to make the big league team and was disappointed when he was sent back to the minors. "I remember when he was sent down he was crying," Padres teammate Benito Santiago recalled in *Sports Illustrated*. "He was crying because he was mad, not because he was sad." But Alomar didn't let his disappointment get him down. "He said to himself, O.K., they sent me down when I can play in the big leagues," Santiago continued, "so I'm going to go down and bust my butt, and when I come back, they'll never send me down again." It took only nine games for the Padres to recall Alomar.

Later in the same season, Sandy, Jr., was called up to the big leagues and the two brothers played together for 47 days during two seasons. Sandy, Jr., found his path to the major leagues blocked by Santiago, the Padres's All-Star catcher. Even though the Padres knew Sandy would be a great defensive catcher, they weren't convinced that he could hit in the major leagues. Finally, in 1989, San Diego traded Sandy to the Cleveland Indians. "It's sad that it worked out that way," Roberto admitted in *Sport*, "but I guess that's the nature of the business."

Alomar had a solid rookie season with the Padres, playing 145 games, batting .266, and stealing 24 bases. On Opening Day of 1989, he was the youngest player in the National

Roberto Alomar

League and was on his way to becoming a star. He batted .295 and stole 42 bases (tied for second in the National League). A great bunter, he led the National League in sacrifices. Alomar had problems, though—he committed 28 errors, the most of any second baseman in the National League that season. "I was too aggressive then because I wanted to make every play," he confessed in *Sports Illustrated.*

ALL-STAR FAMILY. Alomar batted .287 in 1990, hit six home runs, and had 60 RBIs. The Alomar family was thrilled when both sons were named to the All-Star game. Sandy was the starting catcher for the American League and Roberto was a reserve at second base for the National League. "It was an indescribable moment," Sandy, Sr., who was an All-Star only once in his 15-season career, told *Sport.* Roberto did not let success go to his head. "I'm not going to be somebody else just because I made the All-Star team," he told *Sport.* "I don't think my dad taught me that way."

Because Alomar spent so little time in the minor leagues, he often made mental mistakes that cost his team victories. "You try to concentrate on every pitch, but sometimes you get mad and your mind goes away," he admitted in *Sport.* "That's why you have to work on it [concentrating]. Baseball is like going to school. You have to work on it. You have to be real intelligent in this game. I think I'm intelligent, but I know I have a lot to learn." San Diego benched Alomar, hoping he would use the time to think about his mistakes.

BECOMES BLUE JAY. Sandy, Jr., won the American League Rookie of the Year Award in 1990 and was happy he had been traded. "Look at everything I would have missed," he told *Sport.* "The All-Star Game. A chance to be Rookie of the Year." Not all was happy for the Alomar family, though. Sandy, Sr., was released as a coach by the Padres and Roberto was traded, along with outfielder Joe Carter, to the Toronto Blue Jays for first baseman Fred McGriff and shortstop Tony Fernandez.

Alomar discovered that he liked playing in Toronto. He batted .295, drove in 69 runs, and stole 53 bases (second in the American League) in 1991. "He puts pressure on teams in so many ways," Toronto batting coach Larry Hisle told *Sports Illustrated*. On May 10 in a game against the Chicago White Sox, Alomar, a switch-hitter, became the 55th player in major league history to hit home runs from both sides of the plate in the same game.

Alomar improved in the field, winning his first Gold Glove award for fielding excellence at second base, an award he would also win the next two years. In July, Alomar became only the second Blue Jay ever to be voted to start in the All-Star Game. (Outfielder George Bell was the other.) More importantly for Alomar, the Blue Jays were a good team, winning the American League East division title. They faced the Minnesota Twins in the American League Championship Series, and Alomar led both teams in hitting with a .474 average. Despite his great series, the Blue Jays lost to the Twins in five games.

SUPERSTAR

MVP. In 1992 the Blue Jays, a team that had never before reached the World Series, put it all together. Leading the way was Alomar, who for the first time batted over .300 in the major leagues (.310). He also scored 105 runs (third in the American League), drove in 76 more, and stole 49 bases (fifth in the American League). "You can count on him because he wants to be out there," teammate Dave Winfield explained in *Sports Illustrated*. "Some guys don't really enjoy it. They're good at it, but they don't need it. He does." His manager, Cito Gaston, told the same magazine that it would be difficult for Alomar to be a better player. "Let's face it, you can only get so good. How much better would you want him to be?"

OH, CANADA! The 1992 Blue Jays repeated as East division champions in and faced the West division champion Oakland A's in the American League Championship Series. Alomar was a standout, batting .423 with two home runs, and this time

Roberto Alomar goes airborne to turn a double play.

his team won, beating Oakland in six games. Alomar won the series' Most Valuable Player award. The Blue Jays went on to defeat the Atlanta Braves in an extremely close World Series, becoming the first team from outside the United States to win baseball's championship. "This is a great club," Alomar exclaimed to *Sports Illustrated.* "We won like champions."

BEST SEASON. In 1993 Alomar played even better. He set career highs in batting average (.326, third in the American League), hits (192, fourth in the American League), home runs (17), runs scored (109), RBIs (93), and stolen bases (55, second in the American League). He was voted to the All-Star Game for the fourth straight year and hit a home run in the game. For the third consecutive year the Blue Jays won their division and then defeated the Chicago White Sox in six games in the American League Championship Series.

Toronto faced the National League champion Philadelphia Phillies in the World Series, trying to become the first repeat World Series winners since the 1977 and 1978 New York Yankees. In a wild World Series, during which many records for offense were broken, the Blue Jays won when outfielder Joe Carter hit a home run in the bottom of the ninth inning of Game Six. Alomar starred with his bat, hitting .480 for the series, and with his glove, making several outstanding plays, including a diving catch in short right field in Game One that is considered one of the best of all time.

DOME SWEET HOME. Since joining the Blue Jays, Alomar has lived in the Skydome Hotel, a part of the home field Toronto Skydome. "You have to go through all kinds of stuff to get furniture and cable," Alomar told *Sports Illustrated,* explaining why he hasn't gotten a place of his own. "All I really need is a bed, and that's about it. I have cable in the room, I have a fridge. If I need laundry done, I call the laundry, and if I need food, I call room service."

GOLDEN GLOVE

Alomar makes more errors than other second basemen because he reaches balls other players would never touch. "He'll go out in right field and throw you out at first," teammate Joe Carter told *Sports Illustrated.* "Nobody has better range." Cincinnati Reds coach Jackie Moore told *Sport,* "[Alomar's] so good it's frightening. People just don't play that kind of defense." Alomar has made the diving catch his trademark, often throwing baserunners out from a kneeling position. "I anticipate the play more now. People say to me, 'Roberto, you make tough plays look so easy,' but that is the only way I can do it."

OFF THE FIELD. During the off-season, Alomar returns to Puerto Rico. His brother, Sandy, Jr., still plays with the Cleveland Indians, but his career has been slowed down by injuries. When asked what he wanted to do in the future, Alomar had a simple answer. "I want to play," he told *Sport.* "What else is there?"

WHERE TO WRITE

C/O TORONTO BLUE JAYS, 300 BREMNER BLVD.,
SUITE 3200, TORONTO, ONTARIO, CANADA M5V 3B3.

ARTHUR ASHE

1943-1993

"He was doing things, making his point and taking care of business right up until the end, and I guess that sums up everything that he stood for."—tennis champion Jimmy Connors

Arthur Ashe was one of the world's greatest tennis players and made history in 1968 by becoming the first African American male to win the U.S. Open, one of the four major tennis tournaments (the three other tournaments are the Australian Open, French Open, and Wimbledon). He was the first African American male to be the top-ranked men's player in the United States in 1975, a year in which Ashe also became the first black player to win the singles championship at the famous Wimbledon tournament in London, England.

The thin but powerful Ashe was famous for his 115-mile-per-hour serve as well as his gracious and dignified behavior on the tennis court. A true gentleman-athlete, he turned his attention to social issues when he was forced to retire from the game due to heart surgery. He instructed young players and championed the cause of black athletes. Towards the end of his life, he was a tireless advocate of AIDS awareness. Ashe was elected to the Tennis Hall of Fame in 1985 and was chosen *Sports Illustrated* Sportsman of the Year in 1992.

GROWING UP

Arthur Ashe, Jr., was born July 10, 1943, in Richmond, Virginia. His father, Arthur Ashe, Sr., was superintendent of the largest public park for blacks in Richmond during the era of segregation when there were separate facilities for blacks and whites. The Ashe family lived in the caretaker's cottage in the park, and Ashe began playing tennis at the age of seven, the year after his mother died. "Books and sports were my way of bandaging the wound [of his mother's death]," he later said. "I was too light for football and not quite fast enough for track, which left tennis."

SCOREBOARD

ONLY AFRICAN AMERICAN MALE TENNIS PLAYER TO WIN GRAND SLAM TENNIS TOURNAMENTS (U.S. OPEN, 1968, AUSTRALIAN OPEN, 1970, AND WIMBLEDON, 1975).

PIONEER IN OPENING THE SPORT OF TENNIS TO AFRICAN AMERICAN PARTICIPATION.

CHAMPION OF MINORITY RIGHTS AND AIDS AWARENESS.

SEGREGATION. Tennis was not an easy choice for Ashe, since black players rarely entered amateur or professional tennis. With his African American, Mexican, and Native American ancestry, Ashe felt like an intruder in the all-white country clubs. He was very aware of racist attitudes and was often made to feel unwelcome at the tournaments. As the only black person in a crowd of whites, Ashe was very careful of his behavior. Though this made him a very courteous player, it also had a lasting effect on his self-esteem. Later in life, he said that "growing up in the South, you get the impression that the world doesn't like you."

"Drummed into me above all, by my dad, by the whole family, was that without your good name, you would be nothing," Ashe told *Sports Illustrated*. "When some old black lady, maybe your grandmother or maybe a dignified domestic [maid] on her way home from cleaning the white people's houses, saw you or any other black boy doing something wrong, there was one expression she would use that you did not want to hear. It meant you were letting everybody down—your friends, your *history*. And that expression was, 'Boy, you should be *ashamed* of yourself.' Lord, the weight those words carried."

Ashe found encouragement from his hero, Jackie Robinson, the first African American player allowed in major league baseball. His all-black school in Richmond, where he received an excellent education, was also a source of inspiration. "Every day we got the same message drummed into us," he told the *Chicago Tribune*. "'Despite discrimination and lynch mobs [groups of whites who would hang black people for no reason],' teachers told us, 'some black folks have always managed to find a way to succeed. Okay, this may not be the best-equipped school; that just means you're going to have to be a little better prepared than white kids and ready to seize any opportunity that comes your way.'"

EARLY SUCCESS. Despite his difficulties, Ashe excelled in tennis. Ronald Charity, a part-time instructor at the playground, noticed his talent and referred him to Dr. Walter Johnson, a tennis coach and promoter who was an active leader in the development of programs for young African American tennis players. Johnson acted as Ashe's sponsor, overseeing the young player's training, and by the time Ashe was 14 he was playing at the national level. After winning three American Tennis Association (ATA) boy's singles titles, he became the first African American junior player (under 18 years of age) to receive a U.S. Lawn Tennis Association (USLTA) ranking. In 1958 he was ranked number five among all U.S. juniors.

In 1960 Ashe won his first of three consecutive ATA men's singles titles. The same year he moved to St. Louis, Missouri, for his senior year of high school. Dr. Johnson arranged for him to stay with Richard Hudlin, a coach in the St. Louis area. That fall, Ashe won his first USLTA National title, the Junior Indoors. He also became the first African American member of the U.S. Junior Davis Cup Team.

COLLEGE. After high school Ashe enrolled at the University of California, Los Angeles (UCLA) on a tennis scholarship. When Ashe arrived he was told by Coach J. D. Morgan that "UCLA has a long history of black athletic participation beginning with Dr. Ralph Bunche back in the twenties. Even though I never met you before you arrived here on campus, I had you thoroughly checked out and I was satisfied that you would have no academic problems. And your tennis record speaks for itself." During his freshman year, Ashe was intentionally snubbed by a private tennis club because of his race, but for the first time he was meeting and playing with some of the greatest players in the world.

In 1963 Ashe became the first African American player to win the USLTA National Men's Hardcourt title. He also went to Wimbledon in London, England, a trip made possible by donations from members of a local country club. During the summer of 1963, Ashe was the first African American named to the U.S. Davis Cup Team.

SOUTH AFRICA. Ashe continued to win throughout his college years, leading UCLA to the national championship in 1965. In 1966 Ashe joined the U.S. Army, performing his military service as a first lieutenant in the Reserve Officers's Training Corps (ROTC) (1967-69). In 1968 an event occurred that changed Ashe's life. The possibility existed that the U.S.

Davis Cup team would have to play South Africa, a country whose system of apartheid (or racial separation), would prevent Ashe from playing against white South African opponents. Though the United States did not play South Africa in 1968, two years later Ashe was denied permission to enter that country. The experience was a reminder of the unfair treatment he'd received at tournaments in his native Virginia and other areas of the South. In 1970 Ashe helped to get South Africa banned from the Davis Cup tournament because of its racist policies and later worked to reform the laws in that country. In 1985 he was arrested for protesting outside the South African embassy in Washington, D.C.

SUPERSTAR

OPEN VICTORY. Ashe's greatest year in tennis was in 1968. He won the U.S. Amateur tournament in an exciting five-set final and entered the U.S. Open at Forest Hills, New York. Ashe was hot, but no one expected he would win against the more experienced professional players. He surprised the experts in the final match by defeating Tom Okker, 14-12, 5-7, 6-3, 3-6, 6-3. Ashe became the first African American male to win one of the four Grand Slam tournaments, and only the second African American to win one. (Althea Gibson won the women's singles title at the U.S. Championships in 1957.) Ashe also led the U.S. Davis Cup team to victory over Australia. He finished with a 72-10 match record in 1968. In 1969 Ashe turned professional.

WIMBLEDON. Over the next ten years Ashe was in top form, winning many championships, including the 1970 Australian Open, and beating some of the best players in the world. His greatest triumph came in 1975 when he defeated heavily favored Jimmy Connors in the finals at Wimbledon. Changing speeds on his shots, he was able to outfox Connors, winning 6-1, 6-1, 5-7, 6-4. Ashe won nine of 29 tournaments in 1975 and ended the year as the number one ranked player in the United States and the number four ranked player in the world. For 12 years Ashe was in the World Top Ten, reaching his highest ranking of number two in 1975.

GENTLEMAN. Ashe was more than just a brilliant tennis player. His good manners on the court were a notable contrast to the tantrums thrown by other tennis players. Ashe's personal style set an example for all. By the late 1970s black players were finding it easier to get into sports such as tennis, and Ashe, as one of the founders of the National Junior Tennis League, was instrumental in bringing tennis instruction to publics parks and playgrounds. He was also president of the Association of Tennis Professionals (ATP), the male professional players union.

Arthur Ashe at U.S. Open Tennis Championships on August 30, 1979. This was his first public appearance after his heart attack on July 30, 1979.

NEW CHALLENGES. On July 31, 1979, Ashe suffered a heart attack. The next year, following heart bypass surgery, he realized he would no longer be able to compete. He retired as an active player and became the non-playing captain of the U.S. Davis Cup team in 1980. Ashe faced the end of his playing career the way he had faced other challenges—with quiet determination and courage. He changed direction and focused on helping young black athletes through his Safe Passage Foundation, which operates tennis centers in four cities and is committed to improving the graduation rate of minority athletes. To educate young people, he researched and wrote *A Hard Road to Glory,* a three-volume history of African American athletes, published in 1988. Ashe also continued his work to improve conditions for black people in other countries.

AIDS. Though his health was failing, Ashe remained busy working as a television commentator and columnist, writing regularly on tennis for newspapers and magazines, as well as writing books. He had another heart operation in 1983 and in 1988 underwent a brain operation. Tests following his brain surgery revealed that Ashe had AIDS. He had contracted the disease through a blood transfusion during his 1983 surgery.

Ashe told only his wife Jeanne and other close family members at first. Tests showed that neither his wife, Jeanne, nor their daughter, Camera, had contracted the HIV virus responsible for AIDS. Ashe faced his illness bravely and took on additional responsibilities. In 1992 Ashe was forced to make a public announcement about his illness when certain newspapers threatened to release the information. He turned the publicity to good purpose however, educating people about AIDS. In the few months remaining, he lectured widely, organized exhibitions, and set up the Arthur Ashe Foundation for the defeat of AIDS. "He was out doing things, making his point, and taking care of business right up until the end," said former tennis champion Jimmy Connors. "I guess that sums up everything he stood for." For his life work *Sports Illustrated* named Ashe Sportsman of the Year for 1992. Ashe died February 6, 1993, from pneumonia resulting from AIDS.

OKSANA BAIUL

1977—

Everyone has problems and tragedies that they try to overcome. No one would have blamed Oksana Baiul if she had given up, saying enough is enough. In an amazing story, Baiul refused to quit, despite many heartbreaking setbacks. A virtually unknown figure skater in 1992, Baiul tightened her skates and made history in 1993 when she won the World Figure Skating Championship on her first try. She then earned the gold medal at the 1994 Winter Olympics in Lillehammer, Norway, overcoming a serious injury she'd suffered during the competition. Just 16 years old, Baiul has already had more ups and downs in her life than most people will ever have.

GROWING UP

Oksana Baiul was born November 16, 1977, in Dnepropetrovsk, Ukraine. The Russian-speaking Ukraine, formerly part of the Soviet Union, is about the size of Texas. Oksana wanted to be a ballet dancer, but she was chubby when she was young. To help her lose weight, her grandfather bought her a pair of ice skates. She turned out to be a natural figure skater, able to jump and spin easily. By the age of seven Oksana was winning local competitions.

"I like when people are watching. What's the reason for figure skating without spectators watching?"— Oksana Baiul

WON 1993 WORLD FIGURE SKATING
WOMEN'S SINGLES CHAMPIONSHIP
IN HER FIRST TRY.

WON 1994 WINTER OLYMPIC
WOMEN'S SINGLE'S GOLD MEDAL.

HAS OVERCOME INCREDIBLE
OBSTACLES TO BECOME THE BEST
WOMEN'S FIGURE SKATER
IN THE WORLD.

INCREDIBLE TRAGEDY. Baiul has had a very hard life. Her father disappeared when she was only two years old. Her grandmother, who helped raise her, died in 1987 when Baiul was eight, and her grandfather died in 1988. Her mother, Marina, was a French teacher who died in 1991 of cancer when Baiul was just 13. It is still very painful for her to talk about her mother because the two were very close. Skating helped her accept the loss. "It helps me forget," she told *People* magazine. "It helps me get over the pain." Baiul slept for a short time on a cot at the skating rink after her mother died, cooking her food on a hot-plate.

LUCK CHANGES. Baiul suffered another loss when her coach of nine years, Stanislav Koretek, left Ukraine in 1992 to work at the Toronto Skating, Curling and Cricket Club in Toronto, Ontario, Canada. "He just bought a ticket and left," Baiul recalled in *Sports Illustrated*. "He called me afterward to tell me, and I understand his position. Everyone wants to eat." Koretek's leaving was hard on Baiul because she had lived with him after her mother had died and he was the only adult left in her life. Before he left, Koretek asked Galina Zmievskaya to take over Baiul's training. "Oksana had nobody," Zmievskaya told *People*. "I felt chills when I heard [her] story. Zmievskaya coached 1992 men's figure skating Olympic gold medal winner Viktor Petrenko, also of the Ukraine. In fact, Petrenko is married to one of Zmievskaya's daughters, Marina.

Baiul went to live with Zmievskaya in Odessa, about 250 miles from her home town. She shared a room with another of Zmievskaya's daughters, Galina, and Zmievskaya's husband and mother also lived in the three-room apartment. Petrenko, who is like a brother to Baiul, paid for her skates and outfits. This arrangement worked well for Baiul. "God has taken away her family," Zmievskaya told *Sports Illustrated,* "but the skating world is now her family. It's all natural to her, all God-given talent. You tell her something, and she goes, 'Like this?'

She does it all on her own." Zmievskaya, a mother figure to Baiul, is very strict and protects her student, especially from questions about her painful past. Baiul appreciates all Zmievskaya has done for her. "[Coach] Galina is a very special person," Baiul explained to *Sports Illustrated for Kids*. "She is like my mom."

UNKNOWN. It was not at all clear that Baiul would become a star. In 1991 she finished 12th in the national figure skating championships of the Soviet Union. She improved under Zmievskaya's coaching and won the 1993 Ukrainian national figure skating championship to earn the right to compete in the European Figure Skating Championships. To everyone's surprise, Baiul finished second in the 1993 European championships held in Helsinki, Finland, even though she had competed only twice outside of her home country. "I was shocked when she got second at the Europeans," Petrenko told *People*.

Oksana Baiul

MAJOR UPSET. She came to the 1993 World Figure Skating Championships in Prague, Czechoslovakia, a virtual unknown. Since skaters usually aren't very successful in their first world championship competition, she was not expected to do well. In fact, Baiul had never competed in a world junior figure skating championship. Nancy Kerrigan, representing the United States, finished first in the short, or technical, program, but Baiul came in second. In the long, or free skating, program, Kerrigan had problems with her jumps and fell out of contention. Baiul had her chance, and made the most of it. When the final scores were counted up, Baiul won the championship, edging out Surya Bonaly of France—who had defeated her for the European title—for the championship.

"Winning was a big surprise because nobody knew me," Baiul told *Sports Illustrated for Kids*. At 15 she became the youngest woman to win the world championship since the legendary Sonja Henie of Norway won at age 14 in 1927. Baiul was also the first woman from one of the countries of the former Soviet Union to win the singles' world championship. After she won, Baiul wept. "My tears are God's kisses from my mother," she explained after her victory.

CROWD PLEASER. Baiul's success was due in part to her ability to entertain the crowd as well as the figure skating judges. "She needs an audience, even if it's just the maintenance man at the rink," Zmievskaya confided in *People*. "The emotions of an actor are her gift." Baiul skates with a dazzling smile on her face, puts a lot of energy into her performances, and waits after her name is announced before skating to center ice to begin her program. She has a reason for this delay, as she told the *Sporting News*: "I listen to my skates. When they can start, they go to the start." Not a great physical skater, although she can complete all of the difficult triple jumps, Baiul skates extremely well to her music and touches the hearts of audiences and judges with her grace and style.

COMES TO UNITED STATES. After her success in the world championships, Baiul began to train with her idol, three-time U.S. women's figure skating champion Jill Trenery. Baiul looked up to Trenery because although she wasn't a great jumper, Trenery was beautiful on the ice. "The first time she saw me, she gave me a big hug," Trenery recalled in *Sports Illustrated for Kids*. "I was awestruck by her skating." Baiul began a ten-week tour of the United States, the first time she had been in America. As Linda Lever, coach of the 1988 U.S. Olympic team, told *Sports Illustrated*, Baiul enjoyed herself. "She loves everything. She loves staying in hotels. She loves the food. She loves the fans. She loves the bus rides. And she loves to perform." When asked what the biggest difference was between the United States and Ukraine, Baiul told the *Sporting News:* "Cheaper sneakers."

SUPERSTAR

NO PRESSURE. After the tour, Baiul began training for the

Olympics and returned to school (she was in the eleventh grade). She was one of the favorites going into the 1994 Winter Olympics in Lillehammer, Norway, despite finishing second to Bonaly in the 1994 European championships. "It is not important to be always first," she told the *Sporting News* after the European competition. When asked if the pressure of the Olympics would affect her, Baiul told the same magazine: "I don't feel any pressure. I like to compete and show my programs and see how the people will react."

BAD LUCK RETURNS. The women's figure skating competition was much awaited, mainly because Kerrigan had been knocked out of the U.S. Figure Skating Championships when she was attacked by acquaintances of her U.S. teammate, Tonya Harding. Kerrigan worked her way back into shape and won the technical program as the Olympic competition began. Baiul finished second and Bonaly third. A slight stumble on one of her jumps cost Baiul the lead, but the scoring was so close that the long program would decide the competition. Unfortunately Baiul collided with another skater during practice the day before the long program, injuring her back and gashing her leg. It wasn't certain if Baiul would be able to skate in the long program.

OLYMPIC CHAMP. Both Baiul and Kerrigan skated beautifully in the long program, with only a slight stumble by Baiul separating the two skaters. In one of the closest finishes in Olympic figure skating history, Baiul won the gold medal when five of the nine judges gave her a higher score than Kerrigan on her long program. The difference between the two had less to do with skating and more to do with style. "[Baiul] gives emotion to the referees and to the public," men's bronze medalist, Philippe Candeloro of France, observed to the *Sporting News*. And 1992 Olympic men's silver medalist, Paul Wylie, told the same magazine: "Oksana ... plays on a stage. The judges are people, and they appreciate the attention she gives them. She makes them the most important part of her performance."

Baiul broke down in tears when she won. Having overcome so much in her life, and having been injured during the competition, her victory was amazing. She became the youngest Olympic figure skating champion since Henie won in 1928. Baiul's victory was saddened when Petrenko, a favorite for the men's Gold Medal, fell during his short program and finished fourth. Still bothered by her injuries, Baiul decided not to compete in the 1994 world championships. Still only 16 years old, she promises to be a champion for many years to come.

OFF THE ICE. Baiul still lives in Odessa. She loves to shop, collect teddy bears, and talk about boys. She listens to all kinds of music and likes to dance to Madonna and rap star Hammer, and her favorite movies are *The Little Mermaid, Aladdin,* and *Beauty and the Beast.* Baiul keeps a diary about her skating and keeps track of her many accomplishments. Living with two teenagers is not always easy on Zmievskaya, as she told *Sports Illustrated:* "I'm very patient with them. They dance and fall on the ground. They throw pillows. They are starting to put on makeup. They even succeeded in putting makeup on their granny. We have fun together, and when the music is too loud, we have headaches together."

Now famous, Baiul loves to sign autographs. "I don't mind the attention," she told *People.* Sometimes, though, she still feels lonely when she travels around the world. "I miss my coach and friends," she admitted to *People.* Most of all, Baiul wants to continue entertaining skating fans. "I like when people are watching," she told *Sports Illustrated.* "What's the reason for figure skating without spectators watching?"

WHERE TO WRITE

C/O NATIONAL OLYMPIC COMMITTEE OF UKRAINE, ST. ESPLANADNAJ 42, 252023 KIEV, UKRAINE

CHARLES BARKLEY

1963—

At six-feet-four-and-3/4-inches tall and 254 pounds, Charles Barkley is built more like a football lineman than a professional basketball player. His body earned him the nickname, "The Round Mound of Rebound," and his physical style has made many of his opponents wish he did play football. In his nine seasons, "Sir Charles" has established himself as one of the best rebounders in the National Basketball Association (NBA), often having to fight against players who are six to eight inches taller than himself. In 1992 Barkley was named to the U.S. Olympic "Dream Team" and following the 1992-93 season he was named the NBA's Most Valuable Player (MVP). Outspoken and controversial, Barkley has overcome many difficulties to establish himself as one of the NBA's best players.

GROWING UP

Charles Wade Barkley was born February 20, 1963, in Leeds, Alabama, which is ten miles from the capital, Montgomery. At birth he weighed just six pounds. He suffered from anemia (a blood condition that causes a person to feel weak) and required a complete blood transfusion when he was just six weeks old. His

"Everyone is looking for the easy road.... I made up my mind a long time ago to be successful at whatever I did. If you want to be successful, can't nobody stop you."—Charles Barkley

parents were very young when he was born. They divorced while Barkley was still a baby, and he was raised by his mother, stepfather, and grandmother. When Barkley was in grade school, his stepfather was killed in an automobile accident. His mother, Carcey Green, described his childhood to *Sports Illustrated:* "I was quite young when I had Charles, so he and I were almost raised together by my mother [Charles's grandmother]. His father and I were separated when Charles was very young, and then I lost my second husband in an automobile accident ... Charles was very sheltered as a child."

SETS GOALS. None of the problems Barkley faced as a child made him lower his goals. "In the tenth grade, when Barkley stood a chunky [chubby] five-feet-10-inches tall and failed even to make his high school varsity [team], he vowed to anyone who'd listen that he was bound for the NBA," said the *New York Times Magazine.* "He shot baskets by himself into the night, seven nights a week; he jumped back and forth over a four-feet high chain-link fence, for 15 minutes at a stretch." His mom told the *Philadelphia Daily News:* "Other kids were getting new cars and nice clothes, but Charles never complained. He'd say 'One of these days, mama, I'll buy you everything you want.' I'd ask him how and he'd say, 'Basketball.' Other boys signed on at the cement plant down the road, but Charles said he wasn't gonna do that kind of work. He said he was gonna make it in the NBA, nothing was gonna stop him, and he meant it."

FAT GUY. As a high school junior, Barkley was a reserve on the varsity basketball team. Then, during the summer before his senior year, he grew from five-feet-ten-inches tall to six-feet-four-inches. As a senior, Barkley starred for the Leeds High team, averaging 19.1 points and 17.9 rebounds a game and leading his team to a 26-3 record. In the state tournament semifinals, Barkley was a star, scoring 26 points. An assistant coach for

Auburn University head coach Sonny Smith was at the game, and he told Smith he had discovered "a fat guy ... who can play like the wind," according to the *Washington Post*.

Barkley went to Auburn, where he studied business management and earned the nickname "The Round Mound of Rebound." He was better known for his unusual body shape than for his basketball skill. "People concentrated on how much I weighed, not how well I played," Barkley told *People*. "I led the conference in rebounding for three years, but nobody knew it. I was just a fat guy who could play basketball well." During his career Barkley broke the school record for blocked shots (145). As a junior he averaged 14.1 points per game and 9.4 rebounds and was named Southeastern Conference Player of the Year while leading Auburn to a 20-11 season, its second-best win-loss record in 25 years. Auburn was selected to play in the National Collegiate Athletic Association (NCAA) tournament, but was upset in the first round by Richmond, 72-71, even though Barkley scored 23 points.

Charles Barkley

OLYMPIC DISAPPOINTMENT. In 1984 Barkley was invited to the U.S. Olympic basketball trials, where he was one of the final 20 players to be on the team. When the squad was cut to 16, however, Barkley was out. Coach Bobby Knight of Indiana University, known for his tough discipline, did not like Barkley's flashy style and his 360-degree spinning dunks. After his Olympic disappointment, Barkley decided to leave Auburn one year early and join the NBA.

TURNS PRO. The 1984 NBA draft was one of the best in years. Barkley was picked fifth in the draft by the Philadelphia 76ers, chosen after **Hakeem Olajuwon** and **Michael Jordan** (see entries). At the news conference announcing the pick, Philadelphia general manager Pat Williams joked about

Barkley, "He's so fat, his bath tub has stretch marks." More seriously, Williams told the *Los Angeles Times:* "We were concerned about his weight and his work habits.... We asked one question: 'Can this guy play?' The unanimous answer was yes. Fine, we'd start with that. The other stuff we could deal with later."

Barkley was happy to join the 76ers team which starred Hall-of-Fame legend Julius Erving ("Dr. J."), and Moses Malone. In his first season (1984-85) Barkley averaged 14 points and 8.6 rebounds per game, but his attitude began to get him in trouble. He fought with coach Billy Cunningham and Philadelphia fans. "I don't have to please the public to win, I just have to do my job," Barkley told the *Philadelphia Daily News.* Philadelphia won 58 games during the regular season, but lost in the Eastern Conference finals to the Boston Celtics, four games to one.

PROBLEMS. Over the next two seasons, 1985-86 and 1986-87, Barkley became a solid starter for the 76ers. He averaged 20 and 23 points per game and became one of the NBA's best rebounders, averaging 12.8 (second in the NBA) and 14.6 (first in the NBA) rebounds per game. At six-feet-four- and 3/4 inches, Barkley became the shortest player to lead the NBA in rebounding and in 1987 was named to his first All-Star team. (He has been named every year since.) The 76ers win total began to drop, however, and Barkley complained about his teammates, calling the 76ers "a bad team that has to play perfect to win." He was fined $3,000 for his remarks. His comments didn't help the team to win, and in 1987-88 Philadelphia failed to make the playoffs, even though Barkley averaged 28.3 points and 11.9 rebounds per game.

Despite his behavior, experts began to recognize that Barkley was a great player. "There will always be a lot of mouth to Charles Barkley," said Mike Lupica in *Esquire.* "But there is also a lot of talent, the kind of talent only a handful of players will ever have." The secret of Barkley's success is his unique body, which is wide enough to block out larger opponents and quick enough to run by bigger defenders. Barkley claims that his attitude comes from his competitiveness, a desire that enables him to out-battle much taller players. "If I play with emotion I'm a hotdog," Barkley told the *Sporting News*. "That's okay, because I know if I don't play with emotion, I won't play anywhere near my ability."

BUMP AND THUMP. Barkley continued to improve, determined to play his very best, both for the team and for himself. In 1988 to 1989 the 76ers returned to the playoffs, led by Barkley, who scored 25.8 points and grabbed 12.5 rebounds (second in the NBA) per game. Before the 1989-90 season, the 76ers traded for Rick Mahorn, a member of the NBA champion Detroit Pistons "Bad Boys," known for their tough (some said dirty) play. Combining with Barkley, the pair was known as "Bump and Thump," and became one of the most feared set of players in the NBA. The addition of Mahorn, who brought with him the experience of playing for a championship team and who took some rebounding pressure off of Barkley, helped the 76ers win the NBA's Atlantic division title. Barkley scored 25.2 points per game (sixth in the NBA) and grabbed 11.5 rebounds (third in the NBA), but the 76ers lost in the second round of the playoffs to Michael Jordan and the Chicago Bulls, four games to one.

Barkley missed 15 games due to injuries in the 1990-91 season, and the 76ers dropped from 53 to 44 wins. The bottom fell out completely for the 76ers during the 1991-92 season, as the team won only 35 games and missed the playoffs. Barkley's frustration came out when he spit at a fan who was insulting him and accidently hit a young girl. He apologized to the girl, but was fined a large amount of money. He was also arrested for punching a man in Milwaukee, Wisconsin. (A jury later decided that the other man started the fight.)

SUPERSTAR

"DREAM TEAM." In 1992 Barkley was given a second opportunity to represent the United States at the Olympic Games.

He was a member of the first U.S. Olympic men's basketball team to feature professional players. The so-called "Dream Team," made up of the NBA's top stars, was the premier attraction in the 1992 Summer Olympics in Barcelona, Spain. Barkley led the U.S. team in scoring, but also caused more controversy when he elbowed a thin player from Angola and was called for technical fouls for his behavior on the court. Barkley was one of the most popular and most hated players on the U.S. team. The "Dream Team" won the gold medal, but Barkley, along with Michael Jordan, threatened to skip the awards ceremony because the team's outfits were made by Reebok and both players were spokesmen for rival Nike. Barkley and Jordan eventually decided to go to the ceremony, but wore an American flag over the Reebok emblem.

MVP. When Barkley returned to Philadelphia, he began a campaign to be traded, saying he wanted to go to a team that was dedicated to winning. He got his wish when he was traded to the Phoenix Suns for guard Jeff Hornacek, center Andrew Lang, and forward Tim Perry. Nearing the end of his career, Barkley was overjoyed to go to a talented team. The results of the trade were great for both Barkley and the Suns. Barkley proved to be the player Phoenix needed to advance to the NBA championship. He helped motivate his teammates and performed like a man with something to prove, averaging 25.6 points and 12.2 rebounds per game. More importantly, Phoenix finished with 62 wins, the best record in the NBA. When the season ended, Barkley was named the NBA's Most Valuable Player, both for his individual play and his effect on the team.

The Suns won their first three playoff rounds, beating the Seattle Supersonics in the Western Conference finals, four games to three, to reach the NBA finals—the first time Barkley had ever been to the big show. The Suns faced the Chicago Bulls. The Suns were trying for their third straight NBA championship and the spotlight was on Barkley and his friend, Michael Jordan. The Bulls won the first two games in Phoenix—winning Game Two despite 42 points from Barkley. The Suns came back to win Game Three and Game Five in Chicago, but lost the series in Game Six when John Paxson hit a clutch three-point shot with only seconds left on the clock, giving the Bulls a 99-98 victory and the championship. The loss was hard for Barkley to take, as he told the Associated Press: "It's just really difficult, you just hurt."

In training camp before the 1993-94 season, Barkley injured his back, jeopardizing his career. He missed several games at the beginning of the season and the Suns struggled. Barkley's scoring average dropped to 21.6 points per game. Phoenix finished second in the Pacific division behind the Seattle Supersonics and lost in the second round of the play-offs to **Hakeem Olajuwon** and the Houston Rockets, four games to three. Barkley was considering retirement due to his recurring injury problems.

OFF THE COURT. When Michael Jordan retired, Barkley became the best known veteran NBA player. He is spokesperson for McDonald's and Nike, playing basketball with Godzilla, singing opera, and hosting his own talk show in the ads. Barkley lives in Phoenix and has a daughter, Christiana. He writes a column called "Barkley Beat" for the *Arizona Republic* newspaper and hosts his own television show. In his free time, Barkley likes to listen to music, watch television, see movies, and drive his four-wheel-drive truck. When the season is over Barkley often goes home to Leeds. "I'm happiest when I'm home with my family, eating a nice chicken dinner or playing ball with the neighborhood kids across the street," he told the *Philadelphia Daily News.*

Barkley has established himself as an all-time NBA great, in spite of his behavior. "The majority of people in the world don't do what it takes to win," he told the *New York Times Magazine.* "Everyone is looking for the easy road.... I made up my mind a long time ago to be successful at whatever I did. If you want to be successful, can't nobody stop you."

WHERE TO WRITE

C/O PHOENIX SUNS,

2910 N. CENTRAL AVE., PHOENIX, AZ 85012.

LARRY BIRD

1956—

"After God and my father, I respect Larry Bird more than anyone." — Magic Johnson.

When Larry Bird entered the National Basketball Association (NBA) he was the "Hick from French Lick," a country boy coming to live in the big city. When he left 13 seasons later, he was "Larry Legend," one of basketball's all-time greats. Together with **Earvin "Magic" Johnson** (see entry), Bird helped revive the NBA, making basketball the most popular sport in the United States. A three-time NBA Most Valuable Player (MVP) and two-time NBA finals MVP, Bird worked hard to overcome physical limitations and become a star. He did all this after dropping out of college, giving up on basketball, and working as a garbage man.

GROWING UP

Larry Joe Bird was born December 7 (Pearl Harbor day), 1956, in West Baden, Indiana, a small village just outside the slightly larger town of French Lick. Once a famous resort community with highly prized mineral springs, French Lick had fallen on hard times when Bird was a boy. His father, Joe, managed to find factory work in the town, but the family always struggled to make ends meet. His parents were divorced when Bird was still young and his mother, Georgia, supported her children by working as a cook at a restaurant and an aide in a nursing home.

BALL PLAYER. Bird and his brothers were all ball players, and as the next-to-youngest brother, Bird always competed to keep up with the older, bigger boys. This competition helped make him a better player. "Basketball wasn't really my only love," Bird told the *New Yorker.* "We played lots of baseball, softball, rubber ball—we played ball all the time. When we were growing up, before we got a real basketball hoop, we used a coffee can and tried to shoot one of those small sponge-rubber balls through it." Even though Bird played organized basketball from the age of ten, it was not his main sport until he was in high school. When he finally decided on basketball, he began to practice—hard—day and night. "I played when I was cold and my body was aching and I was so tired," he told *Sports Illustrated.* "I don't know why, I just kept playing and playing ... I guess I always wanted to make the most out of it."

GROWTH SPURT. Bird played basketball in one of the most competitive areas of the United States—the Indiana heartland. At Springs Valley High School in French Lick he played guard during his sophomore and junior years, but did not show any outstanding ability. In fact, at six-feet-three inches Bird was not considered very big, but like a lot of teenagers, he grew four inches before his senior year in high school. Bird excelled during his senior season. He averaged 30.6 points and 20 rebounds per game, and colleges around the country expressed interest in him. But Bird decided to stay close to home and attend Indiana University.

Bird lasted only twenty-four days at Indiana. Coming from such a small town, the university campus seemed huge and Bird was uncomfortable. He returned to French Lick and entered Northwood Institute. Within two months he dropped out of that college too and was married. The marriage didn't last long, and

SCOREBOARD

THREE-TIME NBA MVP (1983-84, 1984-85, AND 1985-86).

TWO-TIME NBA FINALS MVP (1984 AND 1986).

LED NBA IN FREE-THROW SHOOTING PERCENTAGE FOUR TIMES.

MEMBER OF THREE BOSTON CELTICS'S NBA CHAMPIONSHIP TEAMS (1981, 1984, AND 1986).

"LARRY LEGEND" IS CONSIDERED ONE OF THE BEST ALL-AROUND PLAYERS IN NBA HISTORY.

Larry Bird

to support himself and his daughter, Bird took a job with the City of French Lick. He drove a garbage truck and did maintenance work for local parks and roadways. He told *Sports Illustrated*. "I loved that job. It was outdoors, you were around your friends ... I felt like I was really accomplishing something.... I had the chance to make my community look better."

RETURNS TO COLLEGE. Tragedy struck the Bird family when his father committed suicide. Instead of letting the death get him down, Bird returned to college, this time at Indiana State University in nearby Terre Haute. By this time he was six-feet-nine and 220 pounds, with better coordination and quickness than other players his size. He was forced to sit out his first season at Indiana State, and without him the Sycamores went 13-12. From 1976 to 1977, his first year on the team, Bird averaged 32.6 points per game and the same Sycamore team earned a 25-3 record—their best in almost 30 years. The following summer Bird played for the U.S. team which won the gold medal at the World University Games in Sophia, Bulgaria.

SYCAMORE SUCCESS. While at Indiana State, Bird became a national collegiate star. A team player, Bird realized that the Sycamores needed him to score and he did, averaging thirty points per game in his second season (1977-78). Indiana State was invited to the National Invitational Tournament (NIT) but lost in the quarterfinals. The Boston Celtics picked Bird in the 1978 draft. But Bird, wanting to finish his degree and play one more season with the Sycamores, decided to stay in school. In his final season the Sycamores won thirty-three straight games—a collegiate record for a single season—and ranked number one at season's end.

Indiana State was invited to play in the National Collegiate Athletic Association (NCAA) tournament where Bird averaged 29.3 points per game as the Sycamores advanced to the national championship finals. There they met the Michigan State Spartans, led by **Earvin "Magic" Johnson** (see entry). In the first game of what became one of basketball's all-time great rivalries, the Spartans, holding Bird to 19 points, won 75-64. Magic won the tournament's MVP trophy, but Bird won most of the major awards given to the season's top collegiate player.

CELTIC SIGNEE. Bird had to make a decision. He could sign with the Celtics or wait to see which team would pick him in the next NBA draft. The Celtics made it an easy decision, giving him the biggest contract ever for a rookie player. Because of his enormous salary, the fans in Boston had high expectations and Bird didn't disappoint them. He led the team with 21.3 points and 10.3 rebounds (10th in the NBA) per game and was named the NBA's Rookie of the Year. The Celtics, who had won only 29 games the year before, won 61, one of the biggest single season improvements in NBA history. Boston won the NBA Atlantic division title and advanced all the way to the Eastern Conference finals, where they lost to the Philadelphia 76ers, four games to one.

NBA CHAMPS. The next season, 1980-81, the Celtics won it all. Adding center Robert Parish and forward Kevin McHale, Boston had a front court that would win three NBA championships in the 1980s. The Celtics won 62 games during regular season and beat the Houston Rockets, four games to two, in the NBA finals. The next year (1981-82) the Celtics won 63 games in regular season, but lost to the 76ers in the Eastern Conference finals. In that year's All-Star game, Bird was named the game's MVP. He was incredibly consistent for these two seasons, scoring 21.2 and 22.9 points per game and averaging 10.9 (fourth in the NBA) and 11 rebounds per contest. Bird increased his scoring average in the 1982-83 season to 23.6 and pulled down 11 rebounds per game. The Celtics's frustration continued, however, as Boston was swept in the second round of the playoffs by the Milwaukee Bucks.

SUPERSTAR

HARD WORK. Larry Bird seemed an unlikely NBA superstar. Not very tall, not very fast, and not able to jump very high, he achieved star status through incredibly hard work. Years and years of practice and study made Bird an expert on the smallest details of basketball. To become a good rebounder, he learned all he could about how the ball bounced off the backboard and rim. He used this knowledge to gain an advantage over bigger and better jumping opponents. Even as an established NBA star, Bird always hustled, diving for loose balls and playing tough defense. Though highly skilled, he always tried to improve, working through the off-season to strengthen his weaknesses. He discovered that in order to win he had to be unselfish and help his teammates play to the best of their ability. In fact, many of Bird's coaches believe that he would rather pass to a teammate than score himself.

MVP. During the 1983-84 season Bird made the Celtics a great team. He averaged 24.2 points (seventh in the NBA), 10.1 rebounds, and 6.6 assists. He also led the NBA in free-throw percentage (.888). His impressive all-around play helped center Robert Parish and forward Kevin McHale become stars. The Celtics won 62 games and the NBA's Atlantic division title. In recognition of his fantastic performance, Bird was named the NBA's MVP.

The NBA finals between Boston and the L.A. Lakers marked the first meeting in the playoffs between Bird and Magic Johnson. The series went back and forth and two games were decided in overtime. In Game Four, won 129-125 in overtime by the Celtics, Bird scored 29 points, (including the game winner over a leaping Magic), and pulled down 21 rebounds. In Game Five, despite temperatures over 100 degrees, he scored 34 points and grabbed 17 rebounds. For the series he averaged 27.4 points and 14 rebounds a game. When Boston won Game Seven (111-102), they won the NBA championship. For his playing and leadership, Bird was named the series' MVP.

MVP REPEAT. The next season (1984-85) was Bird's best season. He scored 28.7 points (second in the NBA) and pulled down 10.5 rebounds per game, and finished second in the league in three-point field goal percentage, making 43 percent of his shots from long range. The Celtics won 63 games and repeated as Atlantic division champs. For the second year in a row Bird was named the league's MVP. Boston and the Lakers met again in the NBA finals, but this time Magic came out on top, four games to two.

GREATEST TEAM. The Celtics won 67 games in the 1985-86 season, and for the third straight year Bird was named the NBA's MVP for the regular season. His scoring and rebounding averages were down (25.8 and 9.8 per game), but his contribution did not always show up in the statistics. The Celtics, one of the greatest teams of all-time, rolled through the playoffs, losing only one game before the finals where Boston faced **Hakeem Olajuwon** (see entry) and the Houston Rockets. The Celtics often played three men on Olajuwon, taking him out of the game. Bird again was a standout, winning his second NBA finals MVP award as Boston defeated Houston, four games to two.

The 1986-87 season marked the last meeting between Bird and Johnson in the NBA playoffs. In the regular season, Johnson broke Bird's streak of MVP titles. Boston again won the Atlantic division, led by Bird's 28.1 points per game. The Celtics barely survived in the playoffs, defeating both the Milwaukee Bucks and Detroit Pistons in seven games. The Lakers had a much easier time reaching the finals, but knew the Celtics were their main competition. In the finals the two teams fought each other fiercely. In the end the Lakers won, four games to two. Bird scored 24 points per game in the series, but it wasn't enough. This would be Bird's last appearance in the NBA finals.

THREE MVP

Since the award was begun in 1956, only seven players have won three or more NBA MVP awards. This list shows those players and the years they won the award.

Player	Number
Kareem Abdul-Jabbar 1971, 1972, 1974, 1976, 1977, and 1980	6
Bill Russell 1958, 1961, 1962, 1963, and 1965	5
Wilt Chamberlain 1960, 1966, 1967, and 1968	4
Moses Malone 1979, 1982, and 1983	3
Larry Bird 1984, 1985, and 1986	3
Magic Johnson 1987, 1989, and 1990	3
Michael Jordan 1988, 1991, and 1992	3

BIRD AND MAGIC

The Bird-Magic rivalry was one of the greatest in NBA history. During the decade of the 1980s these two players and their teams dominated the league. The chart below compares the careers of these two great players.

REGULAR SEASON

	Bird	Johnson
Seasons:	13	12
Games:	897	874
Scoring:	24.3	19.7
Rebounding:	10.0	7.3
Assists:	6.3	11.4

PLAYOFFS

	Bird	Johnson
Seasons:	12	12
Games:	164	186
Scoring:	23.8	19.6
Rebounding:	10.3	7.7
Assists:	6.5	12.5

	Bird	Johnson
Division Titles:	10	10
NBA Finals:	5	9
NBA Championships:	3	5

INJURIES. His last five seasons were frustrating for the Celtics's star. Injuries and age began to catch up with Bird and the entire Boston team. He scored a career-high 29.9 points per game (third in the NBA) in the 1987-88 season, but the Celtics lost to the eventual NBA champion Pistons in the Eastern Conference finals. Bird missed all but six games of the 1988-89 season after heel surgery, and the Celtics were swept by the Pistons in the first round of the playoffs. He returned to All-Star form in the 1989-90 season, scoring 24.3 points per game and leading the NBA in free-throw shooting percentage (93 percent) for the fourth time. But once again the Celtics lost in the first round of the playoffs, this time to the New York Knicks.

RETIRES. In 1990 to 1991 Bird played only 60 games and averaged under 20 points per game for the first time in his career (19.4). Boston won 56 games and the Atlantic division title, but lost in the second round of the playoffs to the Pistons. Prior to the 1991-92 season, Magic Johnson retired from basketball. Bird, after playing only 45 games during the regular season because of back problems, decided to call it quits. The two great stars played together for the first and last time as part of the 1992 U.S. Olympic basketball "Dream Team." With Bird's retirement an historic era in the NBA came to an end. During their careers in the NBA Bird and Johnson played 37 games against each other, with Johnson winning 22 times. When the two entered the league, many teams were close to going bankrupt. When they left, the NBA was the most popular sports league in the United States.

OFF THE COURT. On February 4, 1993, the Celtics held Larry Bird Night and retired his number 33. Bird now works as an executive for the Celtics organization and has been mentioned as a possible NBA head coach. In his free time Bird likes to hunt, fish, swim, and play golf and tennis. He owns a Ford dealership in Bloomington, Indiana, and still lives in French Lick. "I feel comfortable there. People want nothing from me and I want nothing from them. They treat me as just another guy and that's how, more than anything, I want to be treated.

WHERE TO WRITE

C/O BOSTON CELTICS,

151 MERRIMAC ST., BOSTON, MA 02114.

BONNIE BLAIR

1964—

Bonnie Blair, affectionately known as "Bonnie the Blur" because of her speed, is the first woman in U.S. history to win gold medals at three consecutive Olympic Games. More amazingly, in 1994 she became the first American woman to win five gold medals overall in the Olympics, Winter or Summer. Add a bronze medal to her gold and she has won more medals in the Winter Olympics than any other American. Blair is a speed skater who has been competing since she was seven years old. Shorter and less powerful than some of her Olympic rivals, Blair's near-perfect technique helped her set the world record for the 500-meter speed skating race. A true superstar, she remains humble, and happy to be able to participate in a sport that she loves.

GROWING UP

Bonnie Blair was born March 18, 1964, in Cornwall, New York. Her entire family loved to speed skate. The youngest of six children, Blair was born while her brothers and sisters were involved in a local speed skating event. On the way to the race, her father dropped her mother off at the hospital. Bonnie's birth was announced at the rink. The announcement said, "Another speed skater has been born."

By the age of two, Blair was already skating. Because her feet were still so small she had to wear skates over her street shoes. "I can't even remember learning how to skate," she told *Maclean's* magazine. "It comes almost as naturally to me as walking." Her older brothers and sisters were also speed skaters.

GROWING UP. The Blair family moved to Champaign, Illinois, in 1966, a town where skating was very popular. Blair grew up driving from town to town to watch her family members compete, and her dad, a civil engineer, worked at the meets. "We were always a happy family. There were very few times that I was angry or mad, and it's this outlook that I brought with me to sports.... If I put in the physical work and my competitor does the same kind of training, but doesn't have the strong positive mental outlook that I do, then she's going to be beaten." As soon as she was old enough, Blair began to compete, entering her first competition at the age of four. Three years later she raced in the Illinois state championships.

DISCOVERED. Blair was discovered by Cathy Priestner, a former Olympic silver medalist in speed skating from Canada. Priestner convinced Blair to give up pack style racing and work toward qualifying for the Olympics. Priestner saw that Blair had talent. "There's a certain flow you look for," Priestner told *Maclean's,* "and she had it."

BIG WIN. When she was 16 Blair entered her first Olympic-style race at a qualifying meet for the 1980 Olympic trials. She was an immediate sensation. The last competitor at the meet, she was forced to race alone when her competitor did not appear. Blair knew she would have to skate the 500-meters in

> ## SCOREBOARD
>
> FIRST AMERICAN WOMAN TO WIN GOLD MEDALS AT THREE CONSECUTIVE OLYMPICS (500-METERS IN 1988; 500- AND 1000-METERS IN 1992 AND 1994).
>
> ONLY AMERICAN WOMAN TO WIN FIVE GOLD MEDALS IN THE OLYMPICS, WINTER OR SUMMER.
>
> HAS WON MORE MEDALS IN WINTER OLYMPICS THAN ANY OTHER AMERICAN.
>
> WORLD RECORD HOLDER IN THE 500-METER SPRINT.
>
> A FIERCE COMPETITOR WHO OVERCOMES MORE PHYSICALLY GIFTED COMPETITORS WITH HARD WORK AND DETERMINATION.

Blair began by competing in pack style, or short track, races. In pack style, contestants generally run together until they reach the last lap. At that point, each skater tries to break from the pack to reach the finish line first. (Pack style is very similar to track and field running races.) In long track, or metric skating, only two skaters are allowed on the track at one time. The skater with the fastest time in the competition is the winner.

under 47 seconds to win. Coming around the last turn the clock read 42 seconds. "I went as hard as I could," she told *Maclean's,* "and when I came across the line it was 46.7." She wept with happiness when she won. "Here are all these people who had worked years to qualify," she told *Sport Illustrated,* "and I do it the first time I get on the track."

Although she qualified to participate in the Olympic trials, Blair did not make the 1980 Olympic team. At the trials she faced experienced speed skaters Beth Heiden and Sarah Doctor. Refusing to become discouraged, Blair continued to work towards the 1984 Games.

She began to train with Olympic team coach, Mike Crowe, but was soon faced with financial difficulties. It is very expensive to travel to meets in other countries, and both coaches and skating rinks charge large fees. Her parents couldn't afford the costs, but the Champaign police force began collecting money for her in 1982 and continued to do so for almost ten years. They sold t-shirts and bumper stickers that read: "Champaign Policemen's Favorite Speeder: Olympian Bonnie Blair." Beginning in 1986 Blair trained in Butte, Montana, where she worked out with the U.S. men's speed-skating team.

BRAIN OVER BRAWN. Being five-feet-five-inches tall and weighing only 125 pounds, Blair was smaller than her competitors, especially the women from East Germany, so she decided to concentrate less on power and worked to make her technique as perfect as possible. She also developed her "killer instinct," the ability to give the best possible performance she could. Blair qualified for the 1984 Winter Olympics in Sarajevo, Yugoslavia where she finished eighth in the 500-meters, a good finish for a first-time Olympian.

Her Olympic experience made Blair even more determined to win an Olympic medal. She told the *Chicago Tribune* that until 1985 she had been "lazy about training. If I had something else I wanted to do, I did it." Beginning in 1985 Blair began a training program that included long skating sessions, weight training, running, biking, and roller skating. In the 1985-86 World Cup season, an international competition made up of several meets, she placed fourth in the 500-meter, 1000-meter, and 1500-meter events. The following year she broke the world record for the 500-meters with a time of 39.43 seconds and won all but one of the races she entered for that distance. She also won the World Cup championship.

Blair was the U.S. sprint champion from 1985 to 1990. (Sprint races include the 500-, 1000-, and 1500-meter races.) Her chief competition came from other countries—Christa Rothenburger of East Germany, the 1984 Olympic 500-meter gold medalist, and Ye Qiaobo of China. Between 1985 and 1987 Blair and Rothenburger took turns breaking the record for the 500-meter race. The stage was set for an exciting 1988 Olympic encounter between the two in Calgary, Alberta, Canada.

Bonnie Blair

SUPERSTAR

OLYMPIC CHAMPION. Blair was nervous before her first race, and became more so when she watched Rothenburger earn a new world record with a time of 39.12 seconds in the 500-meters. Cheered on by her family, Blair skated the race of her life, once again breaking the world record with a time of 39.10 seconds. Her hero, former Olympic gold medal-winning speed skater Eric Heiden, told *Sports Illustrated:* "What amazed me is that when someone puts a world record up in front of you, it's easy to choke [not perform well because you're nervous], but Bonnie didn't. She showed a lot of poise under pressure." The difference between her and Rothenburger was less than the length of a skate blade. A few days later, Blair won the bronze medal in the 1000-meter sprint.

Talking about her gold medal victory, Blair told *Sports Illustrated:* "The moment I crossed the finish line was the happiest moment of my life. And hearing the national anthem played when I got my medal was probably the second happiest." When she knew she had won, Blair hugged her coaches—Crowe and Priestner—and blew kisses to numerous family members in the stands. Blair's teammates honored her by letting her carry the American flag at the closing ceremonies of the Olympics.

After the 1988 Olympics, Blair gave up speed skating for a short time to compete in cycling. Even though she finished fourth in her first national cycling championship, she soon returned to skating, saying that cycling was too slow. She won her first world sprint championship in 1989, and the following year began to work with a new coach, 1976 Olympic speed skating champion Peter Mueller.

REPEAT. Entering the 1992 Olympics in Albertville, France, Blair was heavily favored to win the 500-meter race, even though bronchitis (a respiratory disease), had slowed her down in 1991. On a track that had begun to melt, Blair defended her Olympic title in a relatively slow time of 40.33 seconds. (She dedicated the medal to her father, who had died in 1989.) With her win, she became the first American woman to win gold medals in two straight Winter Olympics. But Blair was not satisfied with her win in the 500-meters. Facing old rivals, Ye Qiaobo and Christa Rothenburger Luding, Blair was determined to win the 1,000-meter race and won the gold by only .02 of a second over Ye Qiaobo. The crowd sang "My Bonnie Lies over the Ocean," and family members in the crowd were overcome with joy.

RECORD BREAKER. Not satisfied with the Olympic medals she'd already won, Blair continued to train and entered the

1994 Winter Olympics in Lillehammer, Norway, as the favorite to win the 500- and
1000-meter races. Her family was in the
stands again, this time carrying the nickname
"da Blairs." Blair did not disappoint her fans.
She won the 500-meters and, four days later,
the 1000-meters. (She also finished fourth in
the 1500 meters.) In the 1000-meters, she
raced head-to-head with Ye Qiaobo, beating
her by one-and-a-half seconds, a long time
in speed skating. When Blair received her
gold medal for the 1000—meters, she cried
when the "Star-Spangled Banner" was
played because she realized 1994 would be
her last Olympics.

Her victories were record breakers as
she became the first American woman to
win five gold medals in the Olympics, Winter or Summer. (Diver Pat McCormick,
sprinter Evelyn Ashford, and swimmer
Janet Evans [see entry] have won four.)

Bonnie Blair just after
receiving a 1992 Olympic
gold medal.

She also tied her idol, Heiden, as the all-time U.S. leader in
gold medals in the Winter Olympics. When compared to Heiden, Blair reminded the *Sporting News* that "it only took him
one week. It took me six years." About her Olympic accomplishments, she told the same magazine: "Being able to come
away from the Olympics winning five golds and one bronze is
something I definitely would have never dreamed of."

Because the 1995 World Sprint Championships are to be
held in Milwaukee, Wisconsin, her regular training site, Blair
plans to skate at least until then. Although its a thrill to win
Olympic medals, Blair says that's not why she skates. "I don't
think winning means anything in particular," she told *People*
magazine. "It's the satisfaction you get from knowing you did
your best." Bonnie has appeared in commercials for Kellogg's
Corn Flakes and McDonald's, but fame and money are not
important to her, as she told *Sports Illustrated:* "I'm in this
[skating] because I love what I'm doing."

OFF THE ICE. When she is not skating, Blair keeps in shape by running, biking, lifting weights, and roller skating. Her hobbies include reading Danielle Steel novels, watching soap operas, and playing golf. She and her boyfriend, fellow speed skater Dave Cruikshank, plan to be married, but not until her skating career is over. When she retires from competing, Blair hopes to finish her college education and coach other speed skaters because, as she told the *Sporting News,* "It [skating] has brought me a lot of happiness, and I want to return that." She visits Champaign regularly—where she is recognized as a celebrity. Blair confessed to *Sports Illustrated* that she has succeeded as an athlete because she dearly loves her chosen sport. "Skating is joy," she said. "It's a solitary sport, one in which you can claim all the rewards as your own. Nobody makes you do it. It's just you."

WHERE TO WRITE

C/O U.S. INTERNATIONAL. SPEEDSKATING ASSOCIATION.,

2005 N. 84TH ST.,WAUWATOSA, WI 53226.

TYRONE "MUGGSY" BOGUES

1965—

All his life, Tyrone "Muggsy" Bogues has been told to come back to play when he grows up. At five-feet-three inches, he has always been the shortest player on whichever basketball team he joined. He has also been one of the best. When people make fun of his height, Bogues makes them regret it. The shortest player ever in the history of the National Basketball Association (NBA), Bogues has lifted himself to new heights as the starting point guard of the Charlotte Hornets.

"I'm happy the size I am. This is what God wanted."— Tyrone "Muggsy" Bogues

GROWING UP

Tyrone Curtis Bogues was born January 9, 1965. His mother, Elaine, wanted a daughter when she was pregnant with Bogues because she already had two sons and one daughter. "I wasn't disappointed," she told the *Complete Handbook of Pro Basketball* about her youngest child. "He was born healthy. And he had the cutest little nose and the cutest little cheeks." Bogues may get his height from his mom, who is four-feet-eleven inches. His father was five-feet-six inches and worked on the river docks.

TOUGH CHILDHOOD. Bogues grew up in the Lafayette public housing project in East Baltimore, Maryland. Life in the projects was hard. "It was right outside my door—drugs, shootings, people getting killed," he said, describing his neighborhood in the *Handbook*. When Bogues was 12, his father was sentenced to 20 years in prison for armed robbery. "I wasn't proud of what my pops did, but I guess at the time he felt that was his only means of survival," Bogues explained to *Sports Illustrated*. "He used to write me while he was in prison and give me pointers on my [basketball] game." Bogues's mother, who'd dropped out of high school in the 11th grade, learned to type, passed the high school equivalency test, and went to work to support her family.

MUGGSY. Bogues was a childhood friend of two other current NBA players, Reggie Williams of the Denver Nuggets and Hornets teammate David Wingate. Another neighborhood friend gave Bogues the nickname, Muggsy, because Bogues reminded him of a tough-guy character from the Bowery Boys movies and because he always mugged his opponent on defense. Bogues and his friends cut the bottoms out of milk crates and hung them on a fence low enough for slam dunking. Even then, his friends told Bogues to stick to wrestling, another sport at which he excelled, and give up basketball because he was too short. "I can still picture in my mind sitting in the kitchen eating cereal, telling my mom, and her saying, 'Don't believe it. No one can be an expert on your life if they don't know what's inside you,'" Bogues recalled in the *Handbook*.

ROLE MODEL. Bogues and his friends spent most of their time at the Lafayette Court Recreation Center, where they met Leon Howard. A former college basketball player, Howard became the coach and role model for Bogues and his friends. Howard remembers when Bogues was five years old and barely able to climb into a chair at a picnic. His feet weren't even close to the ground and his eyes were barely level with the table. "He was the smallest kid around," Howard told the *Handbook*. But he realized that Bogues was a natural leader. Every day Bogues would insist on holding the flag during the Pledge of Allegiance. "I remember so well him walking out with that flag in his left hand and his right hand over his heart," Howard reminisced in the same publication.

MVP. Bogues began playing organized basketball when he was eight. "You could tell he was going to be a star," Howard told the *Handbook*. "You watch the way a person walks, like a peacock, head up with a little strut. He wasn't afraid of anybody." Bogues starred for Dunbar High School, across the street from his home in Baltimore. Between 1982 and 1983, Dunbar went 59-0 and was the nation's best high school team, producing four future NBA players, Bogues, Williams, Wingate, and the late Boston Celtics star, Reggie Lewis. With teammates like that, Bogues rarely had to shoot, but was still voted the team's Most Valuable Player.

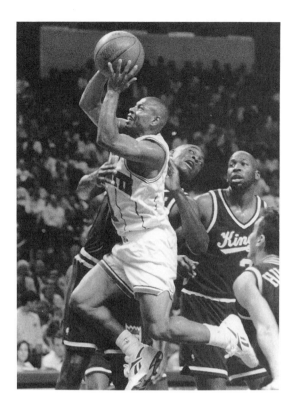

"Muggsy" Bogues

CHOOSES WAKE FOREST. Several colleges offered Bogues scholarships after he graduated from high school. He decided to attend Wake Forest University, where he majored in communications. "Muggsy's the only player I've had who's littler than my wife," his coach at Wake Forest, Bob Staak, joked in *Sports Illustrated*. Away from home for the first time, Bogues had a tough freshman year. He played only ten minutes per game, took only 46 shots all season, and had problems with his schoolwork. He almost decided to quit. "I didn't want to go home and see the disappointment on my mom's face," Bogues told the *Handbook*, explaining his decision to stick it out.

During his last three seasons, Bogues played more minutes and passed for more assists than any player in the Atlantic Coast Conference (ACC). He set ACC career records for assists (781) and steals (275) and had his jersey, number 14,

| **Tyrone "Muggsy" Bogues**

retired by Wake Forest. Despite his accomplishments, Bogues still had to put up with people making fun of his height. During one game at Duke University, the crowd began to yell "stand up" at Bogues. Once again he responded, scoring twelve points and sinking two free throws in overtime that clinched Wake Forest's 91-89 overtime upset of then number-two ranked Duke. Duke fans were more respectful the next time Bogues played there.

In 1986 Bogues was the starting point guard for the U.S. team that won the World Basketball Championships in Spain. He had 10 steals and five assists in a 87-85 U.S. victory over the Soviet Union in the championship game. The newspapers in Spain loved him, and one reporter wrote: "He appears to be a little brother of his teammates; but it is he who orders, commands, and directs." Though Wake Forest was not a very good team during his last two seasons, Bogues was a standout. As *Sports Illustrated* reported: "Critics wondered if he could make it in college ball; it turns out Bogues may have the most talent per inch in the country."

TOO SHORT? Before the NBA draft, Bogues once again heard the critics say he was too short, this time to play in the NBA. "I don't think he'd get a shot off in the pros," Mel Daniels, an assistant coach with the Indiana Pacers, told *Sports Illustrated,* "and defensively he can't stop anybody." Bogues, of course, didn't listen. "In high school," he told the same magazine, "I always heard, 'Muggs, you're too short for the ACC.' Now it's, 'Muggs, you're too short for the NBA.' But the game's not just for seven- or six-feeters. It's for people who can play. And I can play as well as anybody."

SUPERSTAR

SHORTEST EVER. His hometown team, the Washington Bullets, agreed with Bogues. They chose him as the twelfth pick in the first round of the 1987 NBA draft. The first thing Bogues did when he became a pro was buy his mom a new house. He then hired a lawyer to try to get his dad out of jail. In December 1988, his father was paroled and saw his son play basketball in person for the first time. "You always dream of having your mother and father there, watching you participate," Bogues admitted in the *Handbook*. "It was a feeling I will never let leave my memory."

Bogues became the shortest player in NBA history when he played his first game for Washington. It was hard for him to gain respect in the NBA, since many people felt Washington had made a mistake in drafting him. "When I got to the NBA, I was a curiosity," Bogues recalled in *Sports Illustrated*. "People were wondering, can he play? Or is he just a novelty act?" Bogues lasted only one season in Washington. When the new NBA teams, the Charlotte Hornets and the Miami Heat, began drafting players from other NBA rosters, Charlotte picked Bogues.

JOINS HORNETS. The Hornets's team management admitted Bogues was part of the team's publicity program to help sell tickets. His first coach in Charlotte, Dick Harter, had little confidence in Bogues. "I don't think Dick Harter disliked me; he just didn't think a five-three guy could play in the NBA," he explained to *Sports Illustrated*. Most of Bogues's problems were caused by the fact that the Hornets did not play a fast-breaking style, the one best suited to his skills. Harter wanted him traded, but the Hornets fired Harter instead.

The new coach of the Hornets, Allan Bristow, made Bogues his starting point guard and told him to do what he did best—lead a fast-breaking offense. As Bristow told *Sports Illustrated:* "If you set up a half-court offense, that's not Muggsy's game, and he's lost. But if you run it up and down the floor, it doesn't matter if he's five-three or six-three." Bogues has led his team in assists and steals every year since he's been in the NBA, averaging 8.3 assists and nearly two steals per game.

PLAYOFF BOUND. In 1993 the Hornets finally had the players to be a good team. Forward **Larry Johnson** (see entry) and

Tyrone "Muggsy" Bogues

ONE OF THE GUYS

Bogues's biggest fans are children. His wife, Kim, says that neighborhood kids often come to ask if Muggsy can come out to play. "When the kids see the other players, it's always 'Mr. Curry' [for Del Curry] and 'Mr. Mourning' [for Alonzo Mourning]," she told *Sports Illustrated,* "but I have never heard a child call him anything other than Muggsy. They feel like he's one of them." Bogues knows why kids love him. "They think I'm a little kid," he revealed in *Sports Illustrated.* "I guess I'm less intimidating [scary] than a seven-footer." On the way to the locker room following a playoff victory over the Knicks, Bogues took off his shoes, autographed them, and threw them to a teenage fan.

center Alonzo Mourning were drafted, giving Bogues good scorers to pass to. Charlotte made the playoffs for the first time since they entered the league. Bogues starred in the Hornets's playoff win against the Boston Celtics, averaging 8.8 points and 9.8 assists per game. He was even better in their second-round defeat by the New York Knicks. In Game Three against the Knicks, Bogues hit a jump shot, then stole the ball and made two free throws all in the last minute to seal a victory. Knicks guard Doc Rivers told the *Handbook* after the series: "I don't want to ever see Muggsy again. Good riddance."

HOW DOES HE DO IT? What makes Bogues so successful? He is fast, has great quickness, and never seems to get tired. "That's just how I play the game," he explained in the *Handbook.* "I'm always trying to get a steal. I'm always pressuring my opponent, trying to throw them off rhythm. That's where I generate all my energy, trying to cause my opponent problems and hope that he gets distracted. I play each possession like it's the last one of the game. It comes from not wanting to give up. I exert everything I have until exhaustion." Bogues chases opponents all over the court, lunging, swatting, and grabbing at the ball. "Nobody likes playing a guy like that," veteran guard Maurice Cheeks told *Sports Illustrated.* "He's so active, always around you like a mosquito."

Bogues also knows and understands his role with the team. "People say, 'You don't shoot, you've got to shoot more,'" he told the *Handbook.* "If I do that, it'll hurt our team and take away from what these other guys do. I get a great thrill out of passing the ball. That's the ultimate for me. I love seeing my teammates finish [score]."

In many ways, Bogues's height is an advantage. He is a foot or more shorter than the average NBA player. "His size has a lot to do with why he's as effective as he is," Hornets coach Allan Bristow told the *Handbook*. "His center of gravity is very, very low. No one can take the ball away from him. You can't see him. You can't find him. Sometimes it looks like he's two places at once." Because he is so close to the floor, Bogues often scrapes his knuckles when he dribbles. After a hard night's work, his knees have bruises, scars, and scabs.

Charlotte missed the playoffs during the 1993-94 season, due mainly to an injury to Johnson and the trading of guard Kendall Gill to the Seattle Supersonics. After six seasons, Bogues is still the shortest player in the NBA. He is four inches shorter than the two next smallest NBA players, Spud Webb of Sacramento and Greg Grant of Philadelphia. Even with his success, some people still say Bogues is too short. "If that's what they believe, then that's what they believe," he told the *Handbook*. "The only way I can change their mind is on the court." And as he told *Sports Illustrated*: "It's ability that keeps you in the NBA, nothing else. If I hadn't gained the respect of the other players, I would have come and gone by now, like a circus act."

OFF THE COURT. Bogues lives in Charlotte with his wife, Kim, and their son, Tyrone II, and two daughters, Tyisha and Brittney. He likes to play practical jokes, like hiding his teammate's clothes and stealing their hotel keys. He can dunk a volleyball, but his hands are too small to dunk a basketball. He plays golf and softball and runs basketball camps for kids during the summer. Although he knows his job would be easier if he were taller, Bogues isn't complaining. "I'm realistic," he told the *Handbook*. "I don't think about what-ifs. I'm happy the size I am. This is what God wanted."

WHERE TO WRITE

C/O CHARLOTTE HORNETS,

HIVE DR., CHARLOTTE, NC 28217.

"Muggsy" Bogues (5'3")
guarding Yugoslavian forward
Drazen Petrovic (6'10").

BRIAN BOITANO

1963—

Brian Boitano has always set high goals for himself. First, he decided to become a figure skater and practiced on roller skates until his parents agreed to ice skating lessons. Then he decided to win the biggest championship in the sport, the Olympic gold medal, and accomplished that feat at the 1988 Winter Olympics. When he turned professional, he decided he wanted to be the best and he was, winning five professional titles. Finally, he decided he wanted one more chance to skate in the Olympics. In 1994 he achieved this last goal when he took to the ice in Lillehammer, Norway.

GROWING UP

Brian Boitano was born October 22, 1963, in Mountainview, California. The youngest of four children (he has a brother and two sisters), Boitano was raised in the San Francisco suburb of Sunnyvale. His dad, Lew, was a banker who had played minor league baseball, a sport Boitano also played when he was young. The only member of his family to ice skate, Boitano fell in love with the sport when his parents took him to see the Ice Capades when he was eight years old. He tried to do the jumps and spins he had seen in the show on his roller skates, scaring both his neighbors and parents. So that he would receive proper training, his parents took him to a local ice rink for lessons.

QUICK LEARNER. His first and only teacher has been Linda Leaver who spotted Boitano's talent immediately, telling *Sports Illustrated:* "I thought he'd be great right away.... I used to keep charts on every student, with my predictions and expectations for them. Though Boitano was only eight, I went home and told my husband that one day he'd be the world champion." At eight years of age Boitano won first prize in his very first competition. By the age of 12 he had won 17 regional medals. In 1978 he won the U.S. junior men's championship and despite all the practice necessary for competition in figure skating, Boitano was an honors student at Peterson High School.

The first time he competed in the World Figure Skating Championship in 1983, Boitano became the first skater to successfully complete six different triple jumps and finished fifth in the 1984 Winter Olympics in Sarajevo, Yugoslavia. During this time Boitano was the second best male skater in the United States behind 1984 Olympic men's singles champion Scott Hamilton. When Hamilton retired in 1985, Boitano became the number one ranked male skater in the United States, winning the U.S. National title four straight years (1985-88).

WORLD CHAMP. After finishing third in 1985, Boitano won his first world title in 1986, beating Canadian skater Brian Orser, the 1984 Olympic silver medalist. But Orser, a longtime friend of Boitano, took the world title away from him the following year. When trying a quadruple toe loop (a dangerous jump in which a skater has to turn four times in the air), Boitano lost his balance and fell. This mistake alone did not

Brian Boitano

cost him the title, but Boitano lost points to Orser because he was not as artistic in his skating. (In figure skating competitions, a skater receives two scores, one for technical ability and one for the artistry and style of the program. Each part counts for 50 percent of the final score.) A great technical skater, Boitano realized that he needed to work harder on the artistic side of his skating.

KEEPS IMPROVING. In the spring of 1987 Boitano hired Sandra Bezic to help coach him in artistic skating. Bezic changed the music to which he skated and helped him tell a story through his skating, instead of just jumping. Bezic's main goal was to help Boitano use his natural ability to impress the judges. At five-feet-eleven-inches tall, Boitano was much taller than his opponents. "It takes a mature person to skate this way. He's just now learned to get into the music, to feel the emotion and skate from his heart. This was the last piece to come together," Bezic told the *Washington Post*. Boitano introduced his new style at the 1988 U.S. Figure Skating Championships and collected his fourth national men's singles title. "Boitano's short program brought the crowd to its feet and earned perfect marks for composition [artistry] from eight of the nine judges," reported *Sports Illustrated*. The win earned him the right to represent the United States in the 1988 Winter Olympics in Calgary, Alberta, Canada.

SUPERSTAR

OLYMPIC CHAMP. Boitano was not the favorite going into the Olympics. Skating before a home country audience, Orser was expected to win. Boitano had only one goal—to give the best performance of his career. "I didn't care what color medal I got," he told *Newsweek*. "I just wanted to do well." The pressure was on both skaters, and the press called the competition the "Battle of the Brians." Entering the long program, worth 50 percent of the final score, the race between the two skaters was as close as it could be. In his long program Boitano was flawless, skating as close to perfect as he could. Still, Orser could have beaten him if he had skated perfectly. Orser skated brilliantly, but stumbled on a landing to one of his jumps. The minor mistake was enough in a close competition to have five of the nine judges vote for Boitano, giving him the gold medal.

Following his victory, Boitano told the a press that he had fulfilled his personal goal. "I had been told as a child that no one ever skated their best in an Olympic performance. My dream was to change that, to prove it didn't have to be that way. I would have hated to win the gold medal with anything but my best." Boitano went on to win the 1988 world title, then decided he had achieved everything he could as an amateur (unpaid) athlete. He decided to turn professional and joined other figure skaters on a 30-city "Tour of World Figure Skating Champions."

PRO STAR. Boitano teamed up with **Katarina Witt** (see entry), the 1984 and 1988 Olympic women's singles champion, on several projects. The two champions did *Canvas of Ice,* a 1988 television special and a film titled *Carmen on Ice,* which won an Emmy award (given to the best television programs) for outstanding individual achievement in their category of classical music-dance. They eventually started their own figure skating tour, *Katarina Witt and Brian Boitano—Skating,* and performed throughout the United States.

OLYMPIC RETURN. Boitano also continued to compete and was as successful as a professional as he'd been while an amateur. Four times he entered the NutraSweet World Professional Figure Skating Championships and each time he won. In 1992 he decided he would again like to represent the United States in the Olympics and applied to the International Skating Union (ISU) for permission. The ISU said no, claiming that only amateur skaters could compete in the Olympics. Boitano con-

THE 'TANO

Brian Boitano will not only be remembered for the titles he's won, but for developing his own jump, the 'Tano—a difficult triple jump where Boitano raises his left arm over his head and holds his right hand away from his body.

tinued to fight, however, and before the 1994 Winter Olympics in Lillehammer, Norway, the ISU changed its mind and decided to let professional figure skaters back into the Olympics. Boitano was happy about the decision. "I enjoy the training and the challenge of Olympic competition," he told *Sports Illustrated for Kids*. "And I really missed it."

While preparing for the Olympics, Boitano won the 1993 Hershey's Kisses Pro-Am (professional and amateur) competition but still had to earn a place in the Olympics at the 1994 U.S. Figure Skating Championships in Detroit, Michigan. Though used to competition, Boitano admitted he was nervous. "I've never felt pressure like that," he told the *Sporting News*. "I'm proud of myself just for getting out there and standing up. It's never been like that for me." Despite a knee injury that makes it difficult for him to land after jumps, he finished second in the U.S. championships behind amateur Scott Davis, good enough to qualify for the Olympic team.

Entering the 1994 Olympics, Boitano was considered one of the favorites for a medal. At 30 years old, however, he admitted to feeling like a father-figure to his much younger competitors. Asked why he wanted to risk losing after so much success, Boitano told the *Sporting News:* "You either rest on your laurels or you go out and do something else. I'm a risk-taker. You've got to put another log on the fire sometimes." Boitano skated well during the Olympics, but a fall in the short program was too much for him to overcome. His skating was nearly flawless in the long program, but it was only good enough to move him to sixth in the final standings. Though he was disappointed at not winning a medal, he was happy to have had the opportunity to compete.

OFF THE ICE. When not skating, Boitano bike rides and works out with weights. He likes to eat at good restaurants and hopes to open his own Italian restaurant in San Francisco, California. He'll call it "Boitano's." Despite his success, he has always been modest and polite to fans and reporters. In 1988 Boitano was named Young Italian-American of the Year and won the Victor Award for special contributions to sports. He is involved in many charitable activities, donating much of his time to the Starlight Foundation, an organization that grants wishes to terminally ill children. Though his skating career may be nearing an end, Boitano continues to set new goals for himself. It's what he's done all his life.

WHERE TO WRITE

C/O U.S. FIGURE SKATING ASSOCIATION, 20 FIRST ST.,

COLORADO SPRINGS, CO 80906.

Brian Boitano skates to 1988 Olympic gold medal.

BARRY BONDS

1964—

Superstar leftfielder Barry Bonds is the only player to win the National League Most Valuable Player (MVP) award three times. He won the MVP honors in 1990 and 1992 as a member of the Pittsburgh Pirates and again in 1993 as a San Francisco Giant. His talent helped him receive a record-breaking six-year $43.75 million contract to play for the Giants. The investment paid off as Bonds led the team to 103 victories in 1993.

GROWING UP

Barry Bonds was born July 24, 1964, in Riverside, California. He is the oldest son of baseball star Bobby Bonds and the godson of superstar Willie Mays. While other boys could only watch from the stands, Bonds would chase fly balls with his dad and Mays. As he told *Sports Illustrated,* "I was too young to bat with them, but I could compete with them in the field." Bonds may have gotten his speed from his aunt, Rosie Bonds, who held the U.S. women's record for the 80-meter hurdles and was a member of the 1964 U.S. Olympic team.

The elder Bonds was an all-out competitor who encouraged his children to excel. Even before he was old enough to attend school, young Bonds could hit a whiffle ball (a hollow plastic ball with holes in the side) so hard that it could break glass. Bonds told *Sports Illustrated for Kids* that his mom and dad had to replace a lot of windows.

SCHOOL DAYS. As a student at Sierra High School in San Mateo, California, Bonds played baseball, basketball, and football. When he graduated in 1982, he was offered a contract with his father's former team, the San Francisco Giants. Bonds turned down the offer, deciding to go to college instead. At Arizona State University, Bonds played baseball for coach Jim Brock. The young outfielder's talent was obvious from the start and by his junior year he had been named to the all-league team three years in a row. He hit 23 home runs as a junior and compiled a career .347 average. In 1985 he was chosen to the *Sporting News* All-American team.

TURNS PRO. In 1985 Bonds was drafted as the sixth pick in the first round by the Pittsburgh Pirates who sent him to the minor leagues. His first season, Bonds played for the Prince William (Virginia) Pirates of the Carolina League where he batted .299, hit 13 home runs, and was named Player of the Month for July. The following season he played in Hawaii. He batted .311 in just 44 games before being called up to the big league Pirates. He was just 21 when he became a major leaguer.

JOINS PIRATES. Bonds quickly became the starting centerfielder and leadoff hitter for the Pirates. On his second day with the team he smacked a double. Less than a week later he hit his first home run. By year's end he led National League rookies in home runs, runs batted in, stolen bases, and walks.

In 1987 Bonds was switched to left field and moved to fifth in the batting order to take advantage of his multiple skills. He batted .261, hit 25 home runs, and stole 32 bases. The following year a knee injury kept his stolen base total down but did nothing to his average (.283) or home run total (24).

SCOREBOARD

THREE-TIME NATIONAL LEAGUE MOST VALUABLE PLAYER (1990, 1992, AND 1993).

FOUR-TIME WINNER OF RAWLINGS GOLD GLOVE AWARD FOR FIELDING EXCELLENCE (1990-93).

CONSIDERED BY MANY TO BE THE BEST ALL-AROUND PLAYER IN THE MAJOR LEAGUES.

SUPERSTAR

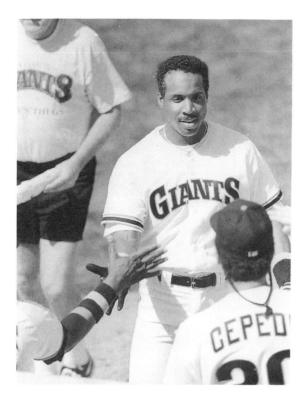

Barry Bonds

MVP. Bonds came into his own in 1990, the year he won his first National League Most Valuable Player award. He hit 32 home runs, stole 52 bases and was awarded the first of four straight Gold Glove Awards for fielding excellence. He became the only player in major league history to bat .300 (.301), hit over 30 home runs, drive in 100 runs (114), score 100 runs (104), and steal 50 bases. Bonds's outstanding season helped lead the Pirates to the National League East division championship. The Pirates lost, however, to the Cincinnati Reds, four games to two in the National League championship series.

In 1991 the Pirates once again advanced to the League championship series. Bonds hit .292, with 25 home runs and 116 runs batted in. He narrowly missed being voted League MVP again, finishing second to Terry Pendleton of the Atlanta Braves. The Pirates also lost to the Braves in the League championship series, four games to three.

FRUSTRATION. In 1992, for the third straight season, Pittsburgh won the National League East division title. Bonds led the way with a .311 batting average, 34 home runs, and 103 runs batted in. These numbers added up to Bonds's second MVP award. The Pirates's post-season downslide continued, as they lost for the second straight year to Atlanta in seven games. Adding to Bonds's frustration was the fact that in the three league championship series in which he'd participated he had batted only .191, with one home run and three RBIs.

PERSONAL PROBLEMS. While with Pittsburgh, Bonds was criticized for being difficult to get along with. He quarreled openly with teammates, managers, and especially reporters who tried to interview him. "I'm not a media person," Bonds explained to the *San Francisco Examiner.* "I don't like to answer the same questions. I just like to play baseball. I'm not into the other stuff. I turn down a lot of interviews. It's the United States of America. I have freedom of choice. It's two different jobs—keeping the media happy, and keeping yourself and your family happy. It's too much for one man."

His father defended his son to the same paper. "For them to say my son is moody is not right. How many days have they spent with my son? How many nights? They've met him for a couple of minutes, and because he might be busy that day, or they don't know his business-like attitude at the ballpark, they say, 'My god, he's got an attitude.' And that's wrong."

BECOMES A GIANT. Following the 1992 season, Bonds became a free agent (able to sign a contract to play with any team). After his problems with teammates and fans, it was clear that Bonds would not be re-signing with the Pirates. The San Francisco Giants offered him a deal that made him the highest-paid player in baseball—$43.75 million for six years. The Giants also hired Bonds's father as a hitting coach. Because his uniform number, 24, worn by the great Willie Mays, had been retired, Bonds chose his dad's old number, 25.

Critics said that no player was worth that much money. Bonds proved them wrong in 1993. He hit a home run in his first at-bat for the Giants, a sign of things to come. Joining a team that had won 72 games in 1992, Bonds helped lead them to 103 victories in 1993. The pennant race came down to the final day of the season, with both teams tied at 103 victories. Atlanta beat the expansion Colorado Rockies and the Giants lost

BACK-TO-BACK MVP TEAM

In baseball history, a player at each position has won back-to-back MVP awards. Put together, the team would look like this:

Position/ Team	Player/ Years
1B Philadelphia A's	Jimmie Foxx 1932-33
2B Cincinnati Reds	Joe Morgan 1975-76
3B Philadelphia Phillies	Mike Schmidt 1980-81
SS Chicago Cubs	Ernie Banks 1958-59
OF Pittsburgh Pirates; San Fran. Giants	Barry Bonds 1992-93
OF New York Yankees	Mickey Mantle 1956-57
OF New York Yankees	Roger Maris 1960-61
C New York Yankees	Yogi Berra 1954-55
P Detroit Tigers	Hal Newhouser 1944-45
DH Atlanta Braves	Dale Murphy 1982-83

THREE-TIME MVPs	
Player Years	**Team**
Yogi Berra 1951, 1954-55	New York Yankees
Barry Bonds 1990, 1992; 1993	Pittsburgh Pirates San Fran. Giants
Joe Dimaggio 1939, 1941, 1947	New York Yankees
Jimmie Foxx 1932-33; 1938	Philadelphia A's Boston Red Sox
Mickey Mantle 1956-57, 1962	New York Yankees

to their longtime rivals, the Los Angeles Dodgers. This combination gave the Braves their third straight Western division title.

THREE-TIME MVP. Bonds had his best season in 1993 and won his third MVP award, batting .336 with 46 home runs and 123 runs batted in. He became only the tenth player to win back-to-back MVP awards and the first to ever accomplish this feat with two different teams. The frustration of another year without a World Series appearance led Bonds to tell *Sports Illustrated,* "Just one time. Just one time." With Bonds, considered by many to be the best all-around player in baseball, in their lineup, the Giants should be contenders for years to come.

OFF THE FIELD. Bonds lives with his wife, Sun, their son, Nikolai, and daughter, Shikari. When he's not playing baseball, Bonds likes to watch basketball and hockey, enjoys playing golf, and works out five or six days a week. Barry and his dad have hit more home runs than any father and son in the major leagues (554), and they are the only father and son to both win Gold Glove awards (Barry 4, Bobby 3). Neither Bonds nor his dad ever won the World Series, and that is one award Barry hopes to add to the family trophy case.

WHERE TO WRITE

C/O SAN FRANCISCO GIANTS, CANDLESTICK PARK, SAN FRANCISCO, CA 94124.

RIDDICK BOWE

1967—

Riddick Bowe faced many obstacles on his way to becoming professional boxing's heavyweight champion of the world. He overcame a childhood of poverty and an up-and-down amateur career to reach the very top of his sport. Critics claimed Bowe lacked desire, that he would never develop the drive required to be a championship contender. He silenced his critics in November of 1992 by winning the heavyweight championship fight against Evander Holyfield, only to lose it to the same boxer a year later.

Bowe proved that a heavyweight champion could also be a good person. He is a committed family man who does not drink, believes in higher education, and invests his money wisely. "By boxing standards, Bowe has done great things," said Wallace Matthews of *Newsday.* "But what Bowe has in mind goes beyond boxing, into the realm of being a true role model, not only symbolically but backed up with real deeds."

GROWING UP

Riddick Lamont Bowe was born in 1967 in Brooklyn, New York. He grew up in a housing project known as "Gunsmoke City" because of the high crime rate. Drug dealers posted

"I knew somehow, someday I would get out of there. I lived there, I survived and I fought my way out, and they said I had no heart."—Riddick Bowe

armed lookouts on every landing of his building and murders were commonplace. A younger child in a family of 13, he was raised singlehandedly by his mother, Dorothy Bowe. Several of his brothers and sisters fell victim to drugs and crime and some have spent time in prison.

ESCAPE. Once a friend named Bugsy stuck a loaded .38 caliber gun in Bowe's hands and told him it was the best way to take care of a neighborhood enemy. Bowe gave the gun back and walked away from a life of crime. "I always tried to be different from everyone else," he told *Newsday* correspondent Wallace Matthews. "Then I found out about boxing. That was the way I could be different from everyone else. I always went against the crowd.... I ain't never been in a jailhouse, not even to visit my brothers. I was always afraid of jail. That's probably why I always stayed out of trouble. That must be a horrible feeling when the doors clang shut behind you."

EARLY TRAINING. As he gained confidence from boxing, Bowe learned to stand up for himself without the aid of weapons. As a teenager he trained at the New Bedford-Stuyvesant Boxing Club in Brooklyn, New York. A close friend introduced him to a young woman named Judy who lived near the club and the two became friends when they discovered that they shared a distaste for the unlawful behavior so common in the neighborhood. "He was so different from the other guys," his future wife Judy told *Sports Illustrated.* "He cared about me, not what he could get from me. He said in the beginning how he felt about me, but he realized that I wasn't into relationships. He was a true friend. If I needed him, he was there. If I didn't need him, he was still there."

FAMILY MAN. After a three-year friendship, the pair began to date. They were married in 1986, just before Bowe graduated from Thomas Jefferson High School. A son, Riddick, Jr., was born shortly after. The Bowes now have one son and two daughters, and, as Bowe told *Sports Illustrated,* they helped teach him responsibility. "Having these kids gave me a reason to live," he said. "In my neighborhood people are always telling you that you are no good, that you can't do this, that you can't do that. But having these kids and knowing they need me, well, that helped me. They are the reason I get up and run in the morning."

OLYMPIAN. The challenge of marriage and fatherhood should have made Bowe take his boxing career more seriously. He was still a teenager, though, and couldn't resist fooling around when he should have been concentrating. Training for the U.S. Olympic Team in 1987, he was sent home when he wouldn't obey his coaches. During the 1988 Olympic Trials, he narrowly defeated U.S. Army boxer Robert Salters in order to qualify for the Olympic team. Despite his victory in the trials, Bowe still did not seem to be taking his boxing seriously.

Riddick Bowe

Bowe's problems continued when he went to the 1988 Olympics in Seoul, South Korea, as the U.S. super-heavyweight contender. Once again he fooled around and clowned for reporters. He was defeated by Lennox Lewis of Canada for the gold medal. This defeat hurt Bowe, especially since critics blamed it on his lack of seriousness. "The talk that I don't have any heart [determination], I have to take that," he later told the *Los Angeles Times.* "Unfortunately, the Lewis fight did take place and it'll follow me around even if I become champion, and long after that."

TURNING POINT. Instead of the hero's welcome he had envisioned at home in New York City, Bowe found only his wife and mother waiting for him at the airport. Worse, boxing promoters and managers were not interested in him as a professional prospect. He was just about to enlist in the Army when he met Rock Newman, a radio commentator-turned-boxing manager from the Washington, D.C., area. Newman was looking for a heavyweight to manage, and on a hunch he visited Bowe in Gunsmoke City.

Newman recalled his first encounter with Bowe's neighborhood to the *Los Angeles Times*. "I wasn't prepared for it, I'd never seen anything like it anywhere," he said. "The building Riddick lived in ... was a dilapidated [run down], six-story building with broken-out windows. It was unlawful. I saw young kids on the rooftops with Uzis [machine guns], working as lookouts for drug dealers. On the first floor of Riddick's building, there was a line of people. I thought at first it was a soup kitchen. It wasn't. They were lined up for crack. The elevator was broken, so I started walking up the stairs. At every other landing there was a kid with an automatic weapon."

Newman said he sat down with Bowe and told him that "for having survived that neighborhood, he was already a champion." Newman invested his own money in Bowe's future. He found a suburban Washington, D.C., home for Bowe's family and placed the boxer on an allowance. Newman contacted Eddie Futch, trainer of 15 world champion boxers, and convinced him to give Bowe a tryout. But the trainer had heard about Bowe's performance in the Olympics, and Futch, in his eighties, was concerned about wasting his time if Bowe wasn't willing to try.

SERIOUS TRAINING. Newman pleaded and Futch agreed to give Bowe a chance. Bowe flew to Futch's training camp near Reno, Nevada, where he began a tough workout schedule that began each day at dawn with Bowe running three miles—all uphill. In order to see if the young boxer was serious, Futch decided to trick him. He told Bowe he was leaving town for a day or two, but early the next morning, Futch waited at the top of the hill to see if Bowe would train on his own. "I looked down that road, and there he was—trudging up that hill by himself, on a very cold, dark morning," Futch told the *Los Angeles Times*. "I knew at that moment the kid had what it took inside. I knew he had the tools. When he got to the top of that hill, he was surprised to see me."

Futch and Newman brought Bowe along slowly. At first he fought only opponents he was sure to beat, while building a 21-0 record with 20 knockouts. He soon began to fight better opponents. In July 1992 Bowe defeated South African Pierre Coetzer. Then-heavyweight champion **Evander Holyfield** (see entry) had agreed to fight the winner of that match, and openly rooted for Bowe, believing him to be the easier opponent to defeat.

SUPERSTAR

GOES ON DIET. Futch thought Bowe had the skills to beat Holyfield. But Bowe's weight and endurance were still sources of concern. The fighter hired former comic Dick Gregory—a self-proclaimed nutrition expert—to help Bowe reduce his weight from 281 to 235 pounds. "Every time Riddick saw me coming he frowned," Gregory told the *Los Angeles Times*. "But it's like I told him ... I don't know anything about boxing, but I can overhaul and clean out his motor. I told him if he got into a long fight with Holyfield, the full benefits of his diet would kick in and make him stronger at the finish, and that's exactly what happened."

BECOMES CHAMPION. On November 13, 1992, Bowe met Holyfield for the undisputed heavyweight championship. The fight was classic heavyweight boxing. As Pat Putnam described it in *Sport Illustrated,* "Neither man danced, and neither took a voluntary step backward.... Through 12 rounds Bowe and Holyfield painted a portrait of courage that will hang forever in the memories of those who watched." The match went the distance and Bowe won a unanimous decision.

HANDLING SUCCESS. Fame and fortune did not change Bowe's outlook on life. "I want to set up drug awareness pro-

BOXING SCORING

A boxing match can end in one of three ways. A fighter can be knocked out, meaning he can not stand up before the referee counts to ten as a result of a punch from the other boxer. A technical knockout occurs when a fighter is not knocked out, but cannot continue in the bout. If neither fighter is knocked out or has suffered a technical knockout, judges, and sometimes the referee, score the fight. A certain number of points are given to each fighter per round, depending on the judge's evaluation of their performance. At the end of the fight, the judges add up the points given each fighter. If a majority of the judges give more points to one boxer, that boxer wins. If there is a tie among the judges, the fight is scored a draw or tie.

grams," he said when asked in the *Los Angeles Times* what he wanted to do as heavyweight champion of the world. "Plus I want to try to do something about world hunger and [the South African system of racial segregation called] Apartheid. There's more to life than boxing and there's a lot I can do to help. I feel like I've been blessed my whole life. I think it's my calling to help people."

The rise of Riddick Bowe brought new interest to boxing's heavyweight division. Late in 1992 Newman negotiated a six-fight deal that could earn the boxer $100 million. Bowe's financial security has allowed him to set up trust funds for his children's education. He has enrolled at Howard University, a traditionally African American college in Washington, D.C., to study business administration and drama.

BOWE-HOLYFIELD II. On November 6, 1993, after successfully defending his title for the second time, Bowe once again faced Holyfield, who had recently come out of retirement. In another classic match, Bowe and Holyfield fought 12 grueling rounds. The bout was interrupted when a parachutist, risking both his life and the safety of the audience, crashed into the ring ropes. The stunt caused Judy Bowe, pregnant at the time, to faint. In an upset, Holyfield won back the title on a decision, but it appears certain that there will be a third match between these two courageous fighters.

OUT OF THE RING. Bowe and his family live in a mansion near Washington, D.C. His mother has her own home nearby. The first thing you see upon entering the house is a framed evaluation from Riddick Jr.'s school that states, "J.R. had a very good day at school today. When he gets home from school give him a big hug."

WHERE TO WRITE

C/O SPENCER PROMOTIONS, 1100 NEW YORK AVENUE, N.W., SUITE 814, WASHINGTON, D.C. 20005-3934.

MICHAEL CHANG

1972—

In 1989 Michael Chang was told he couldn't win the French Open, one of tennis' important Grand Slam tournaments along with the Australian Open, Wimbledon, and the U.S. Open. The players he faced were all bigger and stronger than the five-feet-eight inches, 135-pound Chang. But showing determination and a refusal to quit, he overcame opponents and his own exhaustion to win what people had said he couldn't win. With that victory, Chang became a champion in the truest sense of the word.

GROWING UP

Michael Chang was born February 22, 1972, in Hoboken, New Jersey. Both of his parents, Joe and Betty Chang, were research chemists. His father fled from mainland China to Taiwan after the Communist victory of Mao Tse Tung in the late 1940s. He came to the United States in 1966 and met Betty on a blind date in New York City. They tried to blend their traditional Eastern culture with the Western culture of the United States. "We've taken the best of Western culture and the best of Eastern culture and made it into Chang culture," Betty Chang told *Sports Illustrated*.

Michael Chang "has the head of a champion."— tennis coach Jose Higueras

DEMOCRACY. Chang always felt he could talk to his parents, and says they never pressured him. "My parents never forced me to do anything, except to take my vitamins," he told *Sports Illustrated.* "I could quit tennis tomorrow, and they'd stand behind me." In the Chang household, decisions are made by a vote from every family member. Chang told *Tennis* that this system fits in well with Asian culture. "We tend to put more emphasis on group discussion, and our decisions are more collective [decided by a group]," he said.

COACH DAD. Joe Chang taught himself tennis in 1974 and became his sons' coach. (Michael's older brother, Carl, is also a tennis player.) "My father deserves most of the credit for my accomplishments," Chang admitted to *Sports Illustrated.* He began playing tennis in 1977, after his family moved to St. Paul, Minnesota, and soon both sons were easily beating the local tennis competition. The family moved to Southern California, looking for tougher opponents. "Once the competition is gone, it's time to move," Betty Chang told *Sports Illustrated,* explaining the family's move. "We have a saying in Chinese: *Mung mu san tien.* It means a mother will move many times just for the sake of the child."

Before he was 13, Chang attracted national attention by winning several major amateur (unpaid) titles. In August 1987 he became, at 15 years and five months, the youngest player ever to win the U.S. junior championship, defeating **Jim Courier** (see entry). He won another major tournament by defeating **Pete Sampras** (see entry) in the finals of the United States Tennis Association (USTA) Boys 18-and-under Hardcourt Championship. In September Chang became the youngest player since 1918 to win a match at the U.S. Open, beating Paul McNamee in the first round. In July 1988 he became the youngest player to play on Centre Court, the main stadium at the legendary Wimbledon tournament, since 1927. "I don't mind all that youngest stuff," Chang told *Sports Illustrated.* "I suppose people bring it up so much because they've run out of things to say about me."

TURNS PRO. In January 1988 Chang accepted a multimillion dollar sponsorship deal from Reebok, the athletic equipment manufacturer, and turned professional. He entered the world rankings at number 920. Chang won his first professional match in February and in October won his first tournament as a professional, defeating Johan Kriek in the finals of the Transamerica Open in San Francisco, California. He became the second-youngest male player ever to win a championship with the victory. "He's as quick as anyone on the circuit," Kriek told *Sports Illustrated*. "He gets better every time we play."

By the end of 1988 Chang had risen to number 28 in the world. He knew he would have to be patient in order to get to the top. "As long as I improve, I'll get closer to beating the top guys," he explained in *Sports Illustrated*. "Things have to come gradually. You can't prove everything in a week." Chang was named the Association of Tennis Professionals (ATP) "Newcomer of the Year" for 1988.

TOO SMALL? Small for a tennis player at five-feet-eight inches and 135 pounds, Chang has had to work to compensate for his lack of size. "He's so little that heavy topspin [a high bouncing shot] gives him trouble," a fellow player told *Sports Illustrated*. "He's got to jump in the air and try to hit [the] ball." Chang does not use his size as an excuse. "It's easy to look at the negative side of things," he told *Tennis*. "I think there is always a positive outlook on something. Everybody has a talent, or a certain amount of potential built into himself. You just have to basically dig in there and find it."

Chang's success is based on his reflexes and his speed—he is probably the fastest player on the tour. He also has great defensive ability, which allows him to return every shot and make his opponent feel like he's hitting against a wall. "Chang

Michael Chang

Chang's mom often traveled with her son to tournaments, cooking for him, sewing his shorts, screening his phone calls, and teaching him Chinese. Chang is very close to his family, and says it is difficult for Americans to understand how a Chinese family operates. "[People don't understand] our Asian concept of family bonding," Chang explained in *Tennis.* "In the U.S., kids are almost supposed to leave the nest [home] when they get around college age. But in a Chinese family, it isn't unusual for even a 32-year-old single man to be living with his family."

is a little bit different from other young players," tennis commentator Tony Trabert said. "Too many of them aren't patient and willing to play long points."

Chang makes up for his lack of size by using his head, which his coach, Jose Higueras, calls "the head of a champion." "Tennis is a thinking man's game," Chang explained in *Tennis,* "and the Chinese, who value cleverness, respond to that. In that sense, maybe my background helps my tennis. Overall, my best asset is the ability to move quickly and to think clearly, often at the same time."

SUPERSTAR

BEATS NUMBER ONE. No one expected Chang, ranked 19th in the world, to contend in the 1989 French Open. His mother traveled to Paris with him and cooked noodles in the hotel room. On the court, he faced top-ranked Ivan Lendl in the tournament's fourth round. He lost the first two sets, 6-4, 6-4, and was on the verge of being eliminated from the tournament. But he came back, winning the third set, 6-3. Still facing elimination in the fourth set, Chang began to suffer from cramps, caused by physical exhaustion. Somehow he managed to win the fourth set, 6-3, but was in obvious pain as the fifth, and deciding, set began.

Refusing to quit, Chang gulped water and ate bananas—which are good for tired muscles—between games. Every time it seemed Chang was finished, he found the strength to hit a fantastic shot past the surprised Lendl. Leading 4-3, Chang pulled a trick out of his bag, serving the ball underhanded. The trick worked and Chang won the point and the game. "I was trying to break his concentration," Chang told *Sports Illustrated.* "I would do anything to stay out there. It was the mental thing." When Lendl double-faulted at match-point in the next game, Chang fell to his knees, knowing he had won. "I've never seen a player show such courage on a tennis court," television commentator Tony Trabert said.

MAJOR WIN. Chang's victory over Lendl inspired **Arantxa Sanchez Vicario** (see entry) to defeat number-one ranked **Steffi Graf** (see entry) in the women's singles final. "I see Michael beat Lendl and ask, 'Why not I am beating Number One?,'" Sanchez Vicario asked *Sports Illustrated* in her fractured English. In the men's final Chang faced Stefan Edberg of Sweden, who had won the famous Wimbledon championship the year before. Surprisingly, Chang won the first set, 6-1. Edberg came back quickly, however, winning the next two sets, 6-3 and 6-4. When Edberg took the lead in the fourth set, he appeared to be on his way to the championship. But Chang, with his back to the wall, began to play his best tennis, making great returns on Edberg's serve. He smashed two straight winning shots to take the fourth set, 6-4. Suddenly, the match was all even.

BIG OVERHEAD

Chang is a born-again Christian and his mother says he plays tennis to "spread the word." He credits God for his victories and claims that God helped him in his match against Lendl. "I prayed, and my cramps went away," he told *Sports Illustrated*. "Maybe there are more important things to pray for, but everything that happens in my life is because of Him. I get my strength from Him. He's in control. He keeps me going. I know every time I bring Jesus up, everybody nods and gets sick of it. But it's the truth. He gets all the credit." His grandfather founded a Chinese-American Christian church which Chang still attends. He holds Christian study groups on tour and often reads the Bible with **Andre Agassi** (see entry), who is also a born-again Christian.

Chang's exceptional physical conditioning paid off in the fifth set. Edberg, looking tired, lost a tough game to fall behind 4-1. Chang wasted no time in winning two of the last three games to capture the championship. "I can't really explain what happened to turn it around," an excited Chang told *Sports Illustrated*. "He just keeps coming back," an exhausted Edberg said. "I have to admire him for it." With the victory, Chang became the first American man to win the French Open since Tony Trabert in 1955. He also became the youngest man to ever win a Grand Slam singles title. When given his championship trophy, Chang thanked everyone he could think of in his acceptance speech, including Edberg. "Whatever happens from now on, good or bad," Chang said, "this will stay with me for the rest of my life."

Michael Chang celebrates 1989 French Open title.

IGNORES RACISM. The only thing that took away from Chang's victory was the racism displayed by the French media. One headline, quoting a photographer, read *Le Chinetoque Va Nous Faire Vendre,* which, in English, meant "The Chink Will Sell Us Some Pictures." Another paper referred to him as *notre petit bride,* or "our little slant eyes." Chang didn't let this bother him. "I don't think about the matches and stuff [racism]," he told *Sports Illustrated.*

Chang became the youngest player ever to rank among the top five in the world—he ranked fifth in August 1989. In 1990 he lost to Agassi at the French Open, failing in his attempt to defend his title. He then teamed up with Agassi to help the U.S. team earn the world championship by defeating Australia in the finals of the international Davis Cup tournament. In the 1991 French Open, Chang, seeded fifth, lost in the quarterfinals to unseeded Nicklas Kulti of Sweden in five sets, 7-6, 2-6, 6-3, 3-6, 8-6. Chang fought off eight match points before losing the hard-fought contest. At the U.S. Open Chang lost to Stefan Edberg of Sweden, the eventual champion, in the quarterfinals.

HIGHEST RANK. Chang reached his highest ranking—fourth in the world—in 1992 after winning three tournaments. The highlight of 1992 for Chang was in the semifinals of the U.S. Open. Playing Edberg, the man he'd defeated for his French Open title, Chang endured one of the longest matches in tennis history. After five hours and 26 minutes, Edberg had won 6-7, 7-5, 7-6, 5-7, 6-4, but neither man really lost. 1993 was Chang's best season in terms of tournament wins as he captured five titles. Early in 1994 he had already won two tournaments and was ranked number eight in the world. Chang has won 15 tournaments and over $4 million in his career.

OFF THE COURT. Chang is a bachelor and lives in Henderson,

Nevada. He is a spokesperson for Reebok and Nuprin pain reliever. He quit high school to play tennis, but has since passed the high school equivalency test. He likes to fish and raises and breeds tropical fish in 14 different tanks. "Fishing is more difficult than tennis," he explained to *Sports Illustrated.* "It takes much more preparation and technique." Chang is now coached by his brother, Carl, who played college tennis at the University of California, Berkeley. Even though Chang has not yet reached the very top of his sport, he will continue trying to achieve what others say is impossible.

WHERE TO WRITE

C/O U.S. TENNIS ASSOCIATION,

1212 AVENUE OF THE AMERICAS, NEW YORK, NY 10036.

ROGER CLEMENS

1962—

The speed of Roger Clemens's fastball—usually clocked at 95 to 97 miles an hour—has earned him the nickname "Rocket Man." His fastball (which Rickey Henderson of the Oakland Athletics told the *Providence Journal* "is as difficult to hit as a marble shot out of a cannon"), combined with a sharp breaking curve ball, has established Clemens as the best pitcher in the major leagues. He has won three American League Cy Young Awards (given annually to the league's best pitcher), was named the American League Most Valuable Player (MVP) in 1986, and has won twenty or more games in three different seasons. A fierce competitor, Clemens's temper has often caused him trouble, but his will to win has made him the best.

GROWING UP

William Roger Clemens was born August 4, 1962, in Dayton, Ohio. He is the youngest of Bill (a truck driver) and Bess Clemens's five children (he has two brothers and two sisters). When he was eight years old, Clemens's mother left his father and two years later married Woody Booher, a tool-and-die maker. Five years later Booher died of a heart attack. "I'm sure

[Booher's] death was hard on Clemens, because Woody was the only father he ever knew," his mom told *Sports Illustrated*. "But if he had any problems, he never showed it. When you have adversities [problems] in your life, you have to strive to overcome them." Because his mom worked extra hours to earn money to support the family, Clemens was raised by his grandmother, Myrna Lee. "She always said, 'I made you a man when you were a boy,'" Clemens told *Newsday*.

CHILD STAR. Despite his loss, Clemens had a happy childhood. "I feel as if I was almost spoiled, because I can't ever remember wanting for anything except possibly a father in the stands watching me pitch," Clemens said in his autobiography, *Rocket Man*. At age seven he was the star pitcher in a league of nine-and ten-year-olds. As a teenager he was so much better than other kids his age, his parents had to look for tougher competition for him. During his junior year of high school, Clemens went to live with his brother Randy (a father figure to Roger and a great athlete himself), and his wife in the Houston, Texas, area. He went to school at Spring Woods High School, which had one of the top high school baseball programs in Texas.

Clemens's wife, Debbie, who met him as a teenager, told *Sports Illustrated,* "In high school he was always a good pitcher, but he was never considered the best. The thing was, though, he always felt he was the best. If someone told him he couldn't do something, it just became more of a challenge to him." As a senior, Clemens was 13-5 and set a school record by striking out 18 batters in one game. His dream was to become a major league pitcher like his hero, **Nolan Ryan** (see entry), who played for the Houston Astros.

When he graduated in 1980 Clemens was disappointed that he was not offered a scholarship to play for the University

---

SCOREBOARD

1986 AMERICAN LEAGUE MOST VALUABLE PLAYER.

THREE-TIME AMERICAN LEAGUE CY YOUNG AWARD WINNER (1986, 1987, AND 1991).

1986 ALL-STAR GAME MOST VALUABLE PLAYER.

LED AMERICAN LEAGUE IN WINS TWICE (1986 AND 1987), EARNED RUN AVERAGE FOUR TIMES (1986, 1990, 1991, AND 1992), STRIKEOUTS TWICE (1988 AND 1991), AND SHUTOUTS FIVE TIMES (1987, 1988, 1990, 1991, AND 1992).

DURING HIS CAREER, THE BEST PITCHER IN THE MAJOR LEAGUES.

Roger Clemens

of Texas, a college baseball powerhouse known for developing great pitchers. Though he was offered a contract by the Minnesota Twins, he was not drafted by any major league baseball team. Feeling that he could do better than the Twins, Clemens enrolled at San Jacinto Junior College. He was 18 years old at the time, six-feet-two inches and 220 pounds. "I was a bit overweight and that kept me from having the strength to throw hard," he told the *Los Angeles Times*. "But I still had good control of my pitches."

HARD WORK. At San Jacinto, Clemens put himself on a tough exercise program—lifting weights and running several miles each day—and lost 15 pounds. The exercise helped him improve his fastball from 86 to 90 miles-per-hour. He pitched well enough as a freshman (earning a 9-2 record), for the New York Mets to chose him in the 12th round of the 1981 draft. The Mets offered him $30,000 to sign, but Clemens turned them down when the University of Texas finally offered him a scholarship. "I was very, very close to signing with the Mets," Clemens told the *Dallas Morning News,* "but I knew I could go to school for a couple of more years. Texas was where I'd really wanted to go. It was a national power and a great place to learn how to pitch. I figured if I went to Texas, my chances for becoming a pro would only improve."

TURNS PRO. Clemens pitched two years for the Longhorns, winning 25 games and losing only seven. More impressively, he struck out 241 batters in 275 innings and in June of 1983 he was the winning pitcher in the final game of the College World Series, giving Texas the national title. The Boston Red Sox selected Clemens with the 19th pick of the first round of the 1983 draft. They sent him to their Winter Haven, Florida, minor league team, where he won three of four games and had a terrific 1.24 earned run average (ERA). He was promoted to New Britain, Connecticut, where he won four of five games with a 1.38 ERA. During 81 minor-league innings that season, he struck out 95 batters. In the league playoffs, Clemens pitched a one-hit shutout in the championship game.

INJURY. By spring training before the 1984 season, Clemens was expected to become a star. He combined one of the game's best fastballs with pin-point control and after joining the Red Sox midway through the 1984 season, he won nine games, lost four, and struck out almost a batter per inning. The next season, however, his shoulder hurt so much that he could barely lift his pitching arm. Clemens underwent surgery and some felt that his career might be over. Although it scared him at the time, the injury may have actually helped Clemens. "Maybe it scared him to work even harder," Red Sox pitching coach Bill Fischer told *Newsday.* "A lot of people have athletic ability. But very few make use of every ounce of it the way he does."

SUPERSTAR

MVP. Clemens came back from the injury with a bang. In 1986 he won his first fourteen decisions (one short of the American League record for most wins in a row at the start of the season), led the American League in wins, 24, with only four losses, and ERA at 2.48. On April 29th he struck out 20 Seattle Mariners— at the time the record for a nine-inning game. Fourteen of Clemens's victories came in games after the Red Sox had lost. He started and won the All-Star game and was named the game's MVP, was a unanimous winner of the Cy Young Award (named after Cy Young, the all-time leader in wins with 511), and was named American League Most Valuable Player, the first player ever to win all three awards in one season.

The Red Sox won 95 games and the American League Eastdivision title. In the American League championship series against the California Angels, Clemens started three games, and won the pennant clincher in Game Seven, 8-1, despite having the flu. In the World Series against the National League champion New York Mets, Clemens started two games, but did not earn a win or a loss. Because of a blister on his finger, he was removed from Game Six leading 3-2 in the seventh inning of a game that Boston eventually lost, 6-5, in ten innings. The game is best remembered for an error made by Boston first baseman Bill Buckner that allowed the winning run to score. Boston lost the World Series in Game Seven, 8-5.

CY YOUNG REPEAT. In 1987 Clemens had another standout season. He won 20 games and lost 9, had a 2.97 ERA, struck out 256 batters, and led the major leagues with 18 complete games (when a pitcher pitches the entire game) and seven shutouts. For the second straight season, Clemens won the Cy Young Award, a feat accomplished by only four other pitchers (Sandy Koufax, 1965 and 1966; Denny McLain, 1968 and 1969; Jim Palmer, 1975 and 1976; and **Greg Maddux** (see entry), 1992 and 1993). The Red Sox, however, fell from first, finishing fourth in their division. Boston rebounded in 1988, again winning the American League East title. Clemens, bothered by a strained muscle in his back, won 18 games and lost 12, led the major leagues with 291 strikeouts in 264 innings pitched and shutouts (8), and had an ERA of 3.13. In the American League Championship Series, the Red Sox were swept, four games to none, by the Oakland Athletics.

Clemens, still not completely healthy, won 17 games in 1989 and struck out 230. Back in top form in 1990, he put together another great season. He won 21 games, lost 6, led the major leagues with a 1.93 ERA, and tied for the major league lead with four shutouts. He almost certainly would have won the Cy Young Award for a third time, except that Bob Welch of the Oakland Athletics won 27 games and lost only six. The Red Sox won the American League East division title and faced the Oakland Athletics, going for their third straight American League pennant and the right to go to the World Series.

BAD TEMPER. Boston lost the first three games of the series. Game Four was a must-win. Clemens, losing 2-0 in the second inning, was thrown out of the game when home plate umpire Gerry Cooney claimed the pitcher swore at him. Clemens denied the accusation and was very upset after the game, but during the off-season, Clemens admitted that he'd been wrong, and that he had sworn at Cooney. Always a fierce competitor, the pitcher explained that he'd been frustrated about the Red Sox losing in the playoffs again. Clemens's temper has gotten him in trouble many times, causing problems with his teammates, managers, opposing players, and the news media.

CY YOUNG III. Before the 1991 season the Red Sox signed Clemens to a four-year, $21 million contract. He went out and earned the money as well as his third Cy Young Award, posting an 18-11 record, leading the major leagues in strikeouts (241) and innings pitched (271), and leading the American League in ERA (2.62). In winning his third Cy Young, Clemens became only the fifth pitcher to accomplish this feat.

In 1992 Clemens won 18 games, lost 11, and led the major league in shutouts with five, and the American League in ERA at 2.41. The Red Sox, however, continued to slide, finishing last in the American League East with only 73 victories. Once again bothered by shoulder and arm problems in 1993, Clemens had his first losing season, 11-14, and his first ERA over 4.00 in a full season, 4.46. Clemens has been the subject of trade rumors, but insists he wants to stay in Boston. "All I asked [of the Red Sox]," Clemens told *Sport,* "is that they show me that they're serious about trying to put together a winning team."

TRI-CY

Since 1956 when the Cy Young Award was first given out, only five pitchers have won it three times or more. Here is a list of those pitchers. (From 1956 to 1966 only one Cy Young Award was given out to the best pitcher in the major leagues. Starting in 1967 awards have been given to the best pitcher in the American and the National leagues.)

Player/ Years	Cy Young Awards
Steve Carlton 1972, 1977, 1980, 1982	4
Sandy Koufax 1963, 1965, 1966	3
Tom Seaver 1965, 1966, 1969	3
Jim Palmer 1973, 1975, 1976	3
Roger Clemens 1986, 1987, 1991	3

OFF THE FIELD. During the off-season Clemens lives in Katy, Texas, with his wife, Debbie and their two sons. He visits with children confined to hospitals, gives anti-drug talks to high school groups, and takes part in many other charitable activities. In his spare time, Clemens rides horses and motorcycles. A very private person, Clemens often has a hard time talking about himself and his family. "I don't want to be a superstar," Clemens told *Sports Illustrated.* "I just want to be a regular person."

WHERE TO WRITE

C/O BOSTON RED SOX, FENWAY PARK, BOSTON, MA 02115.

JIM COURIER

1970—

Had he devoted himself to pitching baseballs, he may have been wearing a college jersey and throwing fastballs during the summer of 1991, as his father had done years earlier. Instead, Jim Courier decided at age 13 to put down the bat and glove and go with tennis. Courier trained for seven years, often doubting his own ability. But his hard work paid off in May 1991 when he defeated his one-time camp roommate, **Andre Agassi** (see entry), at the French Open in Paris to win his first Grand Slam title. (The "Grand Slam" is made up of four tournaments: the Australian Open, French Open, U.S. Open, and Wimbledon in London, England.)

Over the next three years he won three more Grand Slam titles and in 1992 became the first American male since John McEnroe in 1985 to finish the year ranked No. 1 in the world. Despite his success, Courier still works to improve. "Jim does one thing that a lot of athletes don't do when they get to the top," fellow player Brad Gilbert once told *Sports Illustrated*. "He works even harder."

> *"Jim does one thing that a lot of athletes don't do when they get to the top. He works even harder."*—Brad Gilbert, professional tennis player

GROWING UP

James Spencer Courier was born August 17, 1970, in Sanford, Florida. His father, an executive at a juice processing plant, had been a scholarship-winning pitcher at Florida State University. His son inherited his gifted arm. But Courier's Little League career was sidetracked when his great-aunt, once a women's tennis coach at the University of Southern California, introduced him to tennis. With an inexpensive department store racquet, Courier learned the basics of the game along with his older sister, Audra.

EARLY TRAINING. By age 11 it was clear that Courier preferred tennis to baseball. He earned the $50 entrance fee he needed to go to tennis camp. His coach, Harry Hopman, was impressed with his game and gave Courier a scholarship to stay at the camp, which he did for two years.

The training paid off. In 1986 Courier won the 14-and-under Orange Bowl championship—the "Super Bowl" of junior tennis. Following his victory, Nick Bollettieri invited him to train at Bolletteri's famous academy in Brandenton, Florida. There Courier practiced with some of the top tennis talents: Andre Agassi, David Wheaton, and MaliVai Washington. But Courier always seemed to be one step behind the best players. According to *Sports Illustrated,* on sunny days, he would take on Agassi outdoors. "Andre always won," Courier said. On rainy days they would slug it out indoors. "Andre always won," Courier said.

Coach Bolletteri was also more supportive of Agassi. The coach's favoritism became clear to Courier when the young player faced Agassi during the third round of the 1989 French Open. "Nick was clapping for Andre, cheering him on," Courier told one reporter. "It kind of hurt me."

EARLY SUCCESS AND STRUGGLES. By this time Courier was ranked No. 24 in the world. His success depended on his strong backcourt playing style. (In a back-court style the player stays behind the end-line of the court and is uncomfortable coming in close to the net.) This style was based on Courier's first love, baseball. "My backhand is definitely developed from a baseball swing," he told the *New York Times*. "And when I serve, I serve like a pitcher. I try to vary speeds and spots and the type of serves I hit. You don't throw a fastball down the middle [in baseball]."

Courier soon discovered that strength alone would not make him a successful player. Between 1989 and 1990 he dropped from No. 24 to No. 25 in the world rankings and was frustrated with his lack of progress. "Last year I didn't have one win that stuck out," he told *Tennis* magazine in 1991. "It seems like I've been wanting it almost too much and maybe that's hurting me a little bit. Maybe I should just kind of let it happen instead of trying to force it."

Jim Courier

NEW COACHES. Just when his career seemed to have stalled, Courier found help from a new coach, Jose Higueras, who quickly discovered the problem with Courier's game. "Jim had only one gear, the fast gear," Higueras told *Sports Illustrated*. "He confused tense with intense. He had never been asked to think, so his game was easy to figure out."

Higueras and college coach Brad Stine worked to redesign Courier's game. Instead of hitting the ball hard from the back of the court, his coaches convinced him to use the whole court. With this new strategy, Courier defeated Agassi in March of 1991. That was, as he later told a journalist, the first match he'd won with his head.

As Courier improved his game, his coaches tried to bring his temper under control. During matches Courier would sometimes explode, yelling at umpires, fans, and himself. After losing in the 1991 Italian Open to a lesser-ranked opponent Courier said, "I'm 21. I'm number 9 in the world, and I'm so unhappy with my life."

After this defeat Coach Stine told Courier to "grow up right now." This time, Courier decided to listen. "I got caught up in the whole winning thing and I forgot about my game," he told *Tennis Illustrated*. "I got it back right then and there and we started working unbelievably hard for the French [Open] the very next day."

SUPERSTAR

WINS FRENCH OPEN. The 1991 French Open was everything Courier had hoped for. He defeated the world's No. 1-ranked player, Stephen Edberg, in the quarterfinals. In the semifinals he eliminated 12th-seeded Michael Stich. And in the finals, Courier faced his longtime rival, Andre Agassi. After a rain delay, he came from behind to defeat Agassi in an exciting, but exhausting, best-three-out-of-five set match, 3-6, 6-4, 2-6, 6-1, 6-4.

BECOMES NUMBER ONE. At Wimbledon (considered the most important tournament in tennis), Courier advanced to the quarterfinals. After losing in the final of the U.S. Open, he claimed the No. 2 ranking at the close of 1991. He started 1992 by winning the Australian Open with a four-set victory over Edberg. A month later, he overtook Edberg again, this time passing him in the rankings. Courier was now ranked No. 1 in the world. "Are we surprised?" Courier's father, Jim, asked the *New York Times* on the eve of his son's crowning as No. 1. "Yes, to put it mildly. We worked with him a little, but my wife and I are not tennis players. You never allow yourself to look too far ahead. Even when he made the top 50, we didn't think of him becoming No. 1."

Courier worked to stay at the top. He successfully defended his French Open title in 1992 and topped the year off by helping the United States defeat Switzerland in the Davis Cup final in December.

Because of his success, the sporting goods company, Nike, began a line of Jim Courier clothing and television advertisements. Courier tried to stay humble despite his celebrity. "[He] comports [behaves] himself in a reasonable, responsible and refreshingly boyish way for a 21-year-old kid who has the world by the tail," *M* magazine reported in the fall of 1992. "He goes for a jog after matches and then hits [balls] with his coach.... When the Prince de Galles hotel offered him a comp [free rent] for a two-bedroom suite for the French Open, he took a one-bedroom and paid in full.... When he got dumped at Wimbledon, he didn't question the umpires, he didn't offer any excuses."

UPS AND DOWNS. Courier had an up and down year in 1993. He began by defeating **Pete Sampras** (see entry) to defend the Australian Open title. This, however, was the high point of his year. He lost his No. 1 ranking to Sampras and in April he was criticized for not playing on the U.S. Davis Cup team. Then, in an upset, he lost in five sets in the finals of the French Open to 10th-seeded [ranked] Sergi Bruguera of Spain.

Because he had trouble playing on the grass surface, Courier had never done well at Wimbledon. Despite this setback, he surprisingly reached the championship match, but lost to Sampras. An early round loss to little known French player Cedric Pioline in the fourth round of the U.S. Open was the lowpoint of the year for Courier; this meant he would not be able to regain the No. 1 ranking. He continued to struggle in early 1994 and failed to defend his Australian Open title for the first time in three years when he lost to Sampras in the semifinals. He defeated Sampras in the quarterfinals of the French Open but lost to Bruguera, the eventual champion, for the second straight year in the semifinals.

Despite losing his number-one ranking, Courier continues to be the hardest-working player on the professional tour.

TENNIS SURFACES

The Grand Slam tournaments are played on three different kinds of surfaces. The French Open is played on clay, Wimbledon on grass, and the Australian and U.S. Opens on hard court surfaces. Most players are more successful on one surface than on others. On clay, the ball travels more slowly and bounces higher. On grass, the ball moves very quickly and often skids on the slick surface. Hard courts are faster than clay, but slower than grass, and the ball bounces in a more predictable way than on grass.

Listening to his coach's advice, Courier also discovered that there is more to life than tennis. He is studying foreign languages and economics, as well as playing the guitar. "I'm getting pretty good at not letting the outside distractions bother me," he told *Tennis Week* at the end of 1992. "I'm getting used to big match situations. You can never control how well or poorly you play. You try and do the best you can."

WHERE TO WRITE

C/O U.S. TENNIS ASSOCIATION,

1212 AVENUE OF THE AMERICAS, NEW YORK, NY 10036.

CLYDE DREXLER

1962—

Portland Trail Blazer guard Clyde "The Glide" Drexler is a different kind of superstar—a superstar who never seeks to call attention to himself. Often compared to **Michael Jordan** (see entry), Drexler has become one of the top players in the National Basketball Association (NBA) and has led his team to two NBA finals appearances. His position in the NBA was recognized when he was named to the 1992 U.S. Olympic "Dream Team." "The Glide is not just a nickname," Mike Bruton commented in the *Philadelphia Inquirer,* "it is what Clyde Drexler does on a basketball court."

> *"The Glide is not just a nickname, it is what Clyde Drexler does on a basketball court."—*
>
> *Mike Bruton, Sportswriter*

GROWING UP

Clyde Drexler was born June 22, 1962, in New Orleans, Louisiana. He grew up in Houston, Texas, in a neighborhood known as South Park. The middle child in a family of seven, Drexler spent hours on the front porch of his home, throwing the ball to his older brother, James. James was a talented basketball player and a good teacher, but his athletic career was cut short because he needed to work. "The funny thing is that James had one of these picture-perfect jump shots, high arc, perfect form, the whole thing," Drexler told *Sports Illustrated.*

"Exactly what my jumper doesn't look like." Drexler's mother told the *Oregonian* of her younger son: "Clyde didn't care about shooting. All he wanted to do is dunk."

"GYM RAT." Drexler told the *Sporting News* that he was a "chubby preteen who was too slow, couldn't jump and was always picked last on his playground in Houston." In order to help himself develop discipline, Drexler enrolled in a martial arts class when he was 12. By the time he entered high school he was a "gym rat," playing whatever sport was in season and doing well in all of them.

It soon became obvious that basketball was his best sport, so Drexler gave up football and baseball. "All you heard back then was to concentrate on one sport, and I think I got caught up in that," he told *Sports Illustrated*. "My one regret is that I didn't get a chance to play two sports at a pro level. Baseball, maybe, or even football, as a quarterback or wide receiver."

Both his mother, Eunice, and his stepfather, Manuel Scott, had full-time jobs, and most of their children went to college. Unlike many athletes, Drexler was not forced to play sports in order to help support his family, although he did give his mom money so she could retire early from her job as a cashier at a supermarket. When Drexler entered the University of Houston, he did it because he wanted to, not because he had to.

COLLEGE. Drexler arrived at the University of Houston in 1980, and helped transform the Cougars into a powerhouse in just two years. He combined with **Hakeem Olajuwon** (see entry) and Larry Micheaux to form a front line that came to be known as "Phi Slamma Jamma," a take-off on college fraternity names. As a sophomore, Drexler was named the team's Most Valuable Player and Houston reached the Final Four of the National Collegiate Athletic Association (NCAA) tournament, losing 68-63 to the University of North Carolina. Averaging 15.9 points as a junior, Drexler was named the South-west Conference Player of the Year. Houston returned to the Final Four, beating the Louisville Cardinals in the semifinal, 94-81, with Drexler scoring 21 points. The Cougars came up short in the finals, though, losing 54-52 to North Carolina State, on a dunk at the buzzer by Lorenzo Charles after a desperation shot.

DRAFT DISAPPOINTMENT. After his junior year of college, Drexler announced his availability for the NBA draft. Though he only played three years at Houston, Drexler set school records with 1,000 points, 900 rebounds, and 300 assists. The Houston Rockets had the first and third picks in the 1983 draft, and Drexler hoped to be chosen by his hometown team. Instead the Rockets picked Ralph Sampson of the University of Virginia and Rodney McCray of the University of Louisville. Drexler was drafted fourteenth in the first round, by a team more than a thousand miles away—the Portland Trail Blazers. "I was upset," Drexler told *The Oregonian*. "I came out [of college] a year early with the idea that the Rockets would grab me. When they didn't, I was disappointed."

Portland seemed like a foreign country to Drexler and he had problems adjusting in his first year. Drexler was "an immature, undisciplined natural talent with just five years of playing experience and an unrealistic opinion of his game," said the *Sporting News*. "Amid the spectacular plays were too many wild shots and too much selfishness." He scored only 7.7 points per game as a rookie.

ALL-STAR. Feeling more at home during the 1984-85 season, Drexler established himself as a solid NBA player, scoring 17.2 points per game. Portland advanced to the Western Conference semifinals, losing to **Earvin "Magic" Johnson** (see entry) and the eventual champion Los Angeles Lakers, four games to one. Drexler's improvement continued the next year, as his scoring

Clyde Drexler

average increased to 18.5 points per game and he was named to the All-Star team for the first time (he has been named every season since). Unfortunately, the Trail Blazers lost to the Denver Nuggets in the first round of the playoffs.

CONFLICT. As his game improved, Drexler began to argue with his coach, Mike Schuler. Schuler "considered Drexler a negative influence on the team, a player who didn't give his all in practice and who, despite streaks of brilliance, made bad decisions on the court," according to *Sports Illustrated*. The Trail Blazers disagreed with Schuler and fired him. "I would never say Clyde didn't practice hard," assistant coach John Wetzel told *Sports Illustrated*. "But I would say he is a little more focused now, more knowledgeable about the right things to do. He doesn't feel he has to prove himself every day, and that's led to a more constructive approach to his game." Under new coach Rick Adelman, Drexler's overall game improved, and he became team captain.

SUPERSTAR

"SILKY SMOOTH." Despite his problems, Drexler continued to dazzle on the court, and his scoring average went up (21.7 in 1986-87, 27.0 in 1987-88, and a Portland record 27.2 in both 1987-88 and 1988-89). The *Philadelphia Inquirer* described Drexler as a player who has a "silky smooth style that ranges from explosiveness when he assaults [goes to] the hoop on the fast break to the utmost finesse when he softly launches a three-pointer or beats his man on a baseline drive." His individual performances, however, did not help the Trail Blazers win. But that all changed during the 1989-90 season. Drexler scored less, 23.3 points per game, but his team won more. The Trail Blazers traded for veteran forward Buck Williams of the New Jersey Nets; young players Terry Porter, Kevin Duckworth, and Jerome Kersey picked up their games; and rookie Cliff Robinson made a big contribution.

Portland won 59 games during the regular season and swept their first playoff series against the Dallas Mavericks three games to none. After a tough series against the San Antonio Spurs and the Phoenix Suns, the Trail Blazers were in the NBA finals for the first time since 1977, when they won the title. Facing the defending champion Detroit Pistons, Portland split the first two games in Detroit, winning Game Two 106-105 in overtime. Heading back to Portland for three straight games, experts felt that Portland had a good chance to become NBA champs. The Pistons had other ideas, however, winning all three games on the Blazers's home court to repeat as champions.

BEST SEASON. Despite winning 63 games and the Pacific division, ending the Los Angeles Lakers's ten-year division reign as champions, the 1990-91 season was a disappointment. Expecting to return to the finals, the Trail Blazers were defeated in the Western Conference finals by the Lakers. Returning more determined than ever, Drexler had his best overall season in 1991-92, averaging 25 points, 6.6 rebounds, and 6.7 assists per game. His accomplishments were recognized as he finished second to Michael Jordan in voting for Most Valuable Player and was named to the All-NBA first team. He would also finish second to Jordan and the Chicago Bulls in the NBA finals, as the Blazers lost a big fourth quarter lead in the sixth and final game to lose the series four games to two. Drexler was disappointed, but didn't let it get him down. "I want to win it all, but I'm not obsessed with it," he said. "It [not winning the championship] won't mar [take away] my accomplishments."

DREAM TEAM. Although Drexler was not originally chosen for the 1992 U.S. Olympic "Dream Team," his outstanding performance in the 1991-92 season made him an obvious choice for the last spot on the team. Clyde gave Portland fans credit for his being named to the squad. "I think the fans on the local level started the whole support system, and that was a great feeling,"

THE GLIDE

Despite his nickname, Drexler says he doesn't just "glide." "From my perspective [point of view], I'm scuffling out there," Drexler told *The Oregonian*. "I'm struggling. I'm barely making it. So when somebody says I make it look easy, that's funny." He also told the *Los Angeles Times* that when he's on the court, "I'm going, 'If I make this move, my ankle's going to kill me, if I make this move my knees may bend wrong.' I'm out there struggling. But I'm trying so hard, before you know it, the play's made. It's like something you've done a million times before, so you just let it happen.... You never have time to think, 'I'm just going to glide.'"

he told the *Los Angeles Times*. "They were behind me all the way and they wanted to see justice done."

Injuries to his hamstring muscle and knee limited Drexler to a career low 49 games in 1992-93. He averaged 19.2 points per game during the 1993-94 season and Portland lost in the first round of the playoffs. During the off-season Drexler lives quietly in Portland with his wife, who is an attorney, and their two children. He studies foreign languages, works on computers, and likes to read. "Each year, I try to expand my learning experience by taking on a new challenge," he told the *Sporting News*. Drexler loves to work with children, who are his biggest fans. "Clyde is the pride of Portland," 12-year-old Trang Nguyen told *Sports Illustrated for Kids*. "He is one player who always stays after games to sign autographs." *Sports Illustrated for Kids* gave Clyde one of its Good Sports Awards for 1992.

OFF THE COURT. His participation on the "Dream Team" made Drexler a household name outside of Portland. Recognition was slow in coming to Drexler, who didn't brag about himself like other players. "I am just uncomfortable talking about myself or my family," he told the *Sporting News*. So far he has few of the high-paying commercial endorsements that other NBA superstars have, although his salary is comparable to other top players. "I've always had recognition, coming out of college. The mega-mega-superstar recognition I haven't had, and that hasn't bothered me at all. I've got a lot of respect from people all across the country, get plenty of fan mail and that's a lot."

WHERE TO WRITE

C/O PORTLAND TRAIL BLAZERS, 700 N.E. MULTNOMAH, SUITE 600, PORTLAND, OR 97232.

LENNY DYKSTRA

1963—

Lenny Dykstra, centerfielder for the Philadelphia Phillies, is one of the fiercest competitors in major league baseball. His intense style of play made him the leader of the Phillies's "worst to first" National League pennant winners of 1993. (The Phillies finished in last place in their division in 1992.) Despite a series of career-threatening injuries—more than a few caused by his own reckless behavior—Dykstra has emerged as a team leader and finished second in the 1993 National League Most Valuable Player voting.

Dykstra does not look the part of a major league baseball player. Modern major leaguers are rarely less that six feet tall; Dykstra is five-feet-ten inches and weighs less than 200 pounds. What has always made Dykstra special is his desire to win. "I grew up with baseball and I remember I always had a plan," Dykstra told the *Philadelphia Daily News*. "Even when I was 12, 14 years old. I knew what I wanted and I went after it. I always knew. No matter what happened or what came along, I knew where I was going to end up: that was in the big leagues."

"He plays like a fire rages, plays every game like it's his last. Intense is too mild a word to describe Dykstra.... He plays baseball like it's football. Fearlessly."—Rick Weinberg, sportswriter

GROWING UP

Dykstra was born February 10, 1963, in Santa Ana, California. His grandfather Pete Leswick was a pro hockey player for the Cleveland Barons (a former National Hockey League team). Two of his great-uncles played on National Hockey League teams. But Dykstra was drawn to baseball because it was the most popular sport in his hometown of Garden Grove, California.

BASEBALL. *Philadelphia Inquirer Magazine* reporter Michael Vitez noted that as a teenager growing up in California, "Dykstra could never drive past a baseball diamond without stopping. He took his glove with him wherever he went. He went to five California Angels games a week. He wrote letters to his favorite players. He made friends with some guy who owned a pitching machine, and hit balls for three hours a day."

Dykstra decorated the walls of his bedroom with posters of ace pitcher **Nolan Ryan** (see entry). He read and reread his favorite book, *Rod Carew on Hitting* (written by Minnesota Twins's and California Angels's Hall-of-Famer Rod Carew). When he and his friends snuck into Anaheim Stadium (home of the California Angels) one Christmas night as a prank, Dykstra practiced running into the outfield wall, chasing make-believe home runs. He was never afraid of physical contact, either with walls, the ground, or other athletes. In high school he played both football and baseball. The *Philadelphia Inquirer Magazine* quoted him as saying: "I loved hitting people, and I enjoyed getting hit.... That made it fun."

By playing the game with such fearlessness, Dykstra was able to overcome problems caused by being small. As a high school senior he was invited one night to take batting practice with the Angels because major league scouts were interested in him. He was also offered a baseball scholarship to Arizona State University, but decided to skip college and go directly into professional baseball.

TURNING PRO. The decision was a tough one, because Dykstra was not drafted until the twelfth round in the June 1981 amateur draft. He had just graduated from high school, and suddenly faced the possibility of working thousands of miles from home all summer as a minor leaguer in the New York Mets organization. He accepted the challenge with confidence. Former Philadelphia teammate Roger McDowell first met Dykstra in the South Atlantic (Sally) League and recalled the experience for *Sports Illustrated:* "The first time I saw him in the Sally League, he was a 12th round draft choice, but he was driving a white Porsche, and he knew he was going to be in the big leagues someday."

Lenny Dykstra

MAJOR LEAGUER. Sure enough, Dykstra progressed rapidly through the Mets's minor league system. In 1983 he was named Carolina League Most Valuable Player for hitting .358 with a Lynchburg, Virginia, farm team. In 1984 he played on a Jackson, Mississippi team, where he met his wife, Terri Peel. In 1985 he batted .310 with the Triple-A (highest minor league) Tidewater Mets and was promoted to the parent team at midseason. In his first major league at-bat, he hit a home run off Cincinnati pitcher Mario Soto.

SERIES HERO. Dykstra's first full year with the Mets (1986) was an important season for the team. As a platoon centerfielder (a left-handed batter, Dykstra only played against right-handed pitchers), he helped New York win the National League Eastern division championship. He became famous in the League Championship Series where the Mets faced the Houston Astros in the best-of-seven series. In Game Three, he stroked a two-run homer in the bottom of the ninth to give the Mets a 6-5 victory. In Game Six he led off the ninth inning with a triple that sparked a Mets rally for the win. New York advanced to the World Series, and Dykstra had four hits—including a leadoff home run—in Game Three. The Mets went on to win an exciting World Series over the Boston Red Sox, four games to three.

Between 1986 and 1989 Dykstra shared Mets centerfielder duties with Mookie Wilson. When New York reached the League Championship Series again in 1988, Dykstra batted .429 with one home run and three runs batted in through four playoff games. This time the Mets lost the Championship Series to the Los Angeles Dodgers, four games to three.

BECOMES A PHILLIE. Dykstra was not particularly happy in New York. As a platoon player, he did not start every day. He felt he would perform better as an everyday player, and let the team know he was unhappy. In reaction to his complaints, the Mets traded Dykstra to the last-place Philadelphia Phillies on June 18, 1989. Phillies general manager Lee Thomas told *Sports Illustrated* that he traded for Dykstra hoping that his leadership would help motivate his under-achieving players. "We did our homework, and even though some of those guys weren't playing regularly, we knew they were winners," Thomas said. "The manager can't motivate a team by himself. He needs guys who will get on their teammates for not showing good work habits."

Before he could motivate others, however, Dykstra had to motivate himself. This proved tough on a losing team. As full-time centerfielder, Dykstra hit over .300 in his first month as a Phillie but finished the year at a mere .237. "People have to keep in mind that I had to make some adjustments to playing every day for a team that was out of it," he told *Sports Illustrated.* In the off-season, Thomas urged Dykstra to help turn the Phillies around. Determined to do so, Dykstra exercised daily to improve his endurance and came to spring training in 1990 ready to lead the team to victory.

SUPERSTAR

BIG SEASON. Dykstra's moment had arrived. He batted better than .400 through May of 1990 and finished the year with a solid .325 average. For the first time he was named starting centerfielder for the National League All-Star team. Dykstra tied for the National League lead in hits with 192, scored 106 runs (fifth in the league, and hit his first inside-the-park home run on July 24).

PERSONAL PROBLEMS. While fearless behavior is welcome on the baseball diamond, it is far less helpful off the field. Dykstra learned this lesson the hard way. On March 10, 1991, a newspaper in Jackson, Mississippi, reported that Dykstra had gambled away more than $50,000 playing poker. He was put on one-year probation by then major league commissioner Fay Vincent.

On May 6, less than two months after the gambling scandal, Dykstra drove his Mercedes-Benz into a tree, severely injuring himself and his passenger, Phillies's catcher Darren Daulton. Blood tests disclosed that Dykstra's blood alcohol level was twice the legal limit—he had spent the evening at a party for teammate John Kruk, who was soon to be married. Dykstra suffered a broken cheekbone and collarbone, and three broken ribs.

LOST SEASONS. Remarkably, Dykstra missed only 61 games following the accident. He returned to action on July 15, 1991, but six weeks later was sidelined again when he ran into an unpadded outfield wall at Riverfront Stadium in Cincinnati, Ohio and re-broke his collarbone. He missed the rest of the season for a total of 99 games lost to injuries.

Dykstra missed part of the 1992 season due to minor injuries. He managed to hit .301, but batted only 345 times. Along with his frustrations on the field, Dykstra continued to be criticized for his off-field behavior. "People always want to focus on the negative," he complained to the *Philadelphia Inquirer*. "People don't know that I gave $40,000 to a children's charity last year. People don't know how well I take care of my family. People don't know about all the autographs I've signed. People don't know about all the hospitals I've visited." Dykstra appeared in a video about drunken driving in which he admitted he was lucky to be alive.

> ## DYKSTRA ON DYKSTRA
>
> "The fans want to see me out on the field. That is how people are going to judge me—how I play baseball."

INJURY FREE. Dykstra returned to action in 1993 determined to silence his critics once and for all. Playing injury-free for the first time in two years, Dykstra had an outstanding season. He batted .305, hit a career-best 19 home runs, scored a league-leading 143 runs, and stole a career-best 37 bases. More important than his statistics, however, was his leadership. The Phillies, who had won only 70 games in 1992, won 97—easily winning the National League Eastern division title. For his effort Dykstra placed second in National League Most Valuable Player voting to winner **Barry Bonds** (see entry) of the San Francisco Giants.

WORLD SERIES. The Phillies were not through. Against the heavily favored Atlanta Braves, winners of 104 games in the regular season, Philadelphia pulled off a major upset, winning the National League Championship Series, four games to two. Dykstra won Game Four, 4-3, with a solo homer in the bottom of the tenth. In the World Series, against the defending champion Toronto Blue Jays, Dykstra was the Phillies's standout. He batted .348, hit four home runs, scored nine runs, and batted in eight. In the wild 15-14 Toronto win in Game Four, Dykstra had two home runs and a double, and also hit a three-run homer in the Sixth, and final, game to give the Phillies their last lead. He would have been the leading candidate for the series' Most Valuable Player if Philadelphia had won. But the Blue Jays managed to pull off a four-games-to-two victory.

Though never claiming to be a saint, Dykstra has worked to reform his off-field behavior, apologizing to those who consider him a role model. "I think people realize I am a human being and human beings screw up," he told the *Philadelphia Daily News.* "I never realized how an athlete reaches people. How he touches them."

WHERE TO WRITE

C/O PHILADELPHIA PHILLIES,

P.O. BOX 7575, PHILADELPHIA, PA 19101.

JOHN ELWAY

1960—

John Elway never quits, even when the odds are against his team, the Denver Broncos. During his eleven-year career, Elway has led the team to over 30 fourth quarter come-from-behind victories, and in the process, has quarterbacked the Broncos to three Super Bowl games as well as four American Football Conference (AFC) championship games. Blessed with one of the strongest arms in the National Football League (NFL), Elway has made the big play his trademark.

GROWING UP

John Albert Elway (along with his twin sister, Jana) was born June 28, 1960, in Port Angeles, Washington. His dad, Jack, was a college football coach, and moved with his family from job to job. When he was a kid Elway's favorite sport was baseball. "I remember Dad was a very hard worker, but when there was time for us to be together, it was always quality time," Elway told the *Orlando Sentinel*. "We'd go out and have batting practice, and those times were very special. Sometimes I'd be [Yankees's great] Mickey Mantle, and other times I'd be [former Giants's star] Willie Mays. It changed every day."

"I've given 110 percent on every play. I always want to win, no matter what it takes."— John Elway

A natural right-handed hitter, Elway was encouraged by his dad to practice left-handed hitting as well.

Elway batted over .500 playing baseball at Granada Hills High School in Los Angeles, California. He led the school to two city football championships and as a senior in 1979, passed for 1,837 yards, 19 touchdowns, and was the most highly sought player in the country by major colleges. He credits his football ability to his dad, who taught him how to run and throw. "He had enormous confidence," his high school coach Jack Neumeier told the *Los Angeles Daily News*. "I don't think I ever coached a competitor like John Elway." In addition to athletics, Elway was a straight-A student.

COLLEGE DAYS. Elway eventually decided to attend Stanford University, where he played on both the football and baseball teams. In his four seasons at Stanford, he threw 77 touchdown passes, was a two-time All-American selection, broke five National Collegiate Athletic Association (NCAA) records, and finished second in the Heisman Trophy balloting in 1983 to Herschel Walker of the University of Georgia. (The Heisman Trophy is awarded annually to the best college football player.) Though Elway quit playing college baseball in his sophomore year, the New York Yankees signed him to play in the minor leagues, where he batted .318. "It was enjoyable," he told the *Akron Beacon Journal*. "I found out what pro baseball was all about—and maybe I could have made it."

COLTS NO, BRONCOS YES. Elway almost got the chance to make baseball his full-time career. In April 1983 the Baltimore Colts, who had finished last among the NFL's 28 clubs the season before, made him the first pick of the draft. Elway who had asked the Colts not to draft him, did not like their coach, Frank Kush, and wanted to play in the West. After the draft he considered giving up football to sign a long-term deal with the

Yankees. A week later, the frustrated Colts traded Elway to the Denver Broncos for two first-round draft picks and quarterback Mark Herrmann. Before he played one down, Elway signed a contract that made him the second-highest paid quarterback in football.

TOUGH ROOKIE YEAR. His rookie year was tough and Elway struggled to meet the high expectations of the team and the fans. He was taken out in each of his first two starts, replaced by veteran Steve DeBerg, and suffered a sprained elbow, making it difficult for him to pass. But Denver coach Dan Reeves stuck with his rookie, and Elway improved enough that season to lead the Broncos to a 9-7 record. His statistics were not impressive: seven touchdowns, and 14 interceptions, with less than half of his passes completed. Fans began to boo when Elway took the field. "That was the first time I realized there were people who hated

John Elway

me," he told the *Boston Globe*. "I just felt terrible. I'd come in and everyone thought I was supposed to walk on water. A young kid is entitled to make mistakes in college but, at this level, you're not entitled to do that."

Elway's playing improved in 1984, and Reeves traded DeBerg—a move designed to show Elway that the quarterback job was his. He responded by completing 56 percent of his passes, throwing for 18 touchdowns, and leading the Broncos to a 13-3 record and the AFC West division title. Denver lost to the Pittsburgh Steelers, 24-17, in the first round of the playoffs, but the Broncos had proven they were a team on the rise.

In 1985 Elway became one of the NFL's top young quarterbacks. He was second in the NFL in completions (327) and passing yards (3,891). He led all AFC quarterbacks in rushing for the second straight year and led the NFL in total yards (passing and rushing yards combined). He threw for more than 250 yards seven times. He had a four-touchdown game, three

three-touchdown games, two two-touchdown games, and finished the season with 22 touchdown passes. The Broncos won 11 games, but did not make the playoffs. As quarterback, Elway took most of the blame from the fans.

SUPERSTAR

"THE DRIVE." In 1986 though Elway's statistics were not the best, he ranked 11th among NFL starting quarterbacks and threw for 3,485 yards and 19 touchdowns. More importantly, he inspired his teammates who won 11 games and the AFC Western division. The Broncos defeated the New England Patriots, 22-17, in the first round of the playoffs. In the AFC Championship game against the Cleveland Browns Elway was a standout. The Broncos trailed the Browns 20-13 and had the ball on their own three-yard line with just 5:32 left to play. Elway, bothered by an injured ankle but showing great control under intense pressure, led the Broncos downfield in what became known as "The Drive." A five-yard pass from Elway to Mark Jackson tied the score, and the Broncos won the game, 23-20, in overtime.

"The Drive ranks as one of the historic events of football history," wrote *Sports Illustrated*. "It was movie stuff—Elway picking apart a loose Cleveland defense like a master locksmith opening a vault." The victory over the Browns put the Broncos into Super Bowl XXI, where they played the New York Giants—a team that had gone 14-2 during the regular season. Denver won the first half, 10-9, but after halftime the Giants took command, outscoring Denver 30-10 on their way to a 39-20 victory.

BACK TO THE BOWL. In 1987 Elway led the Broncos to another AFC Western division title, with Denver earning a 10-4-1 record in a season interrupted by a player's strike. In only 12 games, Elway threw for 3,198 yards and 19 touchdowns. He passed for two touchdowns and ran for one more as the Broncos defeated the Houston Oilers 34-10 in the first round of the playoffs. For the second year in a row Elway crushed the Cleveland Browns's Super Bowl hopes in the AFC Championship game, leading the Broncos to an exciting 38-33 win. Elway threw for 281 yards and three touchdowns. But that was the end of the line for Denver, as they lost 42-10 in the Super Bowl to the Washington Redskins, with Elway throwing three interceptions.

Denver missed the playoffs in 1988, but came back in 1989 to post an 11-5 record and win the AFC Western division. Elway led the Broncos to another come-from-behind victory in the first round of the playoffs. Trailing 23-17 in the fourth quarter, the Broncos marched downfield to score the winning touchdown in a 24-23 victory. The Broncos defeated the Cleveland Browns 37-21 in the AFC Championship game for the third time in four years. Elway threw for 385 yards and three touchdowns in the game.

SUPER ROUT. In the Super Bowl, the Broncos met **Joe Montana** (see entry) and the San Francisco 49ers, who were going for their fourth Super Bowl win. They got it, routing Denver 55-10. Elway had perhaps the worst game of his career, throwing for only 108 yards and two interceptions. Afterward, he was asked what it meant to have been blown out of three Super Bowls in four years. "It means we've lost three times, nothing more," Elway told *Sports Illustrated.* "Can I win the big one? I think I can. Will we be back? I like to think so. Only when I give up will I be a loser."

The Broncos fell to 5-11 in 1990, the first losing record of Elway's career. Things went so badly that a local radio disc jockey sat outside on a billboard until the Broncos won a game. He sat up there for six straight weeks. But in 1991 Denver won 11 games and were once again the AFC Western division champions. With Denver trailing in the fourth quarter, Elway made another legendary comeback, leading the Broncos to a 26-24 victory over the Houston Oilers. For the first time in his career, though, Elway could not lead his team to victory in the AFC Championship game. The Buffalo Bills defeated Denver 10-7 with Elway throwing for only 121 yards.

NEW COACH. During the 1992 season there were hard feelings between Elway and coach Reeves. Elway, who was coming off

THE WHOLE PACKAGE

Elway's rifle arm, which can accurately throw the ball 75 yards, or three quarters of a football field, is responsible for a large part of his success. A fearless opponent, Elway often runs the ball himself when his receivers are covered, and plays his best under pressure. "One of my strengths is my competitiveness!" he told *Inside Sports.* " I can say that, to this day, I've given 110 percent on every play. I always want to win, no matter what it takes."

Elway has a 98-53-1 regular-season record, has taken his team to four AFC championship games and three Super Bowls, and has led the Broncos to over 30 fourth quarter come-from-behind victories. "Every quarterback wants to throw the ball, sure, but you've got to stay within the framework [plan] of what the team is trying to accomplish," Elway told *Sport*. "I respect that. Winning is always much more important than individual statistics."

shoulder surgery, accused Reeves of being too tough on the players and not using Elway's skill to its best advantage. Elway felt he wasn't allowed to throw enough, and that his statistics were not as impressive as they could be because of Reeves's conservative offense that stressed a strong running game instead. After an 8-8 season, during which Elway missed four straight games with an injury, Reeves was fired and replaced by defensive coach Wade Phillips. The new coach put in place a new offense, signed two quality offensive linemen, and convinced Elway to sign a new contract with the Broncos.

In 1993 with the team's new offense in place, Elway had his best individual season ever. He led the NFL with 4,030 yards passing, led the AFC with 25 touchdowns, had only 10 interceptions, was the highest rated quarterback in the AFC, and was named the starting quarterback for the AFC in the Pro Bowl (all-star) game. "I wish I'd been able to run this offense my whole career," Elway told *Sport*. "This offense is perfect for me." Denver finished 9-7, but lost in the first round of the playoffs 42-24 to the Los Angeles Raiders. Despite the loss, Elway was happy with his season.

OFF THE FIELD. Elway and his wife, Janet, live in Aurora, Colorado with their two daughters, Jessica and Jordan. When he's not playing football, he likes to play golf. Though one of the NFL's best quarterbacks, Elway knows that he won't be considered an all-time great until he finally wins a Super Bowl. "All it's going to take is one Super Bowl win, and everything that happened in the past will be wiped out," he told the *Sporting News*. "Just one win."

WHERE TO WRITE

C/O DENVER BRONCOS, 13655 E. DOVE VALLEY PKWY., ENGLEWOOD, CO 80112.

JANET EVANS

1971—

Janet Evans took to the water when she was a year old, and by the time she was 17 she had set three world records. Often considered too small for competition, Evans made up for her lack of size with hard work and determination and in 1988 won three Olympic gold medals. In 1992 she returned to the Olympics, winning another gold and a silver medal to become only the second American woman to win four Olympic gold medals. Despite her record-breaking success, Evans has remained humble and tries to be "Just Janet," a young woman who loves to swim.

GROWING UP

Janet Evans was born August 28, 1971, in Fullerton, California. She is the youngest of three children, and has two older brothers, David and John. Her dad, Paul, is a veterinarian, and her mom, Barbara, is her unofficial coach. While growing up, it was her mom who made sure Evans ate right, went to bed on time, and practiced. She inherited her father's sense of humor. "My dad's good humor gets me through life," she told *Sports Illustrated*. "His philosophy is, you only live once. He tells me to enjoy my swimming successes, to have fun with interviews and to get the most out of being young."

"There are so many people out there in the world, and I have a world record. Why me?"—Janet Evans

By the time she was eight months old Evans was walking, and at just a year old she went in the water at the North Orange County YMCA pool. Her mother remembers her being full of energy, always tagging along to play with her brothers. "When Janet was two, she would stand in the middle of the kitchen, doing the Hula Hoop for 20 minutes nonstop," her mom told *Sports Illustrated*. The only thing that would calmed her down was being in the water, so her mom enrolled her in swimming lessons. A quick learner, Evans was able to do the butterfly and breaststroke by the time she was three years old.

WHO'S TOO SMALL? Coaches quickly realized Evans's talent, and soon she was breaking records on the Swim Team of Placentia. When she was 10, she broke the national record for children 10-and-under in the 200-meter freestyle race. The next year she qualified for the U.S. Junior Olympics and finished 47th out of 81 swimmers. Because she was small for her age, officials wanted Evans to race against younger kids. "Janet fought and fought with one official," Barbara Evans recalled to *Sports Illustrated*. "He said, 'I think you belong with the 10-year-olds,' She said, 'I think you're wrong. This is my race.'"

Evans made up for her size by moving her arms and legs faster than her opponents. "I never saw myself as being small," she told *Sports Illustrated*. "Size doesn't matter as long as you can get to the end of the pool faster than everybody else." She also trained harder than her opponents. Every day she and her parents would get up at five a.m. so that Evans could swim before school started at El Dorado High School. After classes she lifted weights and rode an exercise bike before swimming again in the afternoon. Evans worked hard enough to be able to eat anything she wanted, including her favorite—junk food.

MOVING UP THE CHARTS. The hard work paid off as Evans began to move up in the world rankings. In 1986 she qualified to swim at the Goodwill Games in Moscow, the former Soviet Union. She finished third in both the 800- and 1500-meter freestyle races, and later in the year won the 400- and 800-meter freestyle races and the 400-meter individual medley at the U.S. Open. (In an individual medley, the swimmer uses each of four strokes, starting off with the butterfly, then switching to the backstroke, the breaststroke, and finally the freestyle.) Her victories, at the age of 15, made Evans the best female swimmer in the United States in these events.

WORLD RECORDS. Not satisfied with being the best in the United States, Evans set out to lead the world in 1987. At the U.S. Long Course Championship in July, 1987, she set her first world records, in the 800- and 1500-meter freestyle events. At the U.S. Indoor Championships, she added the 400-meter world record. Evans held world records in the three long-distance freestyle events for women—the second woman ever to accomplish this feat. She also broke her own records in the 800- and 1500-meter freestyle races and won the 400- and 800-meter freestyle races and the 400-meter individual medley at the 1988 U.S. Olympic Trials. She was favored to win each race at the 1988 Summer Olympics in Seoul, South Korea.

OLYMPIC CHAMP. Evans went to the Olympics during her summer vacation from high school. She was the youngest (17) and smallest (five-feet tall and barely 100 pounds) member of the U.S. Olympic women's swim team. She was also the best, blowing away her rivals by winning the 400-meter freestyle in world record time, setting a new American record in the 400-meter individual medley, and a new Olympic record in the 800-meter freestyle. Evans became the fifth woman ever to win three or more individual (not team) gold swimming medals in one Olympics. If women had been allowed to swim

Janet Evans

the 1500-meter freestyle race, Evans would also have been the favorite to win at that distance.

With her Olympic medals and her world records, Evans was the star of the U.S. Olympic women's swim team, the only one to win a medal in an individual event. Her success was a result of hard work and training. "I'm proud of myself for not giving in," Evans said. "I didn't skip workouts. I couldn't have won a gold medal if I did that. Not to be boastful or anything like that, but you have to be proud of yourself if you win an Olympic gold medal. To know all the work paid off. I accomplished my goal." Evans slept with her medals under her pillow.

"JUST JANET." Being a star isn't always easy, especially for a teenager. During the Olympics Evans appeared on national television, magazine covers, radio reports, and the front page of daily newspapers. She was homesick and missed her boyfriend, Aaron Behle, with whom she'd gone to the prom where she was crowned princess of the junior class. Because of her success Evans was afraid her classmates would treat her differently. She wanted to be "Just Janet" again. "I was talking to my friends about meeting me at the airport," she said before leaving Seoul. "And they said, 'When you get off the airplane, there's going to be all kinds of photographers' and I say 'No!' and they say 'Yes there will' and I think, 'Oh, NO!'" Evans was later invited to visit President Bush at the White House.

When Evans returned home, her neighbors threw a block party with barbecued food, banners, and balloons. Evans was asked to be a spokesperson for several products which would have earned her a good deal of money. Instead she decided to attend Stanford University where, for two years, she continued to swim, grew two inches, and gained 15 pounds. Other swimmers began passing her up, especially in the individual medley. Evans didn't get along with her coach at Stanford, and in 1990 transferred to the University of Texas where she joined Texas Aquatics, coached by the U.S. Olympic team coach, Mark Shubert.

TOUGH TIMES. At the Pan Pacific Games in 1989, Evans broke her own world record in the 800-meter freestyle. At the 1992 Goodwill Games she won the 400-, 800-, and 1500-meter freestyle races, and finished second in the 400-meter individual medley. Entering the 1992 U.S. Olympic Trials, Evans was expected to qualify for the team in up to three different events. She easily won the 400- and 800-meter freestyle races, but surprisingly, failed to qualify for the team in the 400-meter individual medley. Evans was disappointed. "She doesn't like to lose," her former Stanford teammate Alex Kostich told *The New York Times Magazine*. "I was always really impressed with how she would talk about winning."

OLYMPIC REPEAT. At the Olympics held in Barcelona, Spain, Evans found it difficult to continue training, but found inspiration from her teammates, especially 15-year old Anita Nall, the world record holder in the 200-meter breaststroke. "I think that she like, re-inspires me," Evans told the *New York Times Magazine*. "I think it's harder the second time around. It's harder to stay on top because people are gunning for you. I like looking at Anita and am just trying to like, have the same attitude because she reminds me exactly of how I was in '88." Evans won the gold medal in the 800-meter freestyle and the silver in the 400-meter freestyle. She became only the third American woman to win four gold Olympic medals (diver Pat McCormick and sprinter Evelyn Ashford were the others), a record broken by speedskater **Bonnie Blair** (see entry), who has now won five.

POOL, NOT PEER, PRESSURE

Evans says that swimming helped her deal with the pressures of the teen years. "I've traveled around the world" she told *Sports Illustrated*. "A lot of kids my age party and try to be cool. They haven't found where they want to be. Most teenagers figure if they don't do what other people do, they won't be accepted. Well, if you like yourself, it doesn't matter what anyone else thinks, as long as you're happy. Twice a day, I push my body to the limit, test my self-discipline. I know what I want out of life. I have a good sense of myself, thanks to swimming."

Evans continued to compete in 1993, but it is doubtful she will swim in the 1996 Olympics in Atlanta, Georgia. When she quits swimming, there will be some things she won't miss. "The chlorine [put into the pool to keep the water clean] makes my feet sore and dries all my skin and I hate that," she told the *Chicago Tribune*. "My hair sometimes gets yucky. I always wanted long hair, but I could never have it. I can do everything I wanted to do as a kid after I quit."

OUT OF THE POOL. Evans loves dancing, going to movies, and shopping. But dating and relationships are not always easy for her. "Yeah, you can always tell when a guy wants to take you out just because you're an Olympic athlete," she said in the *New York Times Magazine*. "They're the ones who just want to talk about swimming. The other ones, they go, 'Oh, you're an Olympic swimmer? Oh, O.K., where do you want to eat?'" Despite her success, Evans hasn't let it go to her head. "There are so many people out there in the world, and I have a world record. Why me?," she asked the *St. Louis Post-Dispatch*. "It's kind of weird. I try not to think about it too much, but it still boggles my mind."

WHERE TO WRITE

C/O U.S. SWIMMING, U.S. OLYMPIC TRAINING CENTER, 1750 E. BOULDER ST., COLORADO SPRINGS, CO 80909.

PATRICK EWING

1962—

Although most basketball players start playing at an early age, Patrick Ewing began playing basketball in high school. Amazingly, by the time he reached his senior year, he had become the best high school player in the country. Overcoming reading and speech problems, Ewing became a solid student and earned his degree from Georgetown University, where he also became the most dominating college basketball player in the United States. Now a National Basketball Association (NBA) superstar and two-time Olympic champion, Ewing has only one major basketball goal he hopes to achieve: winning an NBA world championship.

GROWING UP

Patrick Aloysius Ewing was born August 5, 1962, in Kingston, Jamaica. He was the fifth child in the family of seven children of Carl and Dorothy Ewing. His father was a mechanic in Kingston. Ewing liked to draw when he was young and wanted to become a professional artist. His mother came to the United States in 1971 and worked at Massachusetts General Hospital. The Ewing children and their father followed her over a period of years. Patrick came to America

People think "I'm mean. But I'm not that."—Patrick Ewing

on January 11, 1975. "My coming to America fulfilled a lifelong dream of my mother," Ewing told *Time* magazine. "She told us America is the land of opportunity. I enjoy being an American, but I still miss the natural beauty, the waterfalls and the landscapes of Jamaica."

LEARNS BASKETBALL. In Jamaica Ewing was the goalie on a soccer team and also played cricket. Until he arrived in America Ewing had never seen a basketball game, but liked the sport immediately. His height helped Ewing make his junior high team—he was six-feet-one inch and could dunk the basketball—he was clumsy on the court and unfamiliar with the plays. He made the varsity basketball team at Rindge and Latin High School in Cambridge, Massachusetts, and started to polish his skills. "He was a hard worker, and if he didn't know something, he'd ask you a thousand times until he got it right," his high school coach Mike Jarvis told *New York Newsday.* "He became a star, the tall guy and great player, but he wasn't always a great player. He went through times where he was clumsy and awkward. We had to tell him to be tall, walk tall, be proud of it."

CHOOSES GEORGETOWN. His high school team won three state championships during Ewing's career and he was the first high school player ever invited to play in the U.S. Olympic basketball trials in 1980. Ewing had the talent to be the best high school center in the country, but had problems with his studies, mainly because the English language spoken in the United States is different in many ways from English spoken in Jamaica. When colleges started to recruit Ewing to play for their schools they were told that he would need special educational attention and tutoring, assistance that helped him improve his reading and speaking skills. Ewing finally decided to attend Georgetown University in Washington, D.C., where he played for one of the few African American major college coaches, John Thompson. Thompson had first seen him play when Ewing was a sophomore and knew, even then, that he would be a star.

FIRST FINAL FOUR. During his first year at Georgetown, the Hoyas finished with a 30-7 record and won the championship of the Big East Conference tournament. The team was invited to the National Collegiate Athletic Association (NCAA) and advanced to the national semifinals, defeating the Louisville Cardinals, 50-46. Ewing scored 23 points and grabbed 11 rebounds in the championship game against the North Carolina Tar Heels, but it wasn't enough. **Michael Jordan** (see entry) hit a last-second jump shot to put the Tar Heels ahead, and then Hoya guard Freddie Brown, mistaking Tar Heel James Worthy for one of his own teammates, threw him the ball. This mistake sealed the North Carolina victory. Ewing was named to the all-tournament team.

Patrick Ewing

NATIONAL CHAMPS. In Ewing's second season the Hoya's finished 22-10 in regular season. They were again invited to the NCAA tournament, but lost in the second round, 66-57, to Memphis State. The Hoyas were the most dominant team in college basketball during the next two seasons. Georgetown finished 34-3 in the 1983-84 regular season, winning the Big East and tournament titles. After a first-round scare against Southern Methodist University, which the Hoyas won 37-36, Georgetown began to roll, beating the University of Nevada-Las Vegas, the University of Dayton, and the University of Kentucky on their way to the final game, where they faced **Hakeem Olajuwon** (see entry) and the University of Houston Cougars. Ewing had only 10 points in the final, but pulled down nine rebounds, had four block shots, and played outstanding defense on Olajuwon. The Hoyas won the game, 84-

75, and Ewing was named the tournament's Most Valuable Player.

BIG UPSET. Between his junior and senior seasons, Ewing played on the U.S. Olympic basketball team which won the gold medal at the 1984 Summer Olympics in Los Angeles, California. During his senior season Georgetown was the overwhelming favorite to repeat as national champs. They again won the Big East regular season and tournament championships, finishing 31-2. For the second straight season they won their way to the national championship game, this time against the Villanova Wildcats, a team that barely qualified for the tournament. In one of the biggest upsets of all time, Villanova defeated the powerful Hoyas, 66-64.

ONE FOR MOM. After each of his seasons at Georgetown, professional teams made offers for Ewing to join their teams. But he had promised his mom that he would stay at Georgetown and complete his studies. His mom died in 1983, but Ewing kept his promise, getting his degree in fine arts. "I promised my mother before she died that I would graduate on time, and I'm proud to have fulfilled that promise," Ewing told *Ebony*. Because of the special tutoring he received at Georgetown, some fans and writers criticized Ewing, saying he was only at Georgetown because he could play basketball. A fan at one game wore a T-shirt saying "Ewing Kant Read Dis."

These things hurt Ewing and made him shy around reporters. This shyness, and the intense look he wore on his face during games, made people think he wasn't very friendly. Georgetown also played a tough, physical style of defense, one that often led to fist-fights. Added to this was "Hoya Paranoia," the name given to Coach Thompson's rule that often made his players unavailable for interviews. Thompson's rules didn't bother Ewing, as he told *Interview* magazine: "I didn't want to talk to the press. I just wanted to go about doing things, going to school and hanging out with my friends and enjoying college life."

SUPERSTAR

TOP CHOICE. Ewing graduated from Georgetown as the school's all-time leading rebounder (1,316) and shot blocker (493), and had a career scoring average of 15.3 points per game. In his four seasons the Hoyas compiled a 121-23 record, won one national championship, and played in the national championship game three times. After his senior season Ewing won several national player of the year awards and later was voted best college player of the 1980s. He was so highly sought by professional teams that the NBA started their draft lottery to keep teams from losing deliberately in order to pick him.

ROOKIE OF THE YEAR. In the end the New York Knicks were the team lucky enough to get the first pick in the 1985 draft. They picked Ewing. Knicks fans expected Ewing to be the team's savior and he made an instant contribution, making the All-Star team and leading the Knicks in scoring (20 points per game) and rebounding (nine per game) in his first season (1985-86). The Knicks knew that Ewing was good defensively, but his offensive skills surprised them. As *Ebony* reported: "it's his offensive ability that has everybody talking. He has unveiled a virtually unstoppable 15- to 18-feet jump shot that seems to slip into the basket as softly as a hen sits on her eggs." Ewing injured his knee and missed 32 games, but his performance was impressive enough to win him the NBA Rookie of the Year award.

Even though Ewing was developing into an NBA star, he couldn't turn the Knicks into winners all by himself. In his first two seasons New York finished in last place in the Atlantic Division. They improved in the 1987-88 season, finishing third in their division and qualifying for the playoffs. They lost in the first round to the Boston Celtics, but it was clear they were an improving team. For the third straight year Ewing averaged over 20 points per game (20.2) in the 1987-88 season, but it was the first time he played in all 82 games.

DIVISION CHAMPS. Before the 1988-89 season the Knicks traded center Bill Cartwright to the Chicago Bulls for forward Charles Oakley. The trade was good for Ewing, because he could now move back to his natural center position from forward. Ewing was also happy with the fast-breaking and full-court pressing style employed by Knicks coach Rick Pitino, a style very similar to the one Ewing played at Georgetown. In the 1988-89 season the Knicks won the Atlantic division title, their first since 1971, and Ewing was a big reason, scoring 22.7 points, pulling down 9.2 rebounds, and blocking 3.51 shots (third in the NBA) per game. The Knicks defeated the Philadelphia 76ers in the first round of the playoffs, but lost to **Michael Jordan** (see entry) and the Chicago Bulls.

Ewing had his best individual season in 1989-90, earning a career best in scoring at 28.9 point per game (third in the NBA), pulling down 10.9 rebounds per game (fifth in the NBA), and blocking 3.99 shots (second in the NBA) per contest. For the first time Ewing was a first team All-NBA pick (he was on the second team the previous two years), but the Knicks did not do as well as the season before. Pitino resigned before the season ended to take the coaching job at the University of Kentucky, and the Knicks finished only third in their division. They lost the first two games of their first playoff series against the Boston Celtics, but came back to take the series, 3-2. Ewing scored 33, 44, and 31 points in the games the Knicks won. The Knicks lost the next series, to the eventual NBA champion Detroit Pistons, and once again Ewing's season ended in frustration.

ULTIMATUM. The Knicks fell even further in 1990-91, winning only 38 games and barely qualifying for the playoffs. Ewing continued to play at superstar level, scoring 26.8 points (fifth in the NBA), grabbing 11.2 rebounds (fifth in the NBA), and blocking 3.19 shots (third in the NBA) per game. When the Knicks lost in three straight to the eventual NBA champion Chicago Bulls, Ewing, frustrated by his losing team, tried to become a free agent, which would make it possible for him to sign with any team. He eventually re-signed with the Knicks after the team agreed to make more of an effort to win. The first step in this process was hiring coach Pat Riley, who had guided the Los Angeles Lakers to four NBA championships.

Ewing had another great season in 1991-92, scoring 24 a game (fifth in the NBA) and grabbing 11.2 rebounds per contest, and the Knicks tied for the Atlantic division title with the Boston Celtics. Going into the playoffs the Knicks felt confident that this was their year, but the Bulls had other ideas. In a tough, back and forth series, the Bulls won the Eastern Conference semifinal series, four games to three. The Knicks were disappointed, but felt they were the team to beat in the 1992-93 season.

"DREAM TEAM." During the summer of 1992 Ewing was a member of the U.S. Olympic men's basketball "Dream Team" that routed the competition in Barcelona, Spain. Ewing scored 24.2 points and pulled down a career best 12.1 rebounds per game in the 1992-93 season. The Knicks, who led the NBA in defense, won the Atlantic Division with 60 wins. For the first time in Ewing's professional career the Knicks, who defeated the Indiana Pacers and Charlotte Hornets in the first two rounds of the playoffs, were in the Eastern Conference finals—one step away from the championship round. Unfortunately, they faced their old rivals the Bulls, who again knocked the Knicks out of the playoffs, four games to two. The Knicks repeated as Atlantic division champion in 1993-94. Ewing scored 24.5 points per game and grabbed 11.2 rebounds per contest.

OFF THE COURT. Ewing and his wife, Rita, a Georgetown University law student, live in Potomac, Maryland, a suburb of Washington, D.C. They have one son, Patrick Ewing, Jr. A spokesperson for several products, Ewing also donates much of his time to charities, including the Special Olympics and the Children's Health Fund. When he's not playing basketball, Ewing likes to listen to blues and reggae music, shop, and lift weights. Because he plays so hard on the court and doesn't smile much some people think he's a mean person. "[People

THE CENTERS OF ATTENTION

Ewing began a tradition at Georgetown University, a tradition of great centers. A former center himself, Coach Thompson seems to have a special skill for instructing players on how to play that position. After Ewing left, Alonzo Mourning, now of the Charlotte Hornets, and Dkembe Mutombo, now of the Denver Nuggets, starred at center for the Hoyas. Today, Othella Harrington plays for the Hoyas and carries on the Ewing tradition. The centers, old and young, work out together, the more experienced players passing on advice to the younger stars.

think that] I'm mean. But I'm not that. When I play basketball, they only see that side of me, and when you're on the
court, I still have to be another person. I have to live in the
world around me."

WHERE TO WRITE

C/O NEW YORK KNICKS, MADISON SQUARE GARDEN,

FOUR PENNSYLVANIA PLAZA, NEW YORK, NY 10001.

NICK FALDO

1957—

Nick Faldo decided on a career in golf while watching a televised tournament and has been working to be the best player in the world ever since. As one of the top-ranked golfers in the world, Faldo has had great success in golf's major tournaments—the Masters, British Open, U.S. Open, and Professional Golfer's Association (PGA) Championship—winning three British Opens and two Masters. Early in his career, Faldo was often accused of being too competitive for his own good, but has worked to change. His goal is to be happy as well as successful.

GROWING UP

Nicholas Alexander Faldo was born July 18, 1957, in Welwyn Garden City, Hertfordshire, England. An only child, he grew up in a middle-class home. His father, George, was a book-keeper at a chemical company. His mother, Joyce, wanting to give her son the best of everything, took him to museums and the opera, and enrolled him in dance and piano lessons. Faldo liked this cultural education, except for opera.

LOVE OF SPORTS. It soon became clear to Faldo's mother that her son was more interested in sports than culture. He loved to

"I want people in years to come to say to each other 'Did you ever see Nick Faldo play?' And for those who didn't, to feel sorry they missed out."—Nick Faldo

swim, play soccer, and run track, and was good at all of them. One of his teachers at the Thumbswood primary school wrote on Faldo's report card: "Nick's future will be in sport. He sets his standards high, and dedication will be the key to his success." Faldo excelled in basketball, bicycle racing, canoeing, cricket, rugby, soccer, swimming, and track and field during his years at the Sir Frederic Osborn Comprehensive School. When his parents gave him a bike for his birthday one year, Faldo took it apart and put it back together again, just to see how it worked.

CAREER CHOICE. Faldo first became interested in golf when he saw the legendary Jack Nicklaus playing in the televised Masters tournament. The next day he talked his mother into paying for golf lessons. To save money, Faldo borrowed clubs from neighbors and used stray golf balls from the neighborhood golf course. His mother, who had taken a job as a silk cutter to earn extra money, made him a golf bag. After a few weeks he played his first round of golf, shooting a 78.

After his father took him to the 1973 British Open, Faldo decided to become a professional golfer. He told his parents that when he turned 16 he was quitting school to play golf full-time. His parents didn't like the idea, but Faldo was determined. Instead of taking a low-paying job at a golf course, he spent his time practicing golf, riding his bike to the course almost every morning.

TURNS PRO. In 1975 Faldo won two important tournaments, the British Youth Amateur and the English Amateur Championships. After his successful amateur (unpaid) career, Faldo turned professional in 1976 at the age of 19. An instant success, he was named the European Rookie of the Year in 1977 and became the youngest player ever named to Britain's Ryder Cup team. (The Ryder Cup is a tournament held every two years in which a team of players from the United States plays a team made up of players from Europe.)

Faldo continued to improve over the next several years. He won the British PGA Championship in 1978, 1980, and 1981. He won the European PGA championship in 1981 and finished in the top five at the British Open twice, in 1978 and 1982. He was the leading money winner on the European Tour in 1983 and had 11 top-ten finishes in 16 tournaments. In 1984 Faldo won his first tournament in the United States—the first Englishman to do so in twelve years.

TOO COMPETITIVE? A fierce competitor who stopped at nothing to win, Faldo became one of the most unpopular players on the tour. "If I start smiling," he told one reporter. "I might lose track of what I'm trying to do." His reputation was injured when he turned in another player for a minor rule violation during a tournament, and he was also criticized by other players and tournament officials for his slow play. He practiced alone, complained about playing conditions, and made fun of other players' golf swings. So focused was Faldo on his golfing that he either didn't notice how other players felt about him or he didn't care. When people asked him why he was unpopular, he blamed the press, saying they lied about him. "I don't think I have an image problem with the public," he told *Golf* magazine. "I get a lot of fan mail. My problem is with the press."

In 1985 Faldo divorced his first wife, Melanie, whom he had married when he was 21 years old. Even though they were divorcing, Melanie defended her ex-husband. "I used to read stories about him in the newspapers," she complained in *Golf*. "And I knew this wasn't the real Nick. They'd got it wrong. It was a false picture, as though the real person wasn't getting through."

"FOLDO?" Despite his golfing success, critics said that Faldo couldn't win big tournaments. They gave him the nickname "Foldo," after he faded in the final rounds of three of golf's

Nick Faldo

major tournaments in 1984—the Masters, British Open, and the PGA Championship. Faldo knew that in order to improve he needed help. He turned to a new coach, David Leadbetter, who discovered that Faldo was a strong but incomplete golfer. Faldo and Leadbetter worked on Faldo's swing for two years, attempting to make it perfect. Faldo practiced hard, hitting golf balls until his hands bled. By 1987 he was ready to become a star.

BREAKTHROUGH. In early 1987 Faldo won the Peugeot Spanish Open, his first win since 1984. He was confident entering the 1987 British Open, and played well. Going into the final round, he trailed American Paul Azinger by only one stroke. Showing great concentration and consistency, Faldo parred every hole during his final round. When Azinger bogeyed the last two holes, Faldo won his first major tournament. Following his victory, Faldo was awarded the MBE (Member of the British Parliament) by Queen Elizabeth II.

At the 1987 Ryder Cup tournament, Faldo helped lead the European team to a second straight victory over the United States. In 1988 he continued his great play in the major tournaments. He tied for the lead at the end of regulation at the U.S. Open, but lost in an 18-hole playoff to American Curtis Strange. He finished third in the British Open and fourth in the PGA Championship, and made it clear that he was a player to be reckoned with.

TAKES MASTERS. Faldo continued to make his mark in 1989, scoring his second major win at the Masters tournament. Tied for the lead with the legendary Lee Trevino after two rounds, Faldo shot a 77 in the third round and seemed to be out of contention. Refusing to give up, Faldo shot a 65 in the final round, tying Scott Hoch for the lead at the end of regulation. On the first hole of the sudden-death playoff, Faldo hit the ball into a sand trap. He bogeyed the hole, but Hoch missed a two-feet par putt to keep Faldo in the tournament. On the second hole of the playoff, Faldo sank a 25-feet birdie putt that gave him the win. Faldo was given the famous green jacket that is awarded to the winner of the tournament.

MASTERS REPEAT. Faldo won four other tournaments in 1989, including the World Match Play Championship. As the year ended he was the number-two ranked golfer in the world. In 1990 he repeated as Master's champion, winning once again in a playoff. Down by three strokes entering the final round, Faldo was paired with Jack Nicklaus, the player who had inspired him to take up golf. He birdied three of the last six holes in his final round to make up a four-shot deficit and catch the leader, Raymond Floyd.

On the first hole of the sudden-death playoff against Floyd, Faldo made a clutch four-feet putt to save par. On the second playoff hole, Floyd hit a shot into the water, which cost him valuable strokes. Faldo repeated as Master's champion when he registered a par on the hole. He became only the second player (Jack Nicklaus was the first in 1965 and 1966) to win back-to-back Master's championships. "I was glad when I saw I was paired with Jack [in the final round]," Faldo admitted in *Golf*. "When I won, I was hoping they'd have him put the green jacket on me."

SUPERSTAR

THE BEST. In 1990 Faldo established himself as the best golfer in the world. In June he barely missed qualifying for a playoff in the U.S. Open by missing a 15-feet birdie putt on the last hole. The British Open was played at St. Andrews—the second-oldest golf course in the world. One stroke behind after the first round, Faldo and Australian Greg Norman each tied

---

EQUAL OPPORTUNITY EMPLOYER

Faldo made history in 1990 when he hired Fanny Sunesson as his full-time caddie, the person who carries a player's golf bag and gives advice on what kind of shot to hit. The young woman from Sweden became the first full-time female caddie on the men's professional tour. Female caddies have traditionally had trouble getting jobs, because many people feel they aren't strong enough to carry a golf bag over 18 holes of golf.

the British Open record for 36 holes at 132. Faldo played with Norman in the third round, shooting a 67, while Norman, feeling the pressure, shot 76. Faldo's 54-hole score of 199 set another British Open record. Leading by five strokes going into the final round, Faldo held off American Payne Stewart—who at one point cut the lead to two—and ended up winning by five strokes. His 18-under-par performance broke the British Open record. Faldo considers this the best performance of his career.

THREE-TIME CHAMP. Faldo went into a two-year slump after his 1990 British Open win, and lost his number-one ranking. Early in 1992, however, he improved his play, and made history in the 1992 British Open. Faldo broke his own 54-hole British Open scoring record and headed into the final round with a four-stroke lead. Faldo—known as the Iceman for his ability to concentrate and his behavior toward other players—lost his lead. American John Cook, playing in only his second British Open, caught up with him. Cook then missed short putts on each of the last two holes, giving Faldo a chance.

"I was exploding from the pressure," Faldo told *People*. "I remember thinking, 'My legs are gone. I can hardly stand.'" But he held on, making birdies on two of the last four holes. He earned a par on the 18th hole—good enough to win the tournament. Just before tapping in the winning putt, Faldo looked at his mom, dad, wife, coach, and caddy and wept with joy. He became the first three-time British Open winner since 1948.

Faldo was also a contender in the 1992 PGA Championship, the last major tournament of the year. He led the field after the first two rounds, but shot a 76 in the third round, dropping him too far behind the leader, Nick Price, of South Africa. Faldo shot a final round 67, earning a tie for second behind Price. He was once again the leading money winner on the European Tour in 1992, with four tournament victories. In 1993 Faldo had an off year, with his best finish in a major tournament being third place in the PGA Championship. However, he remained at or near the top of the world rankings.

"LIGHTEN UP!" Along with his improvement on the golf course, Faldo also worked hard to change his reputation. His second wife, Gill, whom he had married in 1986, and his two children have helped him see that golf isn't the most important thing in the world. "I decided to change myself for the good of everyone around me as well as myself," Faldo confessed to *People*. "Before, I never thought about anything except golf. Now I have a family, and they mean the most to me. My two kids have opened up the world, and I'm trying to let other people and activities into my thoughts and life. You know, you get wiser as you get older. I've learned to lighten up."

OFF THE COURSE. Faldo lives in Surrey, England, with his wife, Gill, and their children, Matthew and Natalie. When not playing golf, Faldo enjoys astrology, fly fishing, snooker (a British game similar to pool), and motor sports. He established the Nick Faldo Charity Fund to help deserving causes, has donated part of his prize money to children's charities, and has visits with terminally ill children. He set up golf centers in inner-city areas of England to help disadvantaged youngsters learn to play the game.

Though he tries not to take golf as seriously as he used to, Faldo still works hard to improve himself. "I don't like to think about whether I'm the best player in the game," he told *Golf* magazine. "But when it's over, I'd most like to be remembered as someone who could really play the game. I want people in years to come to say to each other 'Did you ever see Nick Faldo play?' And for those who didn't, to feel sorry they missed out."

WHERE TO WRITE

C/O INTERNATIONAL MANAGEMENT GROUP,

1 ERIEVIEW PLAZA, SUITE 1300, CLEVELAND, OH 44114.

CECIL FIELDER

1963—

Cecil Fielder hits home runs further and more often than any other player in baseball today. In 1990 he became only the eleventh hitter in major league history to hit 50 or more home runs in a single season. From 1990 to 1992, Fielder became the first major leaguer since Babe Ruth (1919-21) to lead the majors in runs batted in for three straight seasons. During that period, he hit 130 homers—easily the best total in baseball.

GROWING UP

Fielder was born September 21, 1963, in Los Angeles, California. Cecil (pronounced *Ceh*-cil) was named after a favorite uncle who stood a towering six-feet-seven inches and weighed 290 pounds. Cecil was always large and always athletic. When he was eight years old, a group of Little League parents demanded he be moved to a higher age group.

Fielder grew up in a close-knit family, lived in a working-class neighborhood, and occasionally got into trouble. "Cecil Fielder could have been a statistic, too," he told the *Boston Globe*. "Thank God my parents kind of put a stop to me hanging with the wrong crowd. Being in a clique, being in a gang, meant something to a lot of people I grew up with. I wasn't in a gang, but I was hanging out with these people."

THREE-SPORT STAR. Instead, his parents directed his energies into sports. Fielder was a three-sport star (baseball, basketball, and football) at Nogales High School in Los Angeles. He was a star point guard on the high school varsity basketball team, leading them to a 29-0 record in his senior year. For a while he thought about becoming a professional basketball player. In football, he played safety and, sometimes, quarterback. During the summers he unloaded produce from a supermarket truck.

TURNS PRO. After high school, Fielder received a scholarship to play baseball at a school known best for basketball—the University of Nevada at Las Vegas (UNLV). After attending college for one year, the Kansas City Royals picked Fielder in the fourth round of the June 1982 amateur draft and he signed a contract for $650 a month with Butte (Montana) of the rookie Pioneer League.

Fielder was an immediate success—hitting .322 with 20 homers—and was named the league's all-star first baseman. But before the next season, the Royals traded him to the Toronto Blue Jays. Fielder worked his way up through the Jays's organization, starring in Class-A and Double-A (minor league) ball. He led the two leagues in home runs and proved to be an adequate defensive player.

JOINS BLUE JAYS. In 1985, after hitting 18 home runs in half a season at Double-A Knoxville (Tennessee), Fielder was promoted to the majors. Just 21 at the time, he ripped a double in his first major league at-bat, and started his career with a five-game hitting streak. In 30 games with Toronto that season, Fielder showed great promise—batting .311 with four home runs.

Cecil Fielder

Despite Fielder's good start, Toronto already had two solid first base prospects, Willie Upshaw and Fred McGriff. Toronto management gave up on Fielder, saying he couldn't hit right-handed pitchers and couldn't play first base. The club also considered him to be undisciplined and overweight.

But he could hit home runs. Fielder crunched 31 homers in 506 major-league at-bats over parts of four seasons between 1985 and 1988. Mostly, though, he sat on the bench. Fielder described these seasons to the *Philadelphia Daily News:* "I wanted to play more, but on the Blue Jay ballclub we had a lot of talent. They knew the frustration I was feeling not playing, and they gave me the opportunity. The Blue Jays came to me and said I had an opportunity to go play in Japan. They asked me to talk to the Japanese people. I didn't even hesitate. I said yes right away."

JAPANESE STAR. The Hanshin Tigers are located in Kobe, Japan. They called Toronto general manager Pat Gillick looking for a first baseman. Gillick agreed to sell them the rights to Fielder's contract—with Fielder's approval. For a salary of $1.05 million and a chance to play every day, the 25-year-old Fielder went to Japan.

During his one season in Japan, Fielder finished third in home runs (38), ninth in batting (.302), and third in RBIs (81). Most importantly, he learned patience. Before heading to Japan, Fielder had gained a reputation as a batter who swung at bad pitches. Pitchers in Japan threw more curve balls than major league pitchers, however, and Fielder taught himself to hold off until a good pitch came his way.

Fielder was a hero in Japan. He was a giant (250 pounds) in a nation of people of smaller physical stature, an African American among people not used to other races, and a friendly, fun-loving person in a country where most stars were not outgoing. Unlike most Americans playing there, he praised the country and its culture. The Japanese nicknamed him "Ogata Senpuki"—the Big Electric Fan—in tribute to his powerful strikeouts.

Though he enjoyed his star status, Fielder never intended to stay in Japan. He had gone to prove he was capable of being an everyday major league player. His excellent season accomplished that and his agent began calling American clubs to see who might be willing to give Fielder a chance.

SUPERSTAR

BECOMES A TIGER. The team that called back was the Detroit Tigers. The Tigers had finished in last place in 1989 and, despite a small ballpark, had no serious home run threat. In January of 1990, then-general manager Bill Lajoie signed Fielder to a two-year, $3 million contract. At the time, no one was impressed. "I didn't know him from Adam," manager Sparky Anderson told the *Philadelphia Inquirer*. "I had no expectations. Little did I know they had sent me an angel."

MONSTER SEASON. Fielder single-handedly revived the Tigers. Detroit climbed from 59 wins in 1989 to 79 in 1990 despite having one of the worst pitching staffs of modern times. He homered against every team and in every American League ballpark and became the first Tiger in history to hit a fair ball over the Tiger Stadium left-field roof. He made the all-star team and led the league in home runs (51), runs batted in (132), and strikeouts. The Associated Press named him the major league player of the year.

Hall-of-Fame slugger Harmon Killebrew described Fielder to the *Philadelphia Daily News*. "Cecil Fielder just has enormous power. He is a great hitter. I have seen him hit home runs that just disappear into the clouds." Killebrew is among the Top 10 home run hitters of all time, but one thing he never accomplished: he never hit 50 home runs in one season. Midway through 1990, it became clear that Fielder had a chance to accomplish the feat that just 10 men before him had achieved.

THE QUEST FOR 50. As Fielder's home run total climbed in 1990, television crews from the United States, Canada, and

50 HOME RUN CLUB

Player	Year(s)	Home Runs
Cecil Fielder	1990	51
George Foster	1977	52
Jimmie Foxx	1932	58
	1938	50
Hank Greenberg	1938	58
Ralph Kiner	1947	51
	1949	54
Mickey Mantle	1956	52
	1961	54
Roger Maris	1961	61
Johnny Mize	1947	51
Willie Mays	1955	52
	1965	52
Babe Ruth	1920	54
	1921	59
	1927	60
	1928	54
Hack Wilson	1930	56

Japan began to follow him. Not since George Foster of the Cincinnati Reds in 1977 had a player hit 50 home runs in one season. Fielder, for his part, tried to downplay the achievement, even as the attention became more intense. "I mean, what's 50, really?" he asked the *Detroit Free Press*. "If some guy hits 49, I'd sure slap him five and say that was a ... [great] year. But if I get 49, people will say, 'Aw, he just missed it.' It's a trip, isn't it?"

Fielder got his 49th run with seven games left in the 1990 season. But then he began to feel the pressure. He went six games without getting close. Finally, in the last game of the season, at Yankee Stadium, he hit not one, but two homers. Typically, he celebrated those homers quietly. Many sluggers pump their fists or cheer for themselves or watch their homers fly. Fielder follows swings by putting his head down and quietly circling the bases. "I don't like to show the pitchers up." he told the *Detroit Free Press*. "If you stand there and watch, it makes them feel bad. You shouldn't do that. They respect you more if you just run around the bases and get out of there."

NO FLUKE. After that great season, Fielder finished second to Rickey Henderson of the Oakland Athletics in balloting for the American League's Most Valuable Player. The question on everyone's mind was whether he could come back with another impressive season in 1991, or whether 1990 was a fluke. "I hear that fluke stuff all the time," Fielder told the *Philadelphia Inquirer*. "I caught a lot of people by surprise last season. Now they're saying, 'OK, this time we're watching, so prove it.'"

Prove it, he did. Fielder came back in 1991 and again led the major leagues in home runs (44) and RBIs (133). Babe

Ruth and Jimmie Foxx were the only two players to accomplish that feat before him. Fielder again made the all-star team and again finished second in MVP balloting, this time to **Cal Ripken, Jr.** (see entry), of the Baltimore Orioles.

BIG REWARD. Fielder played well in 1992. Although he did not make the all-star team, he finished the season with 35 homers. His 124 RBIs led the major leagues for the third consecutive year. Before Fielder, only Babe Ruth had accomplished that. And the Tigers recognized Fielder's value—both as a player and as a fan attraction. Before the 1993 season, they signed him to the highest contract in Tiger team history—$7.3 million a year for five years.

FAST START, THEN FRUSTRATION. The Tigers started fast in 1993. A 43-25 record on June 21 put Detroit in first place. Poor pitching and injuries, however, led to a decline that saw the team finish the season out of the pennant chase. Fielder had another outstanding season. He hit 30 home runs and had 117 RBIs, but for the first time in four seasons Fielder did not lead the major leagues in RBIs and the World Series championship still evaded the big Tiger slugger. He remained a favorite of fans wherever the Tigers played, however, and at the start of the 1994 season a candy bar was named in his honor.

WHERE TO WRITE

C/O DETROIT TIGERS,

2121 TRUMBULL AVE., DETROIT, MI 48216.

EMERSON FITTIPALDI

1946—

"If I had to, I'd pay to drive a racing car."— Emerson Fittipaldi

Since many people change jobs throughout their lives, it's not unusual that Emerson Fittipaldi changed jobs twice. What is unusual is that he drives race cars that travel over 200 miles per hour. Fittipaldi was a world champion driver by the age of 25, but found himself without a racing job in 1980. He came to the United States in 1984 because racing was in his blood. He earned a chance to drive in the most important auto race in the world—the Indianapolis 500. Since then, Fittipaldi has won the 500 twice in five years time.

GROWING UP

Emerson Fittipaldi was born December 12, 1946, in Sao Paulo, Brazil. The youngest of two sons, he grew up in a house dominated by auto racing. His father, Wilson, an Italian immigrant, was a Brazilian motorsport journalist and commentator, and his mother, Juze, raced cars during the 1950s. His brother, Wilson, Jr., also became a race car driver.

Fittipaldi's father first took his son to the race track when he was five years old. At the age of 15, before he could legally drive, he began working as a mechanic and raced motorbikes and go-karts. When he was 17, Fittipaldi designed a leather steering wheel cover that became so popular he hired 15 employees to help him keep up with the orders. (Later, Fittipaldi would design a new steering wheel that is also popular with race car drivers.) Soon he and his brother began building race cars that Fittipaldi drove in races.

YOUNG GUN. Fittipaldi won his first race in 1967, and by 1970 had worked his way up to the big leagues—Formula One racing. He was part of the Lotus team, and won his fist Formula One race at the U.S. Grand Prix at Watkins Glen, New York. Over the next two seasons he proved he was one of the best young drivers in Formula One.

WORLD CHAMP. In 1972 Fittipaldi won five races and earned enough points to win his first Formula One driving championship, considered by many people to be the world championship of auto racing. He was the youngest-ever world champion at age 25. In 1973 he finished second in the points standings to the legendary Jackie Stewart of Scotland. Fittipaldi switched to Team McLaren before the 1974 season, and won his second Formula One driving championship. He is now ranked as one of the greatest drivers of all time. "When Emerson was hot, he was perhaps the greatest driver in the world," Stewart said.

CHANGES JOBS. Now a national hero in Brazil, Fittipaldi looked for new challenges. In 1975 Fittipaldi, in partnership with his brother, Wilson, began his own racing team. At first he was successful, winning the U.S. and the Brazilian Grand Prix, and finishing second in the point standings. That would be his last great Formula One season. After seven years of building his own cars and losing millions of dollars, Fittipaldi realized that operating his own racing team was "the biggest

SCOREBOARD

TWO-TIME FORMULA ONE WORLD DRIVING CHAMPION (1972 AND 1974).

TWO-TIME WINNER OF INDIANAPOLIS 500 (1989 AND 1993). ONE OF ONLY FOUR DRIVERS EVER TO WIN FORMULA ONE DRIVING CHAMPIONSHIP AND INDIANAPOLIS 500.

CHAMPIONSHIP AUTO RACING TEAMS (CART) WORLD SERIES SEASON DRIVING CHAMPION (1991). BECAME ONLY THE SECOND DRIVER TO WIN FORMULA ONE AND CART SEASON DRIVING CHAMPIONSHIPS.

ONE OF THE MOST VERSATILE AND POPULAR RACE CAR DRIVERS IN THE WORLD.

Emerson Fittipaldi

mistake of my life." He would never again win a Formula One race and retired from the sport in 1980. After two more years of struggle, he closed down his team and returned to Brazil.

Fittipaldi returned to Sao Paulo and worked in his family's extensive orange-farming business. He also managed a Mercedes car dealership. "Farming is not very exciting, but it's steady, and the land is always there," he explained in *Sports Illustrated*. Fittipaldi entered a go-kart race for fun, and a Miami promoter, Ralph Sanchez, talked him into racing GTP cars, a smaller version of Indy cars. This experience convinced Fittipaldi to get back into racing, so he moved to the United States in 1983 to drive on the Championship Auto Racing Teams (CART) circuit. "This time I'm going to do it strictly as a driver," Fittipaldi said in *Motor Trend*. "Now, I just want to try to be competitive and enjoy motor racing for what it is."

NEW START. Fittipaldi had to prove he could still drive. He raced in the smaller GTP cars during most of 1984, and in September of that year he was asked to join the Patrick Racing Team. Gordon Johncock had won two Indianapolis 500s for the Patrick team, and it was considered one of the best organizations in Indy racing. Fittipaldi got his chance after another Patrick team driver, Chip Ganassi, crashed at the Michigan 500 and suffered a serious head injury. Ganassi recovered, but his racing career was over. Fittipaldi took his place on the team.

He became the Patrick team's top driver when Johncock decided to retire just before the 1985 Indianapolis 500. Fittipaldi qualified as the fifth-fastest at Indianapolis that year and was a contender in the race before structural failure forced his car to drop out. Two months later, he won his first Indy car race—the Michigan 500. He finished sixth in points on the CART circuit in his first season and had ten top-ten finishes.

In 1986 Fittipaldi won one race and captured the pole position twice as the fastest qualifier. He finished seventh at Indianapolis and ended the year seventh in points. In 1987 he won back-to-back races, at Cleveland, Ohio, and Toronto, Ontario, Canada, and had five other top-ten finishes. 1988 was probably Fittipaldi's best year to that point. He finished second to Rick Mears at Indianapolis and once again earned back-to-back victories at other races.

LEARNING EXPERIENCE. Despite his success, Fittipaldi was unable to repeat his championship seasons from Formula One. He had problems with his cars, which broke down several times when it seemed that he could win. More importantly, he had to learn how to drive Indy cars. "Racing an Indy Car on oval tracks requires a special technique," he explained to *Motor Trend.* "It took me all of five years to be confident in racing with and beating the best Indy Car drivers on oval tracks. It's very difficult, very demanding."

WHAT'S THE DIFFERENCE?

When he came to the United States, Fittipaldi learned there is a world of difference between Formula One racing and driving Indy-style cars. Formula One races are run on winding courses with many turns. A driver must slow down, speed up, and change gears often during the course of one lap. In Indy-style races, cars usually travel on a oval-shaped track. Although there are not as many turns, drivers can go at much faster speeds. Formula One cars are also lighter and less powerful than Indy cars.

SUPERSTAR

INDY CHAMP. In 1989 Fittipaldi, in the car he'd nicknamed *The Flying Beauty,* qualified on the outside of the first row at the Indianapolis 500, beside former Indy champions Mears and Al Unser, Sr. He took the lead at the start and quickly pulled away from the pack and set a one-lap record with a speed of 221.370 miles per hour.

It seemed Fittipaldi would be an easy winner after leading for 156 of the first 195 laps. Making a big mistake, however, his pit crew put too much gas in his car, making it heavier and slower. Soon he could see Al Unser, Jr., son of the former champion, in his rear view mirror. "It was like a nightmare when I saw Al Jr. coming," Fittipaldi recalled in *Motor Trend.* "He was coming, and I knew I had trouble. It was like you

Emerson Fittipaldi and Al Unser, Jr., collide at the Indianapolis 500 in 1989.

dream you're running and you're stuck in the same place and you know someone is going to grab you but you can't move ahead." With only five laps to go, Unser passed Fittipaldi.

CRASH. At that point Fittipaldi decided to make his move. "It was as if someone pushed me from behind and said, 'Emerson, come on. Go for it. You can still do it,'" he said in *Motor Trend*. Going into a turn, Fittipaldi and Unser were side-by-side, with neither driver giving an inch. Suddenly Fittipaldi's tire hit his opponent's, and Unser's car spun out of control.

"At that moment, I was concerned that he had been hurt, and then when I came around I saw him standing at the side of track with his thumbs up," Fittipaldi told *Motor Trend*. Unser applauded Fittipaldi as he took the checkered flag. "I was trying to say to him, 'Damn you're impressive,'" Unser explained to *Sports Illustrated*. Fittipaldi told the same magazine: "When you get two race drivers who want the Indy 500 as bad as we did and they go into a corner, only one is going to come out." Fittipaldi and Unser had collided once before, and that time Unser had won and Fittipaldi had been knocked out of the race.

Fittipaldi sat in the winner's circle after the race with tears in his eyes. "In the winners circle, I had incredible feelings," he revealed to *Motor Trend*. "I think that was one of the most emotional moments of my whole life. After so many years of racing, so many years of hard work, it was a special bonus. There's no doubt it was the most important single win of my career."

RETURNS TO TOP. Fittipaldi won three straight races in June and July of 1989, finished second twice, and wrapped up the CART Indy Car World Series championship in September by defeating his rival, Mears, at a race in Nazareth, Pennsylvania. "I think it all started to come together at the beginning of last year," Fittipaldi explained in *Motor Trend*. The team changed to a more reliable chassis and engine, and Fittipaldi did the rest. "I am driving as well as I ever have," he continued. "Maybe in some ways even better because I have more experience, more knowledge of a wider range of racing than when I was just a Grand Prix [Formula One] driver."

In 1989, Fittipaldi became only the fourth driver (Mario Andretti, Jim Clark, and Graham Hill are the others) to win both the Indianapolis 500 and the Formula One World Championship. Only he, Andretti, and Nigel Mansell have ever won the season-long Formula One and Indy car championships in their careers. Fittipaldi also became the first driver to ever earn over $2 million in prize money in one year.

CHANGES TEAMS. In 1990 Fittipaldi switched to the powerful Penske racing team, joining drivers Rick Mears and Danny Sullivan. He finished third at Indy in 1990 after leading for 115 of the first 117 laps. *The Woman in Red* [his car's nickname] was beautiful today," Fittipaldi said. "She just needed a different pair of shoes." He was referring to his car's tires, which had probably cost him the victory.

In 1991 Fittipaldi was forced out of the Indianapolis 500 with mechanical problems. His teammate, Mears, won the

BELIEVE IT OR NOT

Though he races cars at speeds of over 200 miles an hour, Fittipaldi is not completely fearless. "Many things scare me—heights, roller coasters, sharks—anything you don't have control over," he told *Sports Illustrated*. "But to be a good racing car driver you have to be brave, and you have to be afraid. You have to balance the brave and the afraid." Several times Fittipaldi has been in accidents, but has never been seriously injured. He doesn't like driving on freeways, maybe because he knows that not everyone on the road is a trained, professional driver.

race, and Fittipaldi cried in the garage. "It was a race I felt like I had won," he told *Sports Illustrated*. "That Indianapolis for me is the most emotional race in my career." In 1992 he won four races, finished among the top three in three others, and finished fourth in total points. While these results were good, they were below Fittipaldi's normal standards.

SECOND 500. Fittipaldi phoned his mother in Sao Paulo on the morning of the 1993 Indianapolis 500. She was so nervous about the race that she made Fittipaldi's wife, Theresa, promise to wear her lucky earrings—the same one's she'd worn when Fittipaldi won his first Indy 500. Rick Mears had won at Indy when his wife, Chris, wore the same earrings. With that much history behind them, Theresa decided to wear the charmed jewelry.

Fittipaldi's luck almost wore out midway during the race. In tenth place, trailing leader Mario Andretti, Fittipaldi worked his way to the front. Andretti had car problems, and Fittipaldi took the lead on lap 185. With six laps to go, the race was slowed by an accident with Fittipaldi in the lead and Arie Luyendyk and Nigel Mansell close behind. When the debris was cleared off the track, the cars once again hit top speed. The restart was crucial. "The pressure was on," Fittipaldi explained in *Sports Illustrated*. "I knew Arie and Nigel were like a couple of foxes, that they were going to try to jump me [on the restart] ... I knew I had to hit it just right." He did, forcing the other cars to slow down, then speeding off himself. He never again trailed, winning his second Indy 500.

SO CLOSE. Fittipaldi was the favorite to win the 1994 Indy 500. He qualified to start the race as the third fastest driver and led the field for 145 of the first 185 laps of the famous track. Only 15 laps from victory disaster struck. Fittipaldi attempted to pass teammate Al Unser, Jr., then in second place, and crashed into the wall, knocking him out of the race. He finished a very disappointed seventeenth as Unser, Jr., won the race. "That [the accident] was a shame," Fittipaldi said after the race. "The car was flying. I was very disappointed. I was so close."

OFF THE TRACK. Fittipaldi and his wife, Theresa split their time between Sao Paulo and Key Biscayne, Florida. They have a daughter, Joana, and he has three children from a previous marriage—Juliana, Tatiana, and Jayson. Theresa and Joana travel to all Fittipaldi's races. An international traveler himself, Fittipaldi can speak five languages fluently—English, French, Spanish, Italian, and his native Portuguese. He is an avid jogger and would like to someday compete in a marathon race.

Fittipaldi designs power boats and likes to sail the ocean. He also designs parts for performance boats and cars. He owns his own jet airplane and has said that if he wasn't a race car driver, he would want to be a fighter pilot. Fittipaldi owns a 500,000-acre orange tree farm in Brazil. Despite all his other interests, Fittipaldi continues to race. "Motor racing's been a passion for me all my life," he said. "The feeling of speed, the challenge of driving, controlling a racing car, sliding, the motion you go through. If I had to, I'd pay to drive a racing car."

WHERE TO WRITE

C/O CHAMPIONSHIP AUTO RACING TEAMS,

390 ENTERPRISE CT., BLOOMFIELD HILLS, MI 48302.

GEORGE FOREMAN

1949—

"My opponents didn't worry about losing to me. They worried about getting hurt."—George Foreman

Everyone said that George Foreman was no good when he was young. If not for boxing, he probably would have wound up in prison or dead. Even as heavyweight boxing champion, Foreman didn't know what a good thing he had until he lost everything—his championship, his money, and his family. Only then did he realize that the only way he could be happy was to do things for others. Only then did it become clear that he didn't need a title to be a champion.

GROWING UP

George Edward Foreman was born January 10, 1949, in Marshall, Texas. He grew up in the Fifth Ward, a poor neighborhood on the north side of Houston, Texas, where he had a troubled childhood, and quit school before the ninth grade. By that time he had already gained a reputation as a gang leader, a thief, and a heavy drinker. Former football player Lester Hayes grew up with Foreman, and told *Sports Illustrated* that the young George "was a very, very big kid and had a reputation for savage butt kickings." Foreman told the same magazine that back then he thought a hero was someone with "a big, long scar down his face, a guy who'd come back from prison, a guy [who] maybe killed a man once." He even went so far as to wear bandages on his own face so it would seem like he had a scar.

With no direction, Foreman drifted, spending most of his time on the streets with no idea of how to make a life for himself. "I remember once," he told *Sports Illustrated,* "two boys and myself, we robbed a guy. Threw him down. I could hold the guy because I was strong, and the sneaky fella would grab the money. And then we'd run until we couldn't hear the guy screaming anymore. And then we'd walk home as if we'd just earned some money on a job, counting it. We didn't even know we were criminals."

SAVED BY BOXING. Trying to get his life together, Foreman traveled to Oregon and joined the Jobs Corps where he became involved in a savage fistfight in the town of Pleasanton, California. When the counselors couldn't pull Foreman off of his opponent, they called supervisor Doc Broadus for help. Broadus managed to stop the fight, but realized that Foreman's incredible strength needed to be directed into something constructive.

Broadus had a special talent for developing boxers. He took Foreman to the gym and taught him the art of boxing. Within two years, Foreman had developed into a powerful amateur (unpaid) heavyweight. In 1968 he won the U.S. Olympic Boxing Trials, earning the right to represent the United States in the Summer Olympics in Mexico City, Mexico. Foreman won the gold medal at the Olympics and is remembered for waving an American flag in the ring after his final victory. The Olympic victory remains the highlight of his life. "None of it felt as good as when I was poor and had that gold medal, when I wore it so long I had to have the ribbon restitched," Foreman reminisced in *Sports Illustrated.*

George Foreman

TURNS PRO. Foreman turned professional in 1969 and worked his way toward the championship. He made quick work of his opponents, going undefeated in his first 40 fights and winning more than half of those within *two rounds*. "My opponents didn't worry about losing to me," he told *Sports Illustrated*. "They worried about getting hurt." In January 1973 Foreman fought heavyweight champion, Joe Frazier who had stunned the world by beating Muhammad Ali (see box), and was favored to beat Foreman. "I'm gonna knock Joe Frazier out," Foreman boasted before the fight, and he turned out to be right. He knocked Frazier down six times before the referee stopped the fight. Now it was Foreman who was considered unbeatable.

"ROPE-A-DOPE." One of the most famous fights in boxing history took place on October 30, 1974, in the African nation of Zaire. Foreman, the overpowering champion, faced the legend, Muhammad Ali, who feared no fighter and used a new tactic called the "rope-a-dope" in his fight with Foreman. For the first six rounds Ali leaned against the ropes, daring Foreman to hit him, then covering up his head and body with his arms and his gloves. Foreman threw punch after punch, but they had no effect on Ali. By round seven, Foreman was tired and Ali was still unhurt. In the eighth round, Ali knocked Foreman out to achieve one of the greatest wins in boxing history.

The loss haunted Foreman, who tried to convince Ali to give him a rematch. Losing the title destroyed Foreman's self-esteem and almost ruined his life. "You have to build yourself up [after losing], so you start spending billions of dollars on cars, suits, and anything you can do to make yourself look like the best in the world," Foreman confessed to *Sports Illustrated,* explaining why he had spent his boxing fortune. Always a vicious puncher, Foreman became angry and mean. "After I lost to Ali," he said. "I'd decided I needed more hate."

RETIRES FROM BOXING. Foreman continued to box, and in 1977 lost to Jimmy Young in a 12-round decision. Suffering from extreme dehydration caused by losing so much water during the fight, Foreman lay flat on his back in the training room. "I'm wakin' from the dead," he told a reporter after the fight. "Wait around till midnight, and I will come out of my coffin." After the fight Foreman claimed he had a vision from God. He decided right then to retire from boxing. Foreman became a born-again Christian after his retirement and preached on Houston street corners and in churches. Eventually he opened his own house of worship in a mobile home—the Church of the Lord Jesus Christ. There he built up a small group of believers and tried to avoid publicity.

Despite his religious beliefs, Foreman was still not in control of his life. Between 1981 and 1983 Foreman married and divorced three times. One of his wives flew to the country of Barbados with the couple's two children, and Foreman followed, literally stealing the children back. The turmoil was enough to finally make him stop and examine his life.

FINDS PEACE. Between 1983 and 1986 Foreman seemed to have found peace at last. His small church and a gym he had built next door—the George Foreman Youth and Community Center—filled his days. He remarried and fathered the last of three sons—all of whom he named George. Gradually, however, the cost of running the church and the gym used up the rest of the money Foreman had earned in boxing. At the same time, the oldest of his children were nearing the age when they would need money to go to college.

MUHAMMAD ALI

"Float like a butterfly, and sting like a bee," was the way Muhammad Ali described the way he boxed. Light on his feet and deadly with his fists, Ali was an important person both in and out of the ring. In 1960 Ali, then going by his given name, Cassius Clay, won a gold medal for the United States in the Olympics in Rome, Italy. In 1964 he defeated Sonny Liston to win the heavyweight championship. He then became a follower of the Black Muslim religion and changed his name to Muhammad Ali. In 1966 he was drafted, but after he refused to join the army because of his religious beliefs his titles were taken away from him and he was not allowed to box until 1970. In 1974 he regained his title in the fight against Foreman. In 1978 he lost his championship to Leon Spinks, but regained his crown by beating Spinks in a rematch. Ali is the only fighter to have won the heavyweight championship three times. It just may be that he was, as he often said, the "greatest of all time."

SUPERSTAR

COMEBACK. In 1987, at the age of 40, Foreman returned to boxing. It wasn't an easy decision, because his weight had increased to over 300 pounds since leaving the ring. He trained hard, brought his weight down to 260 pounds, and was soon fighting again. But boxing experts didn't take him seriously because he was only agreeing to matches with fighters he could easily beat. "This is pathetic, it shouldn't be allowed. He's overage, inept," boxing commentator Ferdie Pacheco complained in *Sports Illustrated.*

In the ring, Foreman won 20 straight fights, 19 of them by knockout. "It still only takes me one punch," he said in the *Boston Globe.* "Whump. The power is still there." He also became a fan favorite outside the ring, making jokes about his age, his weight, and his love of junk food. Foreman would always tell reporters that he was coming from or going to a restaurant.

SHOWTIME. The jokes were all part of boxing show business. "I don't even take myself serious," Foreman admitted in *Sport.* "It's a game. It's sports. I can't stand it when athletes take themselves so serious. If people want to hear a joke, they must need a joke. They get plenty of seriousness, plenty of hardship, in their own lives. That's the reason, when I'm on television, I never get serious. When they flip that camera on, it's like 'Showtime.'"

Foreman also joked about being out of shape, but that wasn't the complete truth. "I've gotten to where I am," he told *Sport,* "because I'm the hardest-working fighter in the world. I train all the time, seven days a week." Even though he joked about how much he ate, Foreman actually maintained a very balanced diet. He also had a unique way of jogging. He attached a punching bag to the back of a pickup truck and continually punched the bag while running behind the truck. "I run behind that thing, punching. Sometimes as much as 10 miles, all the time punching and moving." He didn't mind if his opponents didn't believe he trained hard. "It's only to my advantage," he told *Sport.*

TITLE FIGHT. In June 1990 Foreman knocked out Adilson Rodrigues in the 22nd fight of his comeback—his first win over a ranked opponent. Soon he was starting to be taken seriously as a title contender. "Let's cut all this nonsense out," Foreman announced after the fight. "Let's get George Foreman and Mike Tyson [the heavyweight champion] together, once and for all." Foreman would not fight Tyson, who was sent to prison after being convicted on a charge of rape, but on April 19, 1991, Foreman faced the new heavyweight champion, **Evander Holyfield** (see entry). "You're looking at a guy who's been champ of the world, lost the championship of the world. I've had life from every angle," Foreman told *Sport* before the fight. "That's why I'm not ever worried about losing. The only thing that frightens me about fighting Evander Holyfield is that I might hurt him. I don't want to ever hurt anybody."

At 42 years of age, Foreman became the oldest man ever to fight for the heavyweight championship. When he last held the title, Holyfield was 10 years old. Foreman lost a tough 12-round decision, but gained the respect of everyone who watched the fight. In the twelfth round, it was Holyfield, not Foreman, who seemed to be tired. "In that last round, I had him dizzy, I looked in his eyes and it looked like he was asking for mercy," Foreman said after the fight. "The referee said, 'Let him go,' but he wouldn't let go. I should have gotten to him sooner."

"He was strong all the way to the end," said Holyfield. While Foreman hit Holyfield with harder punches, Holyfield hit Foreman with a larger number. Foreman had Holyfield in trouble in the second, fifth, and seventh rounds, but he would not go down. "I hit him a few times, I hit him and he would actually be out," Foreman said. "But the next thing you know, he's [Holyfield's] hitting me." I feel like I'm the victor," Foreman explained in *Jet*. "When you've done your best, and you've given your all, then you're the best person you can be.... He had the points [from the judges], but I made the point," Foreman said after the fight. "If you can live, you can dream."

KEEPS FIGHTING. After the Holyfield fight Foreman's wife, Joan, tried to talk him into retiring. He still wanted one last

KIDS WITH MURDER ON THEIR FACES

After his final fight, Foreman announced that he was going to concentrate on his new career—a television series called "George." In it he played George Foster, a retired boxer who finds new meaning in life helping troubled youths at the school where his wife teaches. The show closely resembled Foreman's own life. With the money he earned from boxing, he was able to build a larger athletic center for underprivileged children in Houston. He plans to spend the rest of his life there, helping others to avoid some of the mistakes he made when he was young. "I want kids with murder on their faces," Foreman told *Sports Illustrated*. "I'll trick 'em with boxing and sports to get them straightened out and going to school."

chance at winning the title, though, and in April 1992 he fought Alex Stewart, thought to be an easy opponent. Foreman knocked him down twice in the second round, but Stewart wouldn't quit. Foreman won the 10-round fight on a decision, but only after a tough battle that left him bruised and bloodied. "Ladies and gentlemen, this is George Foreman. Can you please tell me where the aspirin are?" he joked after the fight.

RETIRES. Foreman's final fight, when he was 44 years old, was against 24-year-old Tommy Morrison, in a 12-round match for the World Boxing Organization (WBO) championship. Morrison, able to move quickly around the ring, was too fast for Foreman to hit. When the bout was over, Morrison had earned a decision. Foreman announced his retirement after the fight. "I've had fun, so much fun this time. I don't think I'm going to box anymore," he declared. "I've got nothing to be ashamed of." Foreman was 27-2 in his comeback and finished his career 72-4 overall.

OUT OF THE RING. Foreman lives in Hayward, California, with his fifth wife, Joan. During his career, Foreman was a spokesperson for Kentucky Fried Chicken and Kraft Foods. Though he never regained his championship, he now has his life in perspective. "I don't never want to be nothin' but a human being that makes mistakes," Foreman told *Sport.* "I just want to live as long as I can and help as many people as I can ease their burdens."

WHERE TO WRITE

C/O TOP RINK, INC., 3900 PARADISE ROAD, SUITE 227
LAS VEGAS, NV 89109.

JUAN GONZALEZ

1969—

Juan Gonzalez of the Texas Rangers is one of the best baseball players in the American League. He has led the league in home runs for two consecutive seasons and has driven in over 100 runs three years in a row. Gonzalez hasn't forgotten where he came from despite the fact that he is now a star. After every season he returns to Puerto Rico and tries to help the poor and the children of his home town achieve the success that he has won. In his generosity, Gonzalez is very much like the greatest baseball player to ever come from Puerto Rico, Roberto Clemente.

GROWING UP

Juan Alberto Gonzalez was born October 20, 1969, in Arecibo, Puerto Rico. He grew up in a rough barrio, or neighborhood, called Alto de Cuba, known for its poverty and criminal activity. Gonzalez's Texas teammate, Ivan Rodriguez, who grew up in Vega Baja, explained to *Sports Illustrated* that he won't go to Alto de Cuba because: "It's too dangerous there.... It's bad. If you go there and the people don't know you, they might shoot at you."

GETS NICKNAME. Gonzalez's father, Juan, was a math teacher, but his son's favorite subject was history. "History is more for

"When Juan only gets a single, you breathe a sigh of relief."—former catcher Carlton Fisk

life," he told *Sports Illustrated*. Gonzalez played baseball barefoot in the street, using a broomstick for a bat and a *chapita* (bottle cap) for a ball. He used paper bags as gloves when he boxed. Outfielder **Dave Winfield** (see entry) was his baseball hero as a child. Gonzalez was given the nickname, "Igor," because of his other childhood idol, The Mighty Igor, a professional wrestler.

SIGNS WITH RANGERS. When he was 13, Gonzalez and his family moved from Alto de Cuba to a safer community nearby. His baseball talent was discovered by scout Luis Rosa after Gonzalez set a Puerto Rican record by hitting 13 home runs in 15 games. Rosa arranged a tryout for the 15-year-old Gonzalez with Sandy Johnson, an assistant general manager with the Texas Rangers, in the spring of 1986. Johnson offered him a $75,000 bonus and Gonzalez accepted. "He looked bigger than he probably was then," Johnson admitted to *Sport*. "He was only 15 and a half years old. I looked at him and thought of Dave Winfield."

Gonzalez spent three years in the minor leagues. His teammates did not speak Spanish and he could not speak English. The Rangers brought Gonzalez to the major leagues in September 1989, but he batted only .150 with one home run and seven RBIs. He spent the entire 1990 season with the Oklahoma City 89ers of the American Association (a top-level minor league) and was named the league's Most Valuable Player after hitting 29 home runs and driving in 101 runs. "People forget that he's only 20," Johnson reminded *Sports Illustrated*. "I hate to use this word, but he's a potential superstar. He hasn't scratched the surface yet." Once again Gonzalez joined the Rangers in September, this time hitting .289, with four home runs and 12 RBIs.

MAJOR LEAGUER. Gonzalez batted .264, hit 27 homers, and drove in 102 runs in his first full season with Texas in 1991. He batted in the middle of a powerful lineup that included outfielder Ruben Sierra, first baseman Rafael Palmeiro, and designated hitter Julio Franco, who won the 1991 American League batting championship with a .341 average. "When they're [the Rangers] clicking, it's a nightmare facing them," pitcher Jimmy Key admitted to *Sport*. Gonzalez impressed his teammates in his first season. "Juan has all the tools in the world," Texas leftfielder Pete Incaviglia raved in *Sports Illustrated*. "Juan's going to be a superstar."

HOME RUN CHAMP. In 1992 Gonzalez batted .260, drove in 109 runs, and became the first Ranger ever to hit over 40 home runs (43) in one season. In accomplishing this feat Gonzalez hit two home runs in a single game six times during the season. In the last five games of the year he hit three home runs to win the major league home run title over Mark McGwire of the Oakland Athletics, who finished with 42. He became the first centerfielder to lead the major leagues in home runs since Willie Mays hit 52 in 1965.

The biggest problem Gonzalez had in his first two seasons was that he sometimes lost his concentration, especially in the field. "He's like a lot of young players," his former manager Toby Harrah explained to *Sport* after the 1992 season. "All he thinks about is his offense." Gonzalez was also criticized for swinging too hard and striking out too much. "If he [Gonzalez] doesn't try to become strictly a home run hitter, he can be the best player in the league," California manager Buck Rodgers told the *Sporting News*.

HOMETOWN HERO. When Gonzalez returned to Puerto Rico after the 1992 season, 5,000 fans greeted him at the airport. More people lined the street on his 23-mile drive home and another 5,000 gathered in the city square in Vega Baja. "I remember I cried," he recalled in *Sports Illustrated*. Gonzalez played 21 games in the Puerto Rican Winter League season

ROBERTO CLEMENTE

Roberto Clemente was the best baseball player to come from Puerto Rico. Clemente, who played for the Pittsburgh Pirates, was the National League Most Valuable Player in 1966 and won four National League batting championships—in 1961, 1964, 1965, and 1967. He batted .317 for his career, hit 240 home runs, and had 1,305 RBIs. Clemente was an excellent rightfielder who won 12 straight Gold Glove Awards for fielding excellence. He died on New Year's Eve, 1972, when his plane crashed while carrying food and medical supplies to earthquake-shaken Nicaragua. In 1973 Clemente became the first Hispanic member of the Baseball Hall of Fame.

and hit seven home runs with 14 RBIs and was named the league's Most Valuable Player.

SUPERSTAR

BEST SEASON. The Rangers considered trading Gonzalez after the 1992 season for **Roger Clemens** (see entry) of the Boston Red Sox. They didn't make the trade and Gonzalez had a great season in 1993. He led the American League for the second straight season with 46 home runs. He had 118 RBIs, scored 105 times, and batted .318—all career bests. "I have surprised myself by hitting .300," he admitted to the *Detroit Free Press*. "I feel more confident at the plate." Gonzalez became the sixth player in American League history to hit three home runs in two separate games in one season. His defense also improved after he moved from center field to left field—an easier position to play. He was named to play in his first All-Star Game in July. Gonzalez has become one of the most feared hitters in the American League. "When Juan only gets a single, you breathe a sigh of relief," former catcher Carlton Fisk revealed to the *Sporting News*.

The Rangers—who moved from Washington, where the team had been named the Senators, after the 1971 season—have not won a pennant during their 21 seasons in Texas. They were in contention for the American League Western division title in 1993, but their chances were hurt when outfielder Jose Canseco injured his arm pitching in a meaningless game. In September the Rangers were only two games behind the division-leading Chicago White Sox, but finished the season eight games out of first place.

ROLE MODEL. Gonzalez makes appearances at schools throughout Puerto Rico. "I want to be an example for you, for Puerto Rico and beyond." Gonzalez announced to a crowd at a Puerto Rican school, according to *Sports Illustrated.* "My priority right now is you: the youth. We as adults must work day by day and hand in hand for a better future for our youth.... After God, education and sports are the best tools to defeat any obstacles in your way." Gonzalez is a hero in Puerto Rico. "It is not just that he's a great athlete. The people here have fondness for him. The children all want to be Igor Gonzalez," Carlos Ayala, a teacher at the school, told the same magazine.

"It makes me feel bad and sad at the same time," Gonzalez confessed to *Sports Illustrated,* while talking about his old neighborhood in Alto de Cuba. "The youth is losing its future to drugs. But I also blame government authorities for not caring for the people of the barrio. There is not a baseball field or a basketball court for them." Gonzalez tries to financially help the poor of his home town. The people of Alto de Cuba appreciate what he does for them, calling him *melao melao,* the "sweetest of the sweet." Stores in the area built shrines to him. "Juan Gonzalez is the perfect guy that, if I was a youngster, I'd want to [be like]," Hall-of-Fame pitcher, Jim Palmer, explained in the *Washington Post.* "He's done everything he possibly can to be the best player he can, and also be a responsible citizen."

OFF THE FIELD. Gonzalez lives in North Arlington, Texas, during the season, and with his parents in Vega Baja during

YOUNGEST HOME RUN KINGS

In 1992 Juan Gonzalez was the sixth-youngest player to ever lead the major leagues in home runs. Below is a list of the youngest players to accomplish this feat.

Season	Player	Age	Home Runs
1901	Sam Crawford	21	16
1953	Eddie Mathews	21	47
1909	Ty Cobb	22	9
1970	Johnny Bench	22	45
1937	Joe Dimaggio	22	46
1992	Juan Gonzalez	22	43

the winter. He has a son, Juan Igor Gonzalez, but is divorced from his wife, Jackeline. He lifts weights to increase his strength. "Each time I lift ... I tell myself that at the end of the season, I'll know all of this work was worth it," he commented in the *Sporting News*. He has also starred in Spanish-language ads for Reebok that are shown in Latin America.

Gonzalez is rather shy and only recently began to learn English. "I let my bat talk for me now," he told *Sport*. He frequently turns down interview requests and always speaks through an interpreter. He would like to be a social worker when his baseball days are done. "When my playing days are over, I will be focused on serving the people of Puerto Rico," he told *Sports Illustrated*. "God gave me a good mind and the ability to succeed in baseball. I understand that I have to give back for what God has given me."

WHERE TO WRITE

C/O TEXAS RANGERS,

1000 BALLPARK WAY, ARLINGTON, TX 76011.

STEFFI GRAF

1969—

In baseball, a grand slam is a home run with the bases loaded and it counts for four runs. In tennis, a Grand Slam is winning the four most important tournaments—the Australian and French Opens, Wimbledon, and the U.S. Open—in one year. While many baseball players hit grand slams, only five players have ever won the Grand Slam in tennis. One of those players is Steffi Graf, who pulled off this feat in 1988. During her career, Graf has been the best women's tennis player in the world, twice spending long periods of time as the game's top-ranked player. And it all began in the living room of her parents' house.

GROWING UP

Stephanie Maria Graf was born June 14, 1969, in Mannheim, West Germany, and grew up in the small German town of Bruhl. Her father, Peter, and mom, Heidi, were both tennis players. When Graf was three years old, she began to drag out her father's racquets and ask to play. Her dad, who was also a well-known soccer player, said he was too busy to teach his daughter the game, but she eventually talked him into it. He sawed off the end of one of his racquets and gave it to Steffi,

"There's nobody else in the world who can do what she does."—tennis player Zina Garrison

who was soon bouncing the ball off walls and breaking the family's lamps.

Graf built her first tennis court in the basement of her home by setting up two chairs and connecting a string to them. Graf and her dad would play on this "court," often for ice cream with hot strawberries. Peter Graf was known for his determination in sports, often playing hard enough to injure himself. He passed along this determination to his daughter, though it took him a while to realize it. "For a long time, I believed that Steffi only wanted to play [tennis] because she loved me and wanted to be with me," he told *Tennis*. "But the evidence of her talent became very strong. Unlike the other children, she did not hit the ball and then look all around at other things. She was always watching the ball until it was not in play anymore."

TURNS PRO. Realizing his daughter had talent, Peter Graf quit his job as an automobile insurance salesmen and opened a tennis club. Graf, with her dad as full-time coach, began to beat other players her age. She was six when she won her first junior tournament, and by the age of 13 had won both the European championships in her age group and the German junior championship in the 18-and-under division. In 1982, at the age of 13, she quit school in the eighth grade and joined the women's professional tour, becoming the second-youngest player ever to be given a ranking, number 124. In 1984 Graf reached the quarterfinals of the legendary Wimbledon tournament and then won a gold medal at the 1984 Summer Olympics in Los Angeles, California. By the end of 1984 she had moved up in the rankings to number 22.

Though she did not win any tournaments in 1985, Graf did reach the semifinals of the U.S. Open, where she lost to **Martina Navratilova** (see entry). Early in 1986 Graf won 24 straight matches, including wins over Navratilova and Ameri-

can star Chris Evert, earning four straight tournament titles, and moving her up to number three in the world. Graf won eight of the 14 tournaments she entered in 1986 and came in second in three others.

BECOMES NUMBER ONE. Despite her success, Graf was not satisfied because she had not won any of the Grand Slam tournaments. Trying to improve, she began a strict training program that included running, weightlifting, jumping rope, and playing tennis. The hard work paid off in 1987 when Graf finally won the French Open, defeating Navratilova in the finals, 6-4, 4-6, 8-6. At the time, she was the youngest-ever French Open champion. She was now ranked number two in the world, trailing only Navratilova, who defeated Graf in the finals at Wimbledon and the U.S. Open. But Graf did well enough in other tournaments to become the number-one ranked player in the world. She lost only two of seventy-two matches she played in 1987 and won 11 of the 13 tournaments she entered.

SUPERSTAR

GRAND SLAMMER. In 1988 Graf made history by becoming only the third woman ever to win all four Grand Slam tourna-

GRAND SLAMMERS

Only four men and seven women have ever won all the Grand Slam tournaments in their careers. Only five players have won all four tournaments in the same year. Here is a list of those players.

Player	Year
Don Budge	1938
Maureen Connolly	1953
Rod Laver	1962 and 1969
Margaret Court	1970
Steffi Graf	1988

ments in the same year. She began with a 6-1, 7-6 win over Chris Evert in the Australian Open. In the finals of the French Open Graf defeated Natalia Zvereva, 6-0, 6-0, the first time in 77 years that a player had shut out their opponent in a Grand Slam final. Graf lost only 20 games in the whole tournament and apologized to the crowd for winning so easily.

In the finals at Wimbledon, Graf prepared for a showdown with Navratilova, who was going for her ninth straight win in that tournament. "This is her [Navratilova's] surface," Graf said. "She can play so much better, so you've go to watch out." Graf was nervous in the first set, making several sloppy shots and losing, 7-5. Navratilova took the first two games of the second set and seemed on her way to victory. Graf did not give up, however, and came back to win 12 of the last 13 games of the match and the championship, taking the last two sets 6-2, 6-1. She also won the tournament's women's doubles competition, teaming up with rival Gabriela Sabatini of Argentina.

With her win at Wimbledon, Graf now had an excellent chance to become the first player to win the Grand Slam in 18 years. All she had to do was win the U.S. Open—a tournament she had never won. Navratilova was upset in the quarterfinals of the tournament, so in the finals Graf faced her doubles partner, Sabatini. Graf won the first set, 6-3, but Sabatini came back to take the second, 6-3. In the third set Sabatini tired and Graf won, 6-1, to win the championship and the Grand Slam. When the final point was over, Graf climbed into the stands to hug her father and other family members. "[W]inning a Slam is amazing—I don't care if it was against old ladies or everybody was sick," male tennis star Ivan Lendl told *Sports Illustrated*.

MAJOR UPSET. A few days after her U.S. Open victory, Graf won a gold medal at the 1988 Summer Olympics in Seoul, South Korea, once again beating Sabatini. Her winning ways continued at the 1989 Australian Open, where she did not lose a set and defeated Helena Sukova in the finals for her fifth straight Grand Slam title. Trying to win a record sixth straight Grand Slam title, Graf entered the French Open as the heavy favorite and easily reached the final match. In the finals, Graf—ill with stomach problems—faced **Arantxa Sanchez Vicario** (see entry)of Spain. Graf won the first set in a tie-breaker, 7-6, then lost the second set, 6-3. Behind 5-3 in the last set, Sanchez Vicario began to play amazingly well, winning four straight games and the championship in a major upset. "She was making some unbelievable shots, so close to the lines," Graf said of the woman who had defeated her.

ANOTHER BIG YEAR. The loss to Sanchez Vicario in the French Open was all that prevented Graf from winning her second straight Grand Slam. Graf defeated Navratilova in the Wimbledon finals for the second year in a row, 6-2, 6-7, 6-1. Her countryman, Boris Becker, won the men's singles championship. The two Germans also won at the U.S. Open, where Graf again defeated Navratilova in the finals, 3-6, 7-5, 6-1. When Graf defeated Mary Joe Fernandez, 6-3, 6-4, in the finals of the 1990 Australian Open, she'd won eight of the last nine Grand Slam tournaments. Between June 1989 and May 1990, Graf won 66 straight matches, the second-longest winning streak in the history of women's tennis (Navratilova won 74 straight in 1984), and won 86 out of 88 matches during the year. "There's nobody else in the world who can do what she does," fellow player Zina Garrison told *Sports Illustrated*.

CHALLENGED. Graf was challenged as the best player in the world by 16-year-old **Monica Seles** (see entry) from Yugoslavia, who defeated Graf, 7-6, 6-4, in the finals of the French Open. Graf lost in the quarterfinals at Wimbledon—ending her record streak of 13 straight Grand Slam finals—and in the finals of the U.S. Open, 6-2, 7-6, to Sabatini. Despite winning 10 tournaments during the year, her hold on the number-one ranking began to slip. "I'm lacking a little bit right now," Graf said. "I'm not hitting the ball like I used to. There's something missing."

1991 started out with more of the same, as Seles won the Australian, French, and U.S. Opens. Graf fell to number two in the world in March after 188 weeks at the top, a record streak. Graf was able to end a year-and-a-half drought in Grand Slam tournaments, and break Seles's Grand Slam streak, by winning the 1991 Wimbledon championships, 6-4, 3-6, 8-6, over Sabatini. The real news of that tournament, however, was that Seles didn't play, claiming a mysterious injury. Still, Graf was happy with the victory. "I needed to win again. I needed it for myself," she said.

In several dramatic head-to-head confrontations in 1992, Seles again got the best of Graf, who missed the Australian Open with the German measles. At the French Open, Seles defeated Graf in the finals, 6-2, 3-6, 10-8, then Graf beat Seles at Wimbledon, crushing her in the finals, 6-2, 6-1. Seles finished the year by winning the U.S. Open (Graf lost in the quarterfinals), winning three of the four Grand Slam tournaments for the second straight year. At the 1992 Summer Olympics in Barcelona, Spain, Graf was upset by American Jennifer Capriati in the gold medal match.

TRAGEDY STRIKES. When Seles again defeated Graf in the finals of the 1993 Australian Open she appeared to be unbeatable—until a terrible tragedy occurred. On April 30, during a tournament in Hamburg, Germany, Seles was stabbed in the back by an unstable spectator as she sat next to the court between games. When asked why he did it, the attacker said he was a big fan of Graf and wanted her to be the number-one ranked player again. Graf felt terrible that someone would do such a thing and was one of the first players to visit Seles in the hospital. Seles missed the rest of 1993 and the beginning of 1994. It is not certain when she will return.

RETURNS TO TOP. Without Seles to challenge her, Graf again dominated women's tennis in 1993. She won the French Open, 4-6, 6-2, 6-4, over American Mary Joe Fernandez. At Wimbledon it appeared Graf would lose in the finals to Jana Novotna of Czechoslovakia, after she fell behind 4-1 in the last set. Feeling the pressure, however, Novotna began to make mistakes, and Graf came from behind to win the set 6-4 and take the championship. Novotna wept after the match, and Graf felt badly for her. "I was very happy in the first few moments after the match," she told *Sports Illustrated*, "but once I saw her face, I knew exactly what was going through her mind. We've all been in that situation. So I really felt bad."

At the U.S. Open, Graf defeated Helen Sukova in the finals, 6-3, 6-3. For the third time, Graf had won at least three of the four Grand Slam tournaments in a single year. She was happy to be back on top, but sad that Seles had been injured. "There's one player who hasn't been around the last three Grand Slams, that's Monica, and let's hope she'll soon be back," Graf told the crowd after her U.S. Open title. She won her fourth straight Grand Slam tournament, the 1994 Australian Open, and seemed to be on her way to a second Grand Slam. She had lost only one match in 1994 as she began the French Open. Graf was the favorite to beat American Mary Piece in the semifinals. In a major upset, Pierce defeated Graf, who was suffering from allergies, 6–2, 6–2. In her career, Graf has won 15 Grand Slam tournaments and finished second seven times. She is fifth on the all-time list in Grand Slam singles titles for women and fourth on the all-time tournament titles list for women. Amazingly, at just 25 years of age, Graf has won over $13 million in her career.

OFF THE COURT. Graf lives in Bruhl, Germany; Boca Raton, Florida; and New York City. Though a fierce competitor on the court, Graf is friendly and fun-loving in private. Because she trains so hard, Graf has not always had time for boyfriends, but now she is serious about race car driver Michael Bartels. Her younger brother, Michael, also races cars. Graf has four dogs—three German Shepherds and one

WHAT MAKES HER SO GOOD?

Steffi Graf has had enormous success. She is always in excellent condition, trains and practices very hard, and is one of the world's fastest players. She has a powerful serve and effective backhand, but her biggest weapon is her forehand. "Her forehand puts fear in everybody," pro player Zina Garrison told *Sports Illustrated*. Her forehand is so good that tennis commentator Bud Collins gave her the nickname "Fraulein Forehand." In addition to her physical talent, Graf is also one of the game's toughest competitors. "She doesn't like to lose a single point," another of her victims, Terry Phelps, told *Sports Illustrated*. "She's always like that, so intense." The combination of tennis talent and mental toughness make Graf a standout. As player Carling Bassett Seguso told *Sports Illustrated:* "Some of the things she does don't seem human."

Boxer. She likes to collect shorts and t-shirts and cook pasta. When not playing tennis Graf enjoys art, listening to all kinds of music, reading, playing cards, watching movies, and photography. She has modeled clothes and is designing tennis fashions for Adidas. In 1991 the Steffi Graf Youth Tennis Center was opened in Leipzig, Germany.

Through all of her ups and downs, Graf's family has always come first. "It doesn't come clear when you are young," Graf told *Sports Illustrated*. "The fights with the brother, when he steals your coat or the other way around. The cleaning the room.... But when you get out into the world, get into difficulty, learn about life, see other families not giving or caring, you realize how important your own [family] is."

WHERE TO WRITE

C/O WOMEN'S TENNIS ASSOCIATION, STOUFFER VINOY RESORT, ONE FOURTH ST., N., ST. PETERSBURG, FL 33701.

WAYNE GRETZKY

1961—

Wayne Gretzky holds so many National Hockey League (NHL) records that it is impossible to list them all. Nine times he has won the Hart Memorial Trophy as the NHL's Most Valuable Player (MVP) and in nine seasons he was the league's leading scorer. Gretzky has more assists (1,563), goals (803), and points (2,328) than any player in NHL history. He has also scored more goals (92), assists (163), and points (215) in a single season than any other player. (No other player has ever earned over 200 points in one season.) A natural leader, Gretzky was the captain of four Edmonton Oilers Stanley Cup winners. No player has ever dominated a sport for as long as Gretzky.

GROWING UP

Wayne Gretzky was born January 26, 1961, in Brantford, Ontario, Canada. Of Russian and Polish descent, he is the oldest of Walter and Phyllis Gretzky's five children. His father, a telephone company employee, bought his son a pair of skates before he was three years old and taught him skating drills on a backyard ice rink. This started a habit of hard work that has stayed with Gretzky his entire career. His father said that hock-

"I approach each game as if I were still a kid, wishing that one day I would play in the NHL."—Wayne Gretzky

ey was Wayne's way of not having to work as hard as his dad to earn a living.

CHILD STAR. When he was young Gretzky played baseball, football, lacrosse, and soccer and says baseball was his favorite sport. He's been a hockey star since the age of 10 and scored 378 goals for the Brantford Nadrofsky Steelers. When he was 14, Gretzky moved to Toronto, Ontario, Canada to escape from his small hometown where the booing of parents from opposing teams and the pressure of being a young celebrity made it hard for him to live a normal life. "We just got to the point where it became uncomfortable to be stared at," Gretzky told the *Los Angeles Herald Examiner.* "More than anything, you always felt like you were on display."

TURNS PRO. At the age of 17, before he finished high school, Gretzky signed a professional contract with the Indianapolis Racers of the World Hockey Association (WHA), a rival league set up to compete with the NHL. It soon became obvious that the Racers were headed for bankruptcy, so they sold Gretzky to the Edmonton Oilers. He was an instant success in the WHA, scoring 46 goals and 110 points (third in the WHA) during the 1978-79 season. The WHA went out of business following Gretzky's first season and the Oilers became one of four teams taken into the NHL.

MVP STRING BEGINS. Many people thought that Gretzky was successful in his first season only because the competition was weak in the WHA. "Everywhere I went they thought I would get killed because of my size," Gretzky, who was five-feet-eleven-inches tall and 165 pounds, said. "I heard a lot of talk then that I'd never get 110 points like I did in the WHA." But he did better than that, leading the NHL with 137 points on 51 goals and 86 assists. At the end of the season Gretzky won the Hart Memorial Trophy as the NHL's MVP and the Lady Byng Trophy as the league's most sportsmanlike player. (He also won the award in 1991 and 1992.)

Realizing that Gretzky might develop into the greatest player of all time, Oilers's owner Peter Pocklington signed the young star to a 21-year contract. "We need a superstar," Pocklington said at the time. "And Wayne is going to be one." The investment paid off as Gretzky led the league in scoring and won the Hart Trophy *eight straight* seasons. During the 1980-81 season Gretzky set a single season record for points with 164 and assists with 109. Still, the Oilers barely qualified for the Stanley Cup playoffs in Gretzky's first two seasons.

Things looked better in the 1981-82 season. The Oilers won the NHL's Smythe Division with 111 points (second best in the league). Having already shattered the scoring record a year earlier, Gretzky went on to destroy it, earning 212 points—an incredible 65 more than anyone else in the league. Included in his total was a record 92 goals, which broke the previous record by 16, and a record 120 assists. But the season ended on a down note when the Oilers lost in the first round of the playoffs to the Los Angeles Kings, the team with the worst record to make the playoffs.

The next season (1982-83) the Oilers reached the Stanley Cup finals against the New York Islanders, a team going for their fourth straight title. Gretzky scored 196 points (71 goals and a record 121 assists) in regular season, winning the scoring title by 72 points, but in the series against the Islanders he was held without a goal and had only four assists. The Islanders swept the Oilers, but it was clear the young Edmonton team would be back.

SUPERSTAR

STANLEY CUP CHAMPS. Edmonton earned an incredible 119 points in the 1983-84 season and Gretzky broke the 200 point

NUMBER 99

Gretzky began wearing the number 99, the highest possible number a hockey player can wear, because the number 9—worn by his idol, former NHL legend Gordie Howe, wasn't available when Gretzky joined a junior team as a teenager.

Wayne Gretzky

mark for the second time (205 points, 87 goals, and 118 assists—79 points more than the second-place scorer). The Oilers swept every playoff game on their way to the Stanley Cup finals where they again faced the Islanders. The high-scoring Oilers won a defensive struggle in Game One, 1-0, then lost Game Two, 6-1. By sweeping the last three games, Edmonton won their first ever Stanley Cup. Gretzky led all scorers in the playoffs with 35 points.

REPEAT. Gretzky broke his own single-season assist record in the 1984-85 season with 135 (he also led the NHL with 73 goals) and the Oilers set a record by going 15 games at the beginning of the season without a loss (12-0-3). On December 19, Gretzky scored his one-thousandth point, breaking the record for reaching this milestone in the fewest games. In the Stanley Cup finals, the Oilers defeated the Philadelphia Flyers, four games to one. Gretzky was given one of the few awards he hadn't already won—the Conn Smythe Trophy as the playoff MVP—breaking NHL playoff records with 30 assists and 47 points.

The Oilers could not three-peat in 1985-86. They were upset in the playoffs by the Calgary Flames when Edmonton defenseman Steve Smith scored into his own net for the winning goal in Game Seven. Breaking records was getting to be routine for Gretzky, so when he broke the single-season records for points (215) and assists (163), no one was surprised. Edmonton returned to the top in the 1986-87 season, defeating the Philadelphia Flyers in the Stanley Cup finals in seven games. Gretzky scored just five goals in the Oilers's 21-game playoff run, but had a playoff-high 34 points.

RECORD-BREAKER. Two streaks ended in the 1987-88 season. For the first time since entering the NHL, Gretzky was not the league MVP and did not lead the NHL in scoring. Both of those honors went to **Mario Lemieux** (see entry) of the Pittsburgh Penguins who finished 19 points ahead of Gretzky, (who missed 16 games with an injury). On March 1 Gretzky earned assist number 1,050, breaking the NHL record held by the legendary Gordie Howe. The Oilers reached the Stanley Cup finals where they faced the Boston Bruins. Edmonton won their fourth championship in five years, sweeping the Bruins in four straight. Gretzky's record 31 assists in one playoff year highlighted the winning of his second Conn Smythe Trophy as the playoff's MVP.

BIG TRADE. By this point in his career, Gretzky was the most popular hockey player in Canada. He married American actress Janet Jones in July 1988, just before the bombshell hit. In an effort to save money, the Oilers traded Gretzky to the Los Angeles Kings for $15 million, three players, and three first-round draft picks. In return, the Kings received Gretzky and three other players. It was the most spectacular trade in the history of the NHL—maybe of all sports. "I hate to leave," Gretzky said. "Sometimes in life you do things that you don't want to do." In Canada hockey fans mourned the loss of their national hero to an American team.

Gretzky had an immediate effect on the Kings, a team that earned only 68 points the season before the trade. In his first season Gretzky finished second in the scoring race to Lemieux (199 points to 168), but he inspired his teammates, lifting the Kings to 91 points in the 1988-89 season. In an emotional series for Gretzky, the Kings played Edmonton in the first round of the playoffs. The Oilers took a 3-1 lead in the series, but the Kings came storming back to win in seven games. The Kings then lost in four straight to the eventual champion Calgary Flames, ending their best season ever.

ALL-TIME POINTS LEADER. The 1989-90 season saw Gretzky's return to the top of the NHL scoring list and another record. He earned 142 points and on October 15, 1989, in Edmonton, Gretzky passed Gordie Howe to become the NHL's all-time leader in points. The record-breaking point was produced when Gretzky scored a goal with 53 seconds left

TOP OF THE CHARTS

Gretzky has shattered most of the NHL's scoring records. The following chart shows the top five in the three major regular season scoring categories: assists, goals, and points.

Player	Assists
Wayne Gretzky	1,655
Gordie Howe	1,049
Marcel Dionne	1,040
Stan Mikita	926
Bryan Trottier	890

Player	Goals
Wayne Gretzky	803
Gordie Howe	801
Marcel Dionne	731
Phil Esposito	717
Bobby Hull	610

Player	Points
Wayne Gretzky	2,458
Gordie Howe	1,850
Marcel Dionne	1,771
Phil Esposito	1,590
Stan Mikita	1,467

in regulation time to tie the score. He then scored in overtime to win the game. The Kings dropped to 75 points and lost in the second round of the playoffs to the Oilers, who were on their way to their first Gretzky-less Stanley Cup.

Early in the 1990-91 season Gretzky scored his 2,000 career point. Asked if he thought he might eventually reach 3,000 points, Gretzky said: "That might be tough. Barring injury and staying healthy, I can probably average 150 points a year, which means seven more years. I don't know if I'll play seven more years." In fact, troubled by his father's illness, Gretzky began to talk about retiring, but not before he led the NHL in scoring in the 1990-91 season with 163 points (41 goals and 122 assists) and the Kings to a Smythe division title. The Kings beat the Vancouver Canucks in the first round of the playoffs, but once again lost to the Oilers in the second round.

CLOSE TO CUP. Gretzky finished third in the scoring race during the 1991-92 season with 121 points, and the Kings were again knocked out of the playoffs early. Then, at the beginning of the 1992-93 season, Gretzky announced that a back injury would force him to miss the first part of the season, perhaps ending his career. Talking about his back injury, Gretzky told the *Sporting News:* "When I was going through those tough times, maybe it was a blessing in disguise. It helped me focus on my priorities, showed me how much I really love this game." He missed 39 games because of his back, but returned in time to help lead the Kings to the Stanley Cup finals for the first time ever, where Los Angeles faced the Montreal Canadiens. The series was extremely close, with three games decided in overtime. In the end, the Kings came up short, losing in five games. Gretzky led the league in playoff scoring with 40 points.

PASSES HOWE. Entering his 15th season in 1993, Gretzky was within range of breaking Howe's all-time goal-scoring record, a record he almost didn't want to break. "I wish I could stop at [800] goals," Gretzky said. Gretzky broke the record on March 23, 1994, when he fired a wrist shot past Vancouver Canucks goalie Kirk McLean. "A lot of things went through my mind— my dad's illness, the four Stanley Cups in Edmonton and much, much more," Gretzky admitted to the *Sporting News.* "But I have to admit, I've never had a greater feeling than when that puck went into the net." Even Howe is amazed by Gretzky's achievements. "He scored 85 more points one year than the next guy," Howe observed in the same magazine. "I scored 85 one year and set a record."

Gretzky ended the 1993-94 season with 38 goals, 92 assists, and 130 points, numbers good enough for him to lead the NHL in scoring for the tenth time. The Kings, however, failed to make the playoffs. It appeared that Gretzky would continue to play as long as physically possible. Always a hard-working player, Gretzky constantly studies hockey and works to improve. For every team he has played with, Gretzky has been the captain. His assist totals show that he works hard to help his teammates score. Gretzky holds 60 NHL records, but he takes the greatest pride in his four Stanley Cup championships with the Oilers and he still has one goal: bringing a Stanley Cup championship to Los Angeles. "You definitely think about running out of chances to win it all," he told the *Sporting News.* "I'm getting older and older, and the time is getting shorter and shorter."

OFF THE ICE. Gretzky and his wife, Janet, live with their daughter, Paulina, and their two sons, Ty and Trevor, in Encino, California. A family man, Gretzky loves to spend time with his children and wants to retire before he is injured too badly to teach them how to play hockey. Gretzky is a spokesperson for cameras, soft drinks, athletic shoes, and rental cars, but says that being famous is not always easy because he is often recognized in public. He is part-owner of champion racehorses and the Toronto Argonauts Canadian Football League team and he collects baseball cards and rare coins. Always polite, Gretzky never turns down an interview request and is the NHL's goodwill ambassador, often giving away his sticks to kids after games. When asked what helps keep him playing by *Sports Illustrated for Kids,* Gretzky said: "I approach each game as if I were still a kid, wishing that one day I would play in the NHL. I play each game knowing that every kid would love to be in my position."

WHERE TO WRITE

C/O LOS ANGELES KINGS, GREAT WESTERN FORUM, 3900 W. MANCHESTER BLVD., INGLEWOOD, CA 90306.

KEN GRIFFEY, JR.

1969—

Ken Griffey, Jr., known as "Junior" and "the Kid," had a hard act to follow when he joined the Seattle Mariners as a 19-year-old rookie. His dad, Ken, Sr., was an all-star outfielder who had played on two World Series championship teams. In his first five seasons, however, "Junior" has shown the kind of ability that might make him one of the best players of all time by the end of his career. In addition to his great talent, Griffey plays baseball with a love that he has carried with him since he was a kid watching his dad play.

GROWING UP

George Kenneth Griffey, Jr., was born November 21, 1969, in Donora, Pennsylvania. The year Griffey was born, his dad, Ken Griffey, Sr., signed a contract to play professional baseball with the Cincinnati Reds organization and started in the minor leagues. During childhood he and his brother followed their dad through a series of minor league towns until 1973, when Griffey, Sr., was called up to play with the major league Cincinnati Reds.

"I just have fun like I did when I was a kid."—Ken Griffey, Jr.

Many kids dream about meeting major-league baseball players, but it was an everyday event for Griffey. His dad was a teammate of great players like Pete Rose, Johnny Bench, Joe Morgan, and Tony Perez, and Griffey often went down on the field with his dad for batting practice and played in father-son games. His dad was a .296 career hitter and three-time All-Star who played for back-to-back World Series champions in 1975 and 1976 before being traded to the New York Yankees after the 1981 season. Griffey, Jr., told *People* magazine: "I watched my dad play for years. I talked to him every day about the game. There isn't one thing I've seen so far that he hasn't told me about beforehand."

NO PRESSURE. The life of a professional baseball player can be hard on their families. When his dad was traded to the Yankees—and then to the Atlanta Braves—the rest of the family remained in Cincinnati. (Griffey's mom, Alberta, was a pretty good hitter herself, and once won a home run hitting contest against other players' wives.) His dad almost always missed Griffey's Little League and high school games, but his mom was always there. Even when his dad did attend his son's sporting events, he had to do so secretly to avoid being mobbed by autograph-seekers. Unlike many fathers, Griffey's dad never pushed his son into baseball. "I don't believe in putting pressure on kids," Griffey, Sr. told *Sports Illustrated for Kids*. "With Junior, you could see it was what he wanted to do."

Griffey had a good relationship with his dad. "If I needed to talk to [my father], I would call him after the game, and we'd talk. If I did something wrong [on the field], he'd fly me to New York and say, 'You can't do that!' Then he would send me home the next day, and I'd play baseball." Hoping to impress him, Griffey often had his worst games when his father was watching. It wasn't until Griffey started to play in the minor leagues that he could hit well while his dad watched. "May dad always told me to have fun, no matter what," Griffey told *Sports Illustrated for Kids*. "I never saw him get upset when he played."

MULTI-SPORT STAR. When he was young, Griffey played football, basketball, and soccer in addition to baseball. He often played with his younger brother, Craig, who is now a minor league baseball player. Baseball scouts who watched Griffey play in Cincinnati were impressed with his talent. At the age of 16 he was invited to join the Connie Mack League, a summer amateur (unpaid) program made up mostly of 18-year-old players. Griffey led the team to the Connie Mack World Series, where he hit three home runs. He was also a star baseball and football player at Moeller High School in Cincinnati, where he hit 20 home runs— three in one game—and set a school record with a .478 batting average as a senior. When he graduated in 1987 at the age of 17, Griffey announced that he would participate in the annual professional baseball draft.

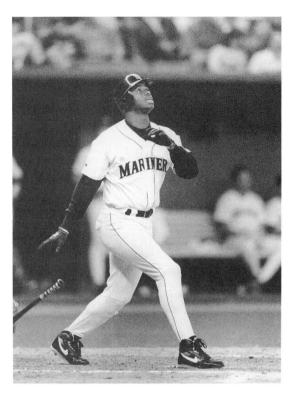

Ken Griffey, Jr.

TURNS PRO. The Seattle Mariners held the first pick in the amateur draft and used it to choose Griffey, who signed a contract and predicted that he would make the major leagues within two or three years. No one expected him to meet that goal—his father had spent four-and-a-half years in the minors, and many good players take even longer to be called up to the big leagues. Griffey got off to a fast start in the minors, batting .320 with 14 home runs and 13 stolen bases, at Bellingham, Washington. He had a hard time adjusting to being away from home for the first time, however, and spent hours on the phone talking long distance with his mom, who visited her son several times.

DUMB THING. Griffey seemed to be a happy young man playing the game he loved, but behind the scenes he was having problems. When he was 17 and playing in Bellingham, he tried to commit suicide by swallowing more than 270 aspirin tablets. Griffey told *Jet* magazine that this suicide attempt—which put him in the local hospital's intensive care unit—was in response to the pressure he felt during his first professional season. "I got depressed, I got angry. I didn't want to live. The aspirin thing was the only time I acted. It was such a dumb thing."

Once he got over his problems, Griffey began to blossom as a hitter and fielder. Despite injuries in his second season in the minors, Griffey was voted the number-one major league prospect in the California League, where he batted .338 and an even better .444 during a late-season promotion to a team in Vermont. As 1989 spring training began, Griffey was determined to find a spot on the big-league Mariners's roster. Working harder to prepare for games and spending more time studying the opposing players, Griffey became focused on his profession.

MAJOR-LEAGUE SON. In 26 spring training games during 1989 Griffey batted .359 with two home runs and 21 runs batted in (RBIs), numbers good enough to earn him a spot on the Mariners's roster. He was 19 at the time, one of the youngest players ever to make the major leagues. Back in Cincinnati Griffey, Sr., was playing in his 20th major league season and reporters rushed to photograph the father and son together. Griffey, who was called "Junior" by the press, tried not to let the publicity affect his on-field concentration. In his first major league at-bat, Griffey doubled. And in his first at-bat before the home fans in Seattle, he hit a home run.

Griffey did so well in his first year that a candy bar was named after him, and only a late-season injury prevented him from winning the American League rookie-of-the-year award. (He finished third in the voting.) Griffey batted .264, hit 16 home runs, had 61 RBIs, and stole 16 bases. He also showed great ability in center field—one of baseball's toughest positions—making leaping catches to rob hitters of home runs and throwing base runners out from the outfield. *Sports Illustrated* called Griffey, "a natural.... The kind of player after whom babies and candy bars are named."

SUPERSTAR

PLAYS WITH DAD. In 1990 Griffey made his first All-Star game appearance, a year in which he led the Mariners in home runs (22) and ranked seventh in the American League in batting average (.300). He also won the first of four straight Golden Glove awards for his defensive excellence. Griffey was thrilled when the Mariners signed his dad, who was nearing the end of his career, and the two Griffeys played together in the Seattle outfield—the first time a father and son had appeared together in the major leagues.

Griffey had an even better year in 1991, batting .327 (fourth in the American League) with 22 home runs and 100 RBIs. His play helped the Mariners to finish 83-79, the first time the team had ever finished with a winning record. At the 1992 All-Star Game Griffey went three-for-three with a home run and won the game's Most Valuable Player (MVP) award. He batted .308 with 27 home runs and 107 RBIs in 1992. His manager, Jim Lefebvre, told *Sports Illustrated* that Griffey's accomplishments "pick up the entire club. He is going to be one of the real marquee [star] players in this league. That's one thing his father, as great as he was, never was." The Mariners tumbled to only 64 wins, however, and Lefebvre was fired as manager.

TIES RECORD. The 1993 season opened with new hope in Seattle as Lou Pinella, who led the Cincinnati Reds to a World Series title in 1990, took over as manager. The Mariners improved to 82-80, mostly as a result of Griffey's performance. He batted .309, had 45 home runs, drove in 109 runs, and scored 113 more. From July 20 through 28 Griffey tied a major league record by hitting home runs in eight straight games. (The two other players to

MAJOR LEAGUE LEADERS BEFORE 24th BIRTHDAY

Player	Hits
Ty Cobb	960
Mel Ott	895
Buddy Lewis	882
Al Kaline	880
Fred Lindstrom	864
Robin Yount	857
Ken Griffey, Jr.	832

Player	HRs
Mel Ott	153
Eddie Mathews	153
Ken Griffey, Jr.	132
Frank Robinson	130
Ted Williams	123
Mickey Mantle	121
Juan Gonzalez	121

Player	RBI
Mel Ott	608
Jimmie Foxx	498
Ted Williams	491
Ty Cobb	478
Ken Griffey, Jr.	453
Al Kaline	450
Mickey Mantle	445

THE WHOLE PACKAGE

Griffey has become a star because of his all-around skill as a player. He bats for a high average, hits home runs, has great speed, and is an outstanding fielder with a strong arm. Griffey makes the game seem easy and has a love for baseball that affects all those who play with him. "I just have fun like I did when I was a kid," Griffey told *Sports Illustrated for Kids*. "No matter where you are playing the game of baseball, you still do everything—hit, run, and catch—the same." That's why some writers call Griffey "the Kid."

accomplish this were Dale Long of the Pirates in 1956 and Don Mattingly of the Yankees in 1987.) In the game that broke his streak, Griffey hit a screaming double and a single. "I like playing in Seattle," he told *Sport*. "I like to just go out there, play, enjoy myself and do the best job that I can do to help this team win."

OFF THE FIELD. Griffey lives in Issaquah, Washington, a suburb of Seattle, with his wife, Melissa, and their son, Trey. Some reporters believe that Griffey is one of the best players of all time and a future Hall-of-Famer, but he knows that it's too soon to tell how good he might become. "I just want to go out there and contribute," Griffey told *Sport* magazine. "No matter what happens, you got to be lucky to get in the Hall of Fame. You got to have a long, healthy career."

WHERE TO WRITE

C/O SEATTLE MARINERS,

411 FIRST AVE., S., P.O. BOX 4100, SEATTLE, WA 98104.

FLORENCE GRIFFITH JOYNER

1959—

In 1988 Florence Griffith Joyner, or Flojo as she is better known, was a blur on the racetrack, winning gold medals in the 100- and 200-meter dashes, and with the U.S. 4 X 100-meter relay team. By doing so, Griffith Joyner became known as "The World's Fastest Woman." She also made news with her unusual track outfits, her long fingernails, her flowing hair, and her bright smile. After she retired from racing, she started new careers in acting, clothes designing, modeling, and writing. Taking on a new challenge in 1993, she accepted President Clinton's invitation to be co-chairperson for the President's Council on Physical Fitness and Sports.

GROWING UP

Delorez Florence Griffith was born December 21, 1959, in Los Angeles, California. One of 11 children, she was raised in the Jordan housing project in the tough Watts section of Los Angeles by her mother, Florence, a seamstress. (Her parents were divorced when she was four.) Her mother had a hard time earning enough money to support her family, but her daughter didn't mind. "We learned something from how we grew up," Griffith Joyner told the *Sporting News*. "It has never been

"Chasing all those records and giving the young kids coming up something to chase, that's what the sport is all about."— Florence Griffith Joyner

easy, and we knew it wouldn't be handed to us, unless we went after it." To avoid being confused with her mother, she was given the nickname "Dee Dee," a name her friends and family still call her today.

HER OWN PERSON. Griffith Joyner showed early signs of becoming her own person. In kindergarten, she braided her hair with one braid sticking straight up. In high school she wore her pet boa constrictor (a very large snake) like a necklace. She read a lot, wrote poetry and kept a diary. "I always wanted a gun set for Christmas, which no other girls wanted," she told the *Chicago Tribune,* "or something in a color no one had." Her mother tried to discipline the young rebel, attention she didn't like at the time but appreciates now. "Everybody in the family survived," she told *Newsweek.* "Nobody does drugs, nobody got shot at. I used to say it was because we were afraid of Mama's voice. We didn't know how poor we were. We were rich as a family."

At the age of seven Griffith Joyner began to compete in 50- and 70-meter dashes at the Sugar Ray Robinson Youth Foundation (named after the famous boxer), a program for poor children. "I would always win," she told the *Chicago Tribune.* In 1973 she won the annual Jesse Owens National Youth Games (named after the legendary track star) and the next year she won again. In 1978 she graduated from Jordan High School in Los Angeles after setting school records in sprint races and the long jump.

WINS OLYMPIC MEDAL. After high school Griffith Joyner attended California State University at Northridge, but ran out of money, quit school, and worked as a bank teller. In college, she met a young track coach named Bobby Kersee, who helped her apply for financial aid. When Kersee changed jobs in 1980 and went to the University of California at Los Ange-

les (UCLA), Griffith Joyner followed him. In 1980 she barely missed qualifying for the Olympic team in the 200-meters and in 1982 she ran the 200-meters in 22.39 seconds for the National Collegiate Athletic Association (NCAA) championship. She was also a threat in the 400-meters, winning the NCAA championship in 1983. She qualified for the Olympic team in 1984, finishing second in the 200-meter race.

Florence Griffith Joyner (third from the left)

TAKES TIME OFF. After the Olympics Griffith Joyner cut back on her training and competing, gaining weight and falling out of shape in the process. She worked as a customer service representative for a bank and as a hair-dresser and nail stylist. At her beauty shop she developed elaborate styles of braiding hair and painting long nails. Griffith Joyner was engaged to be married to Olympic hurdle runner Greg Foster, but broke off the engagement. She then became close to Al Joyner, who had won a gold medal in the triple jump at the 1984 Olympic Summer Games. The two met at the 1980 Olympic trials, began dating in 1986, and married on October 10, 1987 in Las Vegas, Nevada. They later appeared on "The Newlywed Game" TV show.

TRENDSETTER. Griffith Joyner brought her sense of style onto the race track. Her outfits were different, to say the least—she wore white bikini bottoms over most unusual tights. The right leg was completely covered in fabric; the left leg completely bare, except for the shoe on her foot. Her long nails also showed a distinctive style, and the designs she painted on them showed her individualism. "Looking good is almost as important as running well," she once said. "It's part of feeling good about myself."

RECORD BREAKER. In 1987 Griffith Joyner returned to serious competition and began training under Coach Kersee's very strict program. She finished second in the 200-meters at the World Championships in the summer of 1987, and became even more determined to improve. "When you've been second-best for so long, you can either accept it, or try to become the best," she told *Ms.* magazine. "I made the decision to try to be the best." During the U.S. Olympic trials in July of 1988, she shattered the world 100-meter record with a time of 10.49 seconds—.27 seconds better than the previous record held by American sprinter Evelyn Ashford.

SUPERSTAR

OLYMPIC CHAMP. Heading to the Olympics in Seoul, South Korea, Griffith Joyner was favored in the 100- and 200-meter races, and was a member of the U.S. 400- and 1600-meter relay teams. In the 100-meter dash she won with a time of 10.54 seconds. She followed that up by breaking the world record in the 200-meter competition twice—once in the semifinals and again in the finals. In the 400-meter relay, she shared a gold medal with three U.S. teammates in a time of 41.98. Finally, she shared a silver medal with three other teammates in the 1600-meter relay, won by the Soviet Union in a world and Olympic record time of 3:15.18. In both the 100- and 200-meter dashes, Griffith Joyner would have had better times, but she couldn't resist throwing her arms up and flashing a brilliant smile for the cameras.

Florence Griffith Joyner celebrating an Olympic victory.

DRUG-FREE. Following the Olympics, some of Griffith Joyner's competitors claimed she used illegal drugs called steroids to build up her strength. She denied the charges, pointing to her training program as the reason she ran so fast, and passed every drug test she was asked to take. "It [the charges] hurt me, but it didn't bother me," she told *New York Newsday*. "I know that I'm a champion. I am anti-drugs.... Chasing all those records and giving the young kids coming up something to chase, that's what the sport is all about."

With her performance in the Olympics, Griffith Joyner earned the title "The World's Fastest Woman." She was honored with the 1988 Jesse Owens Award as the year's outstanding track and field athlete and the 1988 Sullivan Award as the top American amateur athlete. In February of 1989, she announced that she was retiring from competition to start commercial and entertainment careers. "With all I want to do—

[fashion] designing, writing, acting, modeling—I realized there was no time to train," she told the *Chicago Tribune*. Griffith Joyner became the spokesperson for several products, designed her own line of sportswear for Starter, appeared as an actress in several television shows, and made a fitness video. She also continued her childhood hobby of writing, and is the author of more than 30 books for children.

THE PRESIDENT CALLS. In 1993 President Bill Clinton announced that Griffith Joyner and former NBA basketball star and U.S. Congressman Tom McMillen would be co-chairpersons for the President's Council on Physical Fitness and Sports, which advises the President on ways to promote fitness and sports programs for all Americans. Griffith Joyner hopes to use her new position to help children. "I love working with kids, talking with them and listening to them," she told the *New York Times Magazine*. "I always encourage kids to reach beyond their dreams. Don't try to be like me. Be better than me." As co-chairperson she wants to encourage all Americans, but especially children, to exercise and eat right. But, she admits, nobody is perfect. "I don't always have the best eating habits," she told the *New York Times Magazine*. "I like butter and ice cream. There are days I should work out and I don't. But it's never too late to change old habits."

OFF THE TRACK. Griffith Joyner and her husband have a daughter, Mary Ruth. Though she no longer competes in track and field, she is training to run in the marathon at the 1996 Olympics in Atlanta, Georgia. A very religious woman, Griffith Joyner reads the Bible every day, says a prayer before every meal, and calls her mom twice a day. She recently began Flojo International, a foundation through which she works with inner-city youth. Remembering her childhood, running at the Sugar Ray Robinson Foundation, Griffith Joyner's ultimate goal, as she told the *New York Times Magazine* is to "make sports and athletics available to every youth in America, not just one day a week like it was for me, but every day."

WHERE TO WRITE

C/O PRESIDENT'S COUNCIL ON PHYSICAL FITNESS AND SPORTS, JUDICIARY PLAZA, SUITE 7103, 450 FIFTH STREET, N.W., WASHINGTON, D.C. 20001.

EVANDER HOLYFIELD

1962—

> "I don't believe that you have to be mean to be successful in the ring.... In boxing, two athletes compete against one another. When it's over, you hug."—Evander Holyfield

Evander Holyfield worked long and hard to earn the title of undisputed heavyweight boxing champion of the world. He spent two years on top, before losing his title to **Riddick Bowe** (see entry), in November, 1992, in a hard-fought 12-round fight. Although he announced his retirement after losing his crown, his desire to regain his title brought him back to the ring. One year after losing his crown, Holyfield regained it by defeating Bowe, once again in 12 rounds, in November 1993.

Holyfield became champion despite the fact that he is not as big as many of his opponents. He has entered each fight with the idea that he is the "little guy," the underdog, the one who has to fight harder because he is smaller. "All my life, I've been fighting people who didn't think I could make it," Holyfield told the *Philadelphia Inquirer*. Holyfield has made it, and despite losing his title to Michael Moorer, he was a role model of disciplined and dignified behavior during his reign as heavyweight champion.

GROWING UP

Holyfield was born October, 19, 1962, in Atmore, Georgia and grew up in nearby Atlanta. The youngest of eight children, he credits his mother, Annie, with much of his success—she taught him the importance of hard work and provided him with Christian values. Holyfield's Christian faith kept him out of trouble as a youth and has helped him throughout his career. To support her four sons and four daughters, Annie Holyfield worked 12 hours a day as a cook and at an Atlanta hotel. She suffered a heart attack when Evander was ten, and could no longer work. In order to keep food on the table, all the children worked to help their mother financially.

STARTS BOXING. When he was eight, Holyfield began to box at the Warren Memorial Boys Club in Atlanta, a place where he could escape the bad influences of his run-down, inner-city neighborhood. Carter Morgan, the club's boxing coach, saw potential in Holyfield and liked his determination. Soon the youngster was fighting in peewee boxing tournaments, going undefeated for two years. "I always went out in the ring feeling I was the best," Holyfield said. "The only reason you fight is to prove it. As a kid, I loved to say, 'I'm a boxer.' But to tell you the truth, when the fights started I'd think, 'How'd I get myself into this?'"

DON'T QUIT. Holyfield also liked to swim and play football. He was an excellent linebacker on the Warren Boys Club team and hoped to be a star for Fulton High School. He made the team as a sophomore, but at five-feet-four-inches tall and 115 pounds, he was small for a football player. He didn't play much, and became disappointed that the coaches overlooked him. "So little Evander Holyfield ... sat on the bench," *Boston Globe* reporter Ron Borges wrote. "Game after humiliating game. He wanted to quit. Once he even suggested it to his mother, Annie, who had raised eight Holyfields with no intention of any of them quitting when troubled waters arose. She told him four simple words that ended their conversation: 'You finish it out.'"

When Holyfield was young, his mother called him "Chubby." She described her son to *Current Biography*: "Chubby paid all his own clothes and extras by the age of eleven, running errands, working a concession at the ballpark.... [He was] just a naturally hard worker. But there were times when I was afraid Chubby might be almost goody-good. I mean, and this may sound funny, but he really hated to fight. Sometimes he'd come home to complain about being bullied. I'd tell him you can't always run away. Sometimes you've got to stand up for your rights."

Holyfield didn't quit. When he finally got his chance, he made the most of it. In a regional championship game, he starred at cornerback. Even though the team lost, the coaches praised the play of Holyfield. Unfortunately for the coaches, that would be Holyfield's last football game. "It kind of hurt my feelings when the coach said I was too small," he told the *Boston Globe*. "So I just gave up on football and told myself, 'Evander, stick to boxing.' Football was important, but once I saw I wouldn't get a fair chance, I went back to what I did best."

ROLE MODEL. Holyfield suffered a setback when Carter Morgan died of emphysema, a lung disease. Having never known his father, Holyfield had looked up to Morgan as a male role model. "I missed him," Holyfield told *People* magazine, "but all of a sudden, I thought, 'I don't have to box anymore because I ain't got nobody to please.'" Holyfield's "retirement" from boxing lasted only three months before he returned to the gym, training with Morgan's son, Ted Morgan. "You could show him how to do something, and he could do it immediately, where other kids would have to work on it for months," Morgan told the *Chicago Tribune*. "When he came in the gym, he came in and worked."

Watching the 1980 Olympic boxing trials, held in Atlanta, Holyfield began to believe he could be an Olympic champion. He realized, seeing his competition close-up, that he could contend for an Olympic gold medal. After graduating from high school Holyfield worked two jobs, one as a lifeguard and the other fueling planes at the Dekalb-Peachtree Airport. During his time off, he trained, often getting up at four o'clock in the morning to jog before leaving for work at six o'clock. He was dedicated to training, rarely missing a workout and resting only on Sundays.

Evander Holyfield gives Riddick Bowe a left fist to the face during the first round at Caesar's Palace in Las Vegas on November 6, 1993.

OLYMPICS. Between 1980 and 1984 Holyfield compiled an impressive record of 160 wins and 14 losses as an amateur boxer, with 75 of the wins coming by knockout. He won the national Golden Gloves amateur title, the National Sports Festival boxing title in 1983, and qualified for the 1984 U.S. Olympic team as a light-heavyweight. The Olympics were a disappointment, however, as Holyfield was disqualified in the semifinal match. During the fight the referee claimed that Holyfield hit his opponent after he was told not to, something that many people who saw the fight say never happened. He was given the bronze medal for third place, but to Holyfield the medal was a badge of shame. "I still use it as a motivating thing," he told the *Boston Globe*. "People aren't going to let me forget it anyway. No matter how many fights I win, they'll always ask about what happened at the Olympics."

TURNS PRO. After the Olympics, Holyfield decided to turn professional. As a professional he fought first as a light-heavyweight, then moved to the cruiserweight (190-pound maximum weight) division, where for the first time he faced fighters who were naturally bigger than he was. Despite that obstacle, Holyfield was the first of the 1984 Olympians to win a championship when he defeated Dwight Muhammad Qawi in a tough 15-round decision on July 12, 1986. By winning that fight, Holyfield became the champion of the World Boxing Association (WBA) and the International Boxing Federation (IBF). He later became the undisputed cruiserweight champion by knocking out the World Boxing Council's (WBC) top contender, Carlos DeLeon.

Despite his success, Holyfield knew he would not win large amounts of money or be considered a great champion unless he joined the heavyweight division. With the support of his trainers—father-and-son team Lou and Dan Duva—he announced his intention to fight as a heavyweight beginning in 1989. Many observers opposed the decision, saying that Holyfield, who rarely weighed more than 212 pounds, could not fight with men who weighed 230 pounds or more.

Wanting to prove people wrong, Holyfield began "Project Omega," an intense training program. He worked on his agility, endurance, and speed. Most impressively, he improved his strength and increased his weight through weightlifting. Month after month he endured three workouts a day, six days a week—workouts that included running, swimming, weightlifting, and aerobic exercise to improve his stamina. The "Project" worked, and Holyfield proved it by reaching the finals of television's "Superstars" competition, in which athletes from many different sports participated in several different athletic events.

Holyfield won his first six fights as a heavyweight, all against opponents who were heavier and, supposedly, stronger than him. What his opponents didn't have was his desire to win. "You can't just fight for money because if you do, after the first round you can think you don't need to take all the punishment," he commented in the *Boston Globe*. "You've got the money now. You fight for the belt plus the pride."

SUPERSTAR

HEAVYWEIGHT CHAMP. After defeating former champion Michael Dokes in March 1989, Holyfield was considered a worthy challenger to heavyweight champion Mike Tyson. Negotiations had begun to set up a Tyson-Holyfield bout when "Iron Mike," as Tyson was known, was defeated in a major upset by

James "Buster" Douglas. Because Holyfield was the number-one ranked contender for the heavyweight championship, Douglas agreed to fight him, rather than fighting a rematch against Tyson. A Holyfield-Douglas showdown was set for October 25, 1990, with the champion to receive $23.5 million and the challenger $8.5 million.

Douglas came into the fight out of shape, weighing 246 pounds, while Holyfield was in top shape at 208 pounds. Holyfield, along with his trainer, Lou Duva, had analyzed Douglas's style and had a plan to defeat him. In the third round, Holyfield hit Douglas with a big right handed punch, knocking Douglas to the floor. Douglas made little attempt to get up, and when the referee counted to ten Holyfield was the champion.

Rather than fighting Mike Tyson, Holyfield defended his title in April 1991 against **George Foreman** (see entry). The 42-year-old Foreman, who had lost his heavyweight title to Muhammad Ali in 1974, was making a comeback in which he had won 24 straight fights. Although Holyfield could not knock Foreman out, he did win a unanimous decision. Holyfield was then set to meet Tyson, but the bout was canceled when Tyson was sent to prison after being convicted of rape.

To substitute for Tyson, Holyfield decided to fight Bert Cooper in Atlanta. Showing off for his home-town crowd, Holyfield was sloppy, and in the third round, he was knocked down for the first time in his professional career. Holyfield came back to knock out Cooper in the seventh round, but many people looked at the bout as a defeat for Holyfield. In June 1992 Holyfield fought another 42-year-old former champion Larry Holmes. Again he was unable to knock the older man out, winning by a decision. Holyfield's critics once again said that Holyfield was not an impressive champion.

LOSES TITLE. On November 13, 1992, Holyfield fought **Riddick Bowe** (see entry), an undefeated fighter who was taller,

FAITH

Despite being a boxer, Holyfield is a gentle man who strongly believes in his Christian faith. When he signs autographs he adds the Biblical citation "John 3:16." After regaining his title from Riddick Bowe, Holyfield took the championship belt and hurried to the airport so he could go to church the next morning.

Evander Holyfield strikes a pose.

heavier, and younger than the champion. The fight was a classic, with both fighters slugging it out for 12 rounds. Bowe knocked Holyfield down in the 11th round, and in the end the judges awarded the fight to the challenger. Despite losing his title, Holyfield proved that he could go the distance with a more powerful fighter, earning him respect, even among his critics. The day after the fight, as Bowe told *Sports Illustrated*, the new champion called Holyfield and told him "You always were a class act."

Immediately after the fight, Holyfield said he was retiring, claiming he no longer wanted to box. He changed his mind in January 1993, announcing his return to boxing. About his decision, Holyfield said, "My mother told me, 'Do it [box] until you have filled your heart.'" He also announced that his new promoter would be rap star Hammer and his new trainer would be Emanual Steward, who would try to change Holyfield's style to give him more power. Holyfield's first fight after his return was June 26, 1993, against Alex Stewart, who Holyfield defeated, but not impressively.

BOWE-HOLYFIELD II. On November 6, 1993, after twice successfully defending his title, Bowe once again faced Holyfield. In another classic match, Bowe and Holyfield fought for 12 grueling rounds. In this fight, however, Holyfield did not slug it out with Bowe, trying instead to use his speed to avoid heavy punches. The bout was interrupted in the seventh round when a parachutist risked his life and those of the audience by crashing into the ring ropes. The stunt interrupted the fight and caused Judy Bowe, Riddick's pregnant wife, to faint. In an upset, Holyfield won back his title on a decision. One judge scored the fight even, while the other two said that Holyfield had won.

RETIRES. Holyfield defended his title on May 6, 1994, against challenger Michael Moorer. The champion knocked down

Moorer during the fight, but when the judges reached their final decision after 12 grueling rounds Holyfield had lost his title. Holyfield announced after the fight that his doctors had advised him to retire due to a heart condition. The boxing world mourned the loss of a great champion.

OUTSIDE THE RING. Holyfield lives just outside of Atlanta and bought a home nearby for his mother. He still donates money to the Warren Memorial Boys Club and visits often. His hobbies include basketball, dancing, and listening to music, and he is a spokesperson for Diet Coke. Talking about boxing in the *Philadelphia Daily News*, Holyfield said, "I don't believe you have to be mean to be successful in the ring.... In boxing, two athletes compete against one another. When it's over, you hug."

WHERE TO WRITE

C/O MAIN EVENTS,

811 TOTAWA ROAD, SUITE 100, TOTAWA, NJ 07512

BRETT HULL

1964—

Brett Hull inherited two things from his father—a famous hockey name and an awesome slap shot. Hull, the record-setting right winger for the St. Louis Blues, is the son of Bobby Hull, a member of the National Hockey League (NHL) Hall of Fame and one of the greatest players in hockey history. In the 1989-90 season, Brett scored 72 goals, leading the NHL and breaking the all-time record for goals by a winger (a winger is a forward in hockey who does not play center). To prove he wasn't a one-year wonder, in the 1990-91 season Brett scored 86 goals and won the Hart Memorial Trophy as the league's Most Valuable Player. In his first six full seasons, Hull has averaged 59 goals and 100 points.

GROWING UP

Brett Andrew Hull was born August 8, 1964, in Belleville, Ontario, Canada. As a young child growing up, first in Chicago (where his dad played with the Black Hawks) then in Winnipeg, Manitoba, Canada (where his dad played with the Jets), Hull would stay after practice and play hockey with the other hockey players' children. At first Hull refused to wear skates, playing in gym shoes, but before long his father forced them on his feet and he has skated ever since.

Hull told *People* magazine that his father "never taught me anything directly. He just said, 'Watch me.' I figured out the game by watching what he did." Hull's parents never pushed him into playing hockey, afraid that he would be compared to his dad. "Kids would say, 'Oh, you're a hot dog, Hull, you're not as good as your father," his mom, Joanne, a former professional figure skater, told the *Los Angeles Times*. "He wouldn't even answer. He'd just say, 'Mom, the only way to get even with them is to put the puck in their net.'"

PARENTS DIVORCE. When Hull was 12 his parents separated, divorcing two years later. Hull, the third of five children, went to live with his mother in Vancouver, British Columbia, Canada. For years after that, he lost contact with his father. "The man never came to see him at all," his mom told the *Los Angeles Times*. "Never sent a Christmas card or a postcard or anything else. He seemed to wash his hands of the kids. We never heard from him." Only in the mid-1980s, as Hull began his professional career, did he get back together with his dad.

"HUGGY BEAR." As a teenager, Hull's nicknames were "Pickle" and "Huggy Bear," because he was overweight at five-feet-nine-inches tall and 220 pounds. Hull described himself to the *St. Louis Post-Dispatch* as "naturally lazy and easygoing." In those days he played hockey just for fun, never thinking about playing professionally. He quit hockey at 18, but his mother—angry that he had already quit baseball after being considered a good prospect—talked him back into playing. Hockey scouts considered Hull as a teenager to be too fat and lazy to be a professional prospect. They were impressed, however, with his booming slap shot. A scouting report on him at age 17 said, "He is tubby, but he can score."

When Hull finished midget hockey at age 17, no junior teams wanted him to play for them. He did play with a lower level team in Penticton, British Columbia, Canada, in 1983. In his second season with Penticton he scored a remarkable 105 goals and 83 assists for 188 points in only 56 games. His performance in Penticton won him a scholarship to play for the University of Minnesota-Duluth. As a freshman, Hull scored 32 goals in 48 games and. As a sophomore, he had 52 goals in 42 games. Hull was finalist (in his sophmore year) for the Hobey Baker Award, given to the best player in college hockey in the United States. Hull then led the U.S. team in scoring at the world championships in Moscow, Soviet Union.

TURNS PRO. Hull accomplished much of this even though he was still out of shape. Because of his lack of fitness, pro scouts still weren't impressed with Hull. His mother wanted Hull to stay in college, but he decided to sign with the NHL's Calgary Flames, who had drafted him in 1984. Hull's first two NHL games were in the Stanley Cup finals against the Montreal Canadiens. When Hull reported to training camp before the 1986-87 season out of shape, the Flames sent him to the minors. Hull scored 50 goals and had 92 points for the Flames farm team in Moncton, New Brunswick, Canada, and made the American Hockey League All-Star team. Still, his coaches wanted him to work harder, especially on defense. The next season, 1987-88, Hull was promoted to the NHL. In his first full season he scored 26 goals and 50 points in 52 games.

JOINS ST. LOUIS. On March 17, 1988, Hull, then 23, was traded to the St. Louis Blues in return for defenseman Rob Ramage and goalie Rick Wamsley. When Hull arrived, the Blues were near the bottom of the NHL, but were rebuilding by using young players. In 1988-89, Hull made the All-Star team, scoring 41 goals and 43 assists, but his sometimes selfish play did not help the Blues win. After the season his coach, Brian Sutter, talked to Hull, telling him that if he wanted to be a great player he had to play defense, help his teammates, and become a leader. "It was a turning point for me," Hull told *People*. After the coach's lecture, Hull cut back on his partying, ate better food, and began running and doing aerobics in the off-season. He came to training camp before the 1989-90 season ten pounds lighter and more muscular.

SUPERSTAR

RECORD SETTER. The results of Hull's training program could be seen in his skating ability and the quickness with which he could shoot. Hull's dream season was 1989-90, when he scored 72 goals and had 41 assists. The 72 goals broke the NHL record for a winger. At the end of the season, Hull, who had just ten penalty minutes all season long, was awarded the NHL's Lady Byng trophy for excellence combined with good sportsmanship. In the playoffs, Hull scored 13 goals and had eight assists in 12 games, but the Blues lost a hard-fought seven-game series to the Chicago Black Hawks in the second round.

Brett Hull

Following the 1989-90 season, Hull signed a four-year, $7.1 million contract. He went out and earned his money during the 1990-91 season, scoring 86 goals, six short of the all-time record of 92, set in the 1981-82 season by **Wayne Gretzky** (see entry), when he was playing with the Edmonton Oilers. The Blues, behind Hull, moved up in the standings, earning 105 points (in the NHL, teams earn two points for a victory and one point for a tie), second-best in the league. Hull was rewarded with the Hart Trophy as the NHL's MVP. In the Stanley Cup playoffs, the Blues defeated the Detroit Red Wings in a tough first-round series. St. Louis was heavily favored to beat the lowly Minnesota North Stars, a team that earned only 68 points in the regular season, in the second round. But in a major upset, the North Stars stunned the Blues, winning four games to two. A secret to Minnesota's success was using two players to guard Hull.

Hull continued his scoring dominance during the 1991-92 season, netting 70 goals, 16 more than the second-place scorer. In the NHL All-Star game, Hull had two goals and one assist and was named the game's Most Valuable Player. The Blues, however, slipped to 83 points that season, and traded away center Adam Oates, Hull's friend and linemate, who set up many of his goals. Angry over the trade, unhappy about his contract, and fighting with his coach, Hull started out slowly in 1992-93. There were rumors that Hull would be traded, but during the season he was signed to a contract worth approximately $5 million per season. Despite his problems, Hull still scored 54 goals and 101 points. He continued to be one of the NHL's top guns during the 1993-94 season. Hull scored 57 goals and earned 40 assists. The Blues, however, were eliminated in the first round of the NHL playoffs.

BOBBY AND BRETT. Now that Hull is a star, people compare him to his father, Bobby. "The most noticeable difference, other than Bobby's having a lefthanded shot and Brett a righthanded one, is in physique," said *Sports Illustrated*. "Bobby, now a cattle rancher in Ontario [Canada], looks like Popeye after a jolt of spinach, his chest stretching the seams of his sweater. Brett's build [body] is less impressive." Bobby Hull was known as a tough player and fast skater, while Brett is not known for his skating ability or physical play. (In fact, Brett rarely fights on the ice.) What they have in common is being able to score large numbers of goals. "Until I get 610 goals, 1170 points [Bobby Hull's NHL statistics], and win a couple of Hart [Most Valuable Player] trophies and ... get voted into the Hall of Fame, I'll still be Bobby Hull's son. Even if I did all that, I'd still be Bobby Hull's kid. I kind of like that."

OFF THE ICE. A citizen of both the United States and Canada, Hull lives in Warson Woods, Missouri, a suburb of St. Louis, during the season, and in Pike Lake, Minnesota, during the off-season. In his spare time Hull plays golf, donates his time to amateur (unpaid) hockey organizations in the St. Louis area, and does commercials for Coca-Cola. Describing his feelings about hockey, Hull told the *Sporting News*: "You've got to have fun with all this. If you don't have a sense of humor about it all, you're going to get lost in it all. You have to prepare yourself mentally every game to deal with it. If I'm uptight, I can't play. If I'm relaxed, I'm on my game."

WHERE TO WRITE

C/O ST. LOUIS BLUES, ST.

LOUIS ARENA, 5700 OAKLAND AVE., ST. LOUIS, MO 63110.

MIGUEL INDURÁIN

1964—

Induráin is a "special organism made for cycling"— Induráin's coach, Jose-Miguel Echavarri

Miguel Induráin grew up working on a farm in the countryside of Spain. This early training paid off when it came time to begin his career in one of the most physically demanding sports in the world—long-distance bicycle racing. Despite early disappointments, Induráin kept working and eventually won the most important bicycle race in the world—the Tour de France—three years in a row. A national hero in Spain, Induráin has achieved his success through single-minded devotion to his sport.

GROWING UP

Miguel Angel Induráin-Larraya was born July 16, 1964, in Villava, Navarre Province, Spain. He grew up with his brother and three sisters on the family farm. Induráin would probably have taken over the farming business from his father had he not become a bicycle racer. "It's [cycling is] a way of getting out of a certain environment," he told *Bicycling* magazine, "of knowing another life." He began bicycle racing at the age of 11, but quit to play soccer and run track in school. Five years later he was biking again. "Cycling was always in my head," Induráin explained in *Bicycling,* "so I started again when I was 16."

By 1983, shortly after starting a training program with Eusebio Unzue, coach of the local racing team, the 19-year-old Induráin won his first amateur (unpaid) race in the Spanish championships. He later told *Bicycling* magazine that his coach had a lot to do with his success. "He taught me how to be realistic: 'Don't run before you can walk,' he always said." Induráin won 14 races in 1984 and decided to turn professional.

NEW COACH. Induráin joined a team in the nearby city of Pamplona, put together by Jose-Miguel Echavarri, former Spanish national team coach. Induráin lost ten pounds under Echavarri's coaching and trained almost exclusively on his bike. No running, no aerobics, and no soccer. "The important thing is to get kilometers into his legs, to stay in form," Echavarri commented in *Bicycling* magazine.

It took two years for Induráin to qualify for his first Tour de France, in 1985. Once in the race, however, he failed to complete the course, dropping out after the twelfth stage, or lap, of the race. It was a similar story the next year, as he went further but still couldn't finish. 1987 marked the first year that Induráin cycled down the Champs Elysees, the main street of Paris and the Tour's finish line. He was 95th. Slowly over the next three years he improved his performance in the Tour and won five other prestigious races.

FIRST WIN. Then came the 1991 Tour de France. Defending champion Greg LeMond (see box) of the United States led the pack after the first week, as expected. Induráin and Dutch racer, Erik Breukink, followed close behind. But Breukink and his entire team had to drop out of the race because of bad food supplements that made them ill.

With the Dutchmen out of the race, the Tour headed into the Pyrenees mountains. Induráin, considered an excellent hill climber, finished second in this stage, but took the overall lead in the race. With this accomplishment, Induráin was able to

Miguel Induráin

wear the famed yellow jersey. "Winning this jersey is my childhood dream," he told the crowd of fans gathered in the mountain town of Val Louran. When the race was over, Induráin was still in first place. His victory, only the fourth for a Spaniard since the race began in 1903, began what author Sam Abt called the "Age of Induráin."

REPEAT. It wasn't until 1992 that most observers began to realize Induráin's extraordinary talent. Weeks before the Tour, he became the first Spaniard to win the prestigious Giro d'Italia race and won the Spanish national championship. The 1992 Tour de France seemed to be made for Induráin because it was made up of two long climbs in the Alps mountains. But Induráin tried not to be overconfident, as he told one journalist at the time: "I'm in form. I've worked hard ... I'm no Superman.... The Tour is so difficult."

Induráin stayed near the front at the start of the race, and when the Tour reached the country of Luxembourg he made his move, winning the stage by over three minutes. He took over the yellow jersey as the Tour passed through the Alps. The day Induráin took the lead the course climbed nearly 6,000 feet and covered 158 miles. LeMond fell behind Induráin during this climb and dropped out of the race for the first time in his career. With his rival out of the Tour, Induráin cruised into Paris, claiming his second Tour victory in the fastest race in history. The racers averaged 24.49 miles per hour over the 2,490 mile course, and Induráin was the fastest of them all.

PERFECT STYLE. On the course, Induráin has almost perfect form. "His style is all grace and beauty," wrote *Bicycling* magazine. "He rarely grimaces [shows pain], gets out of the saddle [seat], or allows his back to inchworm painfully upward like that of other racers." Induráin told the same magazine: "Everybody tells me that I never look as if I'm suffering. But when I watch videotapes of a race, I remember the pain I endured." Induráin is very quiet and shy, and little is known about his private life. "I was his roommate for years," former teammate Pedro Delgado told *Sports Illustrated*. "And even I don't know him."

Induráin has always lived close to his home town. He trains with his younger brother, Prudencio, on road and mountain bikes during the late fall and early winter. In January, he joins the other members of his Banestro team to train under Echavarri. "I trust him entirely," Induráin once confided to *Sports Illustrated*. "He's directed my career perfectly and given me only good advice. Whatever he asks of me, I'll do it. Whatever he decided is fine with me."

PHYSICAL GIFTS AND HARD WORK. Blessed with great physical talent, Induráin has natural advantages over his rivals. At six-feet-two inches, he is much taller than his opponents and his legs are perfect for long uphill climbs. In tests, his heart and lungs have proven to be exceptional. The whole package results, as *Sports Illustrated* said, in "a motor that's simply bigger than anyone else's." His coach calls Induráin a "special organism made for cycling."

Induráin trains very hard, avoids activities not related to racing, and watches his weight. During the off-season he often puts on ten pounds, and the weight, according to his coach, "is his only enemy." He has few other weaknesses. "You have to know what you want in life," Induráin once said. "I race to become always stronger, always better, to get better results. So I make sacrifices. I live a strict life. Lots of things interest me but I didn't have the right to let them get mixed up with my racing. Later, when I've finished racing, I'll make time for them."

SUPERSTAR

THREEPEAT. That large motor undoubtedly helped Induráin win his third Tour de France in 1993. The course featured 21 long climbs through both the Pyrenees and Alps mountains. Once again, Induráin not only defeated his competitors, he blew them away. "I've never seen [anyone] like him," former Tour champion, Felice Gimondi, stated. "[Induráin] calculates everything he's going to do. He has an exceptional sense of the race." According to LeMond, who also won three Tour de France races, Induráin is "unreal."

Induráin remains humble despite his success. He never humiliates his opponents, and often lets other racers win stages, or parts, of his races. "That has the pack [of racers] saying to itself, 'If I'm nice to Miguel, maybe he'll let me win a stage,' which is about all most people can hope for," American rider Andy Hampsten admitted to *Sports Illustrated.*

His attitude comes from his coach and father-figure, Echavarri, who told Sam Abt, author of *Bicycle Racing in the Age of Induráin:* "I always dreamed about making Miguel a champion, but above all, I wanted to make [him] a man. Like [five-time Tour champion Jacques Anquetil], who was a fabulous man, whose philosophy was 'Live and let live.' You have to think of yourself but you should never humiliate others." As Induráin observed in *Bicycling* magazine: "Win or lose, I try to remain the same person. I'm proud of what I've done in the Tour, but you have to keep your perspective. It's just a bicycle race after all."

OFF THE COURSE. Induráin lives in the village of Villava, in Navarre Province, Spain, only a mile from his family's farm. In 1992 he married his longtime sweetheart, Marisa Lopez de Goicoechea. A national hero in Spain, Induráin is a spokesperson for many products and is a partner in a sporting goods store. Only 29 years old, Induráin might be able to tie or break the record for consecutive Tour de France victories, four, and the overall record of five victories. But even if he doesn't, he already, according to *Sports Illustrated,* "must be considered among the best cyclists ever."

BO JACKSON

1962—

Throughout his life, Bo Jackson has known bad times, like when he used to get in trouble as a teenager and when he injured his hip in 1991. He has also known good times, like when he won the Heisman Trophy in 1986 as the best college football player in the United States and in 1989 when he became the first athlete ever to play in all-star games in two professional sports. Overcoming many obstacles, Jackson has earned a reputation as one of the best and most versatile athletes of all time. When he took the field for the Chicago White Sox in 1993, following career-threatening hip surgery, he also proved that Bo knows miracles.

"Don't run life too fast. You only have one."—Bo Jackson

GROWING UP

Vincent Edward Jackson was born November 30, 1962, in Bessemer, Alabama. He was the eighth of ten children. His mother, Florence Jackson Bond, worked as a maid and raised her children alone in the small town of Raimond. His dad, A.D. Adams, was a steelworker who never married Jackson's mom. "He [his father] had his own family on the other side of town," Jackson said in his autobiography, *Bo Knows Bo.*

"He'd come by sometimes and give me a little money, but then I wouldn't see him again for months."

TROUBLEMAKER. "We didn't have [anything], and what we did have we had to work hard for," Jackson said in the *New York Times,* describing his tough childhood. He and his brothers and sisters had to share beds or sleep on the floor. "Trouble's been haunting me since I can remember," Jackson admitted to *Sports Illustrated,* and by the time he reached the third grade he was stealing lunch money from sixth graders, throwing rocks, and fighting at the drop of a hat. He admits that twice he almost shot kids who had "crossed him." His toughness as a child earned Jackson the nickname he carries today. "Bo" is short for "boar hog," the only animal Jackson's four brothers felt was as tough as Jackson.

LEARNS LESSON. His mother tried to discipline her son, whipping him with a stick, but Jackson didn't listen. When he was 13, Jackson and a group of friends killed some pigs owned by a local minister. One of the farm workers recognized Jackson, who was in danger of being sent to reform school. It was this incident that convinced him to change his behavior. "I guess that's when I said to myself, 'I'm gonna have to straighten up,'" Jackson confessed to *People.* Given the chance to repay the owner of the pigs rather than be sent to reform school, Jackson worked until he had paid his debt. He then turned his energy to athletics. "[Sports] left me too tired to run with my old friends," he told *People.* "Plus I made new friends that didn't get into trouble."

HIGH SCHOOL STAR. Jackson's first sport was track. When he was 13 he was pitcher and catcher in an adult men's baseball league. Jackson became a multi-sport star at McAdory High School, where he set state records in the 60- and 100-yard dashes, the 60- and 100-yard hurdles, and the long and high jumps. He also won the state decathlon title in both his junior and senior years. (The decathlon is the hardest track and field competition because athletes must compete in ten different events.) As a member of the football team he did everything—playing offense and defense and kicking extra points and field goals. He gained 1,173 yards in his senior year, earning all-state honors.

It was in baseball, however, that Jackson made his biggest mark. As a senior he hit .493, set a national high school record with 20 home runs, and pitched two no-hitters. His performance earned him $250,000 offer from the New York Yankees to begin playing professionally right out of high school. When Jackson decided to attend college instead, many major schools were interested in him. Wanting to stay close to home, his first choice was the University of Alabama, but the school would not guarantee he could play football until his junior year. Jackson received a better offer from Alabama's long-time rival, Auburn University.

COLLEGE DAYS. Jackson immediately impressed the Auburn football coaches, gaining 123 yards and scoring two touchdowns in his first game. His coaches told him he needed to practice harder, and Jackson decided to call it quits. He got as far as the local bus station and was going to go home, but decided to stick it out. Later in the year Jackson scored the winning touchdown against Alabama as Auburn defeated the Crimson Tide for the first time in 10 years. For the season Jackson gained 829 yards and was named to the All-Southeastern Conference (SEC) team.

In his sophomore year, Jackson ran for 1,213 yards, gaining 256 in a victory over Alabama, a win that earned Auburn the SEC championship and a place in the Sugar Bowl. Jackson was named the Sugar Bowl's Most Valuable Player in a 9-7

ROLE MODEL

In high school Jackson met Dick Atchison, the coach of the football and track teams. "He was as close as I came to having a father," Jackson said in his autobiography. "I couldn't have become the human being I am without him.... He taught me how to control my temper ... [he] taught me how to turn that meanness around, to wait until after school and take that meanness out on running the hurdles or high jumping."

Bo Jackson

Auburn victory over the University of Michigan. But he was slowed down by a separated shoulder in his junior season and gained only 475 yards in six games. He was upset when he learned surgery was needed to repair his injury. "I cried like a baby," Jackson told *Sports Illustrated.* "I had never been in the hospital before."

BEST IN THE COUNTRY. Jackson entered his senior season as the favorite for the Heisman Trophy. He gained more than 200 yards rushing in three of his first four games, but several muscle pulls restricted his performances in losses to Tennessee and Florida. He finished the season with 1,786 yards and won the Heisman Trophy. "Bo is the best football player in America at his position," his college football coach, Pat Dye, said in the *New York Times*. "There can't be anybody better." Jackson finished his career as the all-time leading rusher at Auburn and the second leading rusher in SEC history.

Even off the football field, Jackson was a star at Auburn. He had outstanding speed and power and was the first athlete in 20 years to letter (participate) in three different sports in the SEC—baseball, football, and track and field. Auburn's baseball coach, Hal Baird, stated in the *New York Times:* "I think it's safe to say that nobody who has played [baseball] in the modern era could run like he can or throw or hit for power like he can. It's such a rare combination."

TOUGH CHOICE. When it came time to become a professional, Jackson had to chose between baseball and football. Or maybe he didn't. "I wish I could do both [football and baseball]," he told *Sports Illustrated.* "At least, I'd like to try it to see if I liked it." If Jackson played football it would be for the Tampa Bay Buccaneers, who chose the Heisman Trophy winner with the top pick in the National Football League draft. Instead, he decided to play baseball and signed with the Kansas City Royals for much less money than he would have received from Tampa Bay. Jackson explained at a press conference announcing his decision: "My first love is baseball, and it's always been a dream of mine to be a major-leaguer." In his contract with the Royals, however, Jackson included a clause that allowed him to play football if baseball didn't work out.

Jackson began his professional baseball career in the minor leagues with the Memphis [Tennessee] Chicks. He batted only .089 in his first 45 at-bats, and the media began to say that he had made a bad decision. Soon, however, Jackson exploded, eventually batting .277 for Memphis and showing great power—including a 554-foot home run. He hit a home run in his first major league game with the Royals on September 2, 1986, but ended up batting only .207 and striking out 34 times in 82 at bats the rest of the season.

FOOTBALL, TOO? Believing they could talk Jackson into playing football, the Los Angeles Raiders chose him in the 1987 NFL draft. Jackson stunned the sports world when he signed a contract to play with the Raiders after the end of the baseball season. Many people said he did it as a publicity stunt, especially when he described football as a hobby. But he was serious. Pointing out that he had played both sports since he was in high school, Jackson felt he could play at the professional level. "I can honestly say I've never felt physically fatigued [tired]," he told *USA Today*. "At my age, why should I? I can't stand idle [free] time. I have the rest of my life to rest and relax. Now is the time for me to do what I can do."

1987 was Jackson's first two-professional-sport season. He batted .235 with 22 home runs for the Royals, but also struck out 159 times in only 396 at-bats. When the Royals's season ended, Jackson joined the Raiders. He gained 554 yards and averaged 6.8 yards per carry in his rookie season and set a team record with 221 yards in one game. In 1988 Jackson became the first Royal to hit 25 home runs and steal more than 25 bases (27) in one season, but his batting average was a disappointing .246. He was less successful on the football field, gaining 580 yards but averaging a career-low 4.3 yards per carry.

Bo Jackson playing his "hobby" with the Los Angeles Raiders.

SUPERSTAR

ALL-STAR TIMES TWO. Jackson had his best seasons in both baseball and football in 1989. In baseball he finished fourth in the American League in both home runs (32) and runs batted in (105). For the first time he was named to the All-Star squad, hitting a 448-foot home run, getting two other hits, and stealing a base. He was named the game's Most Valuable Player. Jackson also had his best season for the Raiders, gaining 950 yards. When he was named to the NFL Pro-Bowl (all-star) team, he became the first player in history ever to play in the all-star game of two different professional sports.

Jackson missed five-and-a-half weeks of the Royals's season in 1990 after suffering a dislocated shoulder—his first major injury in professional sports. Playing only 111 games, Jackson had a career high .272 average and hit 28 home runs. Returning to the Raiders, he gained 698 yards and helped lead Los Angeles to the American Football Conference (AFC)

Western division title. He gained 77 yards and averaged 12.8 yards per carry in his first professional playoff game—a 20-10 victory over the Cincinnati Bengals. During the game, however, Jackson tried to gain a few extra yards and injured his hip. He missed the next playoff game as the Raiders season came to a disappointing end with a 51-3 loss to the Buffalo Bills.

CAREER OVER? It soon became clear that the hip injury Jackson had suffered was serious and would likely end both his baseball and football careers. The Royals decided to release him, but the Chicago White Sox took a chance and signed him. Training harder than he ever had in his life, Jackson worked to get his hip in shape. He was sent to the minor leagues and by the end of the season was called back to the majors. He hit .225 and had three home runs and 14 RBIs in 71 at bats. But he limped badly and his great speed was gone.

Though Jackson thought he could still play football, he flunked a physical with the Raiders. He has not played the sport professionally since. His doctors advised him that he would have to have his hip replaced with an artificial joint. On April 4, 1992, Jackson underwent surgery, missing the entire baseball season. Most people thought his career was over, but those people didn't know Bo. His mother died three weeks after his surgery and Jackson had promised her that he would play baseball again. He worked incredibly hard to keep that promise and was at spring training with the White Sox in 1993. Though he no longer limped, it was clear that he could not run the way he used to.

COMEBACK. Jackson made the White Sox team, an amazing feat in itself, overcoming a tremendous obstacle through hard work. He hit a home run in his first at bat, batted .232, hit 16 home runs, had 45 RBIs, and was able to play the outfield with little or no difficulty. More importantly for Jackson, the White

BO KNOWS EVERYTHING

Even though Bo Jackson was an amazing athlete, he became even more famous off the field. His "Bo Knows" ads for Nike were among the most popular of all time. The ads featured Jackson in many different sports, including auto racing, basketball, and golf. He even got on stage and played guitar (he can't really play the instrument) with bluesman Bo Diddley. The ads helped to make Nike the biggest athletic equipment manufacturer in the world, and raised their shoe sales from 80 million to 280 million pairs.

Sox were a good team, and won the American League West division title for the first time since 1983. They faced the Toronto Blue Jays in the American League Championship series, but lost, four games to two. Jackson had a frustrating series, going 0-10. When the season ended the White Sox released Jackson, and he signed a contract to play for the California Angels in 1994. No one knows how long he can play, but Bo knows he will never stop trying.

OFF THE FIELD. Jackson and his wife, Linda, a psychologist, have three children: Garrett, Nicholas, and Morgan. "The smartest thing I've ever done was to get married and start a family," Jackson told *Ebony.* "When I leave the ballpark, I leave everything there. When I hit the driveway, I become a husband and father." He likes to hunt and fish and would someday like to get his pilot's license. Jackson, who neither drinks nor smokes, talks to school groups and he has good advice for kids. "Don't run life too fast," he was quoted as saying in *Sports Illustrated.* "You only have one."

WHERE TO WRITE

C/O CALIFORNIA ANGELS,

P.O. BOX 2000, ANAHEIM, CA 92803.

DAN JANSEN

1965—

Pressure is part of competing in the Olympics, an international event where the best athletes in the world give their best performances. Probably no athlete has ever faced as much pressure in the Olympics as speedskater Dan Jansen. The world record holder in the 500-meter sprint race and the winner of many international competitions, Jansen suffered both disappointment and tragedy in his attempts to win an Olympic medal. After suffering defeats in three straight Winter Olympics, Jansen stood at the starting line of his last Olympic race, not knowing if his dream would ever come true.

GROWING UP

Dan Jansen was born June 17, 1965, in Milwaukee, Wisconsin, the youngest of nine children of Harry, a police lieutenant, and Gerry Jansen, a nurse. He grew up in West Allis, Wisconsin, with his five sisters and three brothers. The Jansen house was only a block away from the rink where the annual North American Speedskating Championships were held. All of the Jansens were speed skaters, and his brother Mike and sister Jane were world-class competitors. Dan began to skate at age four. "We couldn't afford a babysitter, so we took the little

"If you try and try, you'll have a gold medal."—Norwegian speed skater Adne Sondral

ones along as well," his dad recalled in *People*. When his parents went out, they dropped Dan at the skating rink.

FIRST OLYMPICS. His dad told *People* that Jansen was "no better than anyone else in the family. He had real wobbly ankles and had to work very hard on them." Jansen did work hard, and by the age of eight he began to win. First he won regional meets, but by the time he was 12 he was also winning national competitions. In 1984 Jansen earned the right to represent the United States at the Winter Olympics in Sarajevo, Yugoslavia. He took fourth place in the 500-meters and 16th in the 1,000-meter race. "I was 18," he told *People,* "and I just missed a bronze medal. I was so excited. Then I came home, and the reporters were saying, 'That's too bad [about finishing fourth].' That's when I started to feel [that too big a deal is made out of] medals."

FAMILY TRAGEDY. Jansen's sister, Jane Bere, learned in January, 1987, that she had leukemia, a form of cancer. Doctors said her only chance of surviving was a bone marrow transplant. Only Dan and his other sister, Joanne, had the same kind of bone marrow. (Marrow is the substance inside of bones. Leukemia is a form of cancer that attacks this substance.) Jansen was ready to go ahead with the procedure, even though it might have ended his skating career. But Jane, who realized how important skating was to her brother, said no, and Joanne donated the bone marrow.

Jane seemed to be doing better in September 1988 after the surgery, but in December, she reentered the hospital. "It hurt to leave her," Jansen told the *Sporting News* after arriving at the 1988 Winter Olympics in Calgary, Alberta, Canada. "It makes all this [skating] seem unimportant." Jane was featured on a television special just before the Olympics began in which she described her close relationship with her brother. "I want to go out there and do well for her because she's fought so hard," Jansen told a reporter.

THE FALLS. On February 14, 1988, Jansen, then 22, was favored to win the 500-meter race. In 1987 he had won the world sprint championships and was skating as well as he ever had. On the morning of the race however, his brother Mike called at six in the morning to tell him that Jane was dying and wanted to say goodbye. A speedskater herself, Jane had urged Jansen to compete in the Olympics even though her health was worsening. Jansen talked to her, but Jane was unable to respond because of the oxygen mask that covered her mouth. An hour later she died.

Dan Jansen

Television cameras, looking for a reaction to his sister's death, followed Jansen as he warmed up for his race. He had decided earlier that if he won the gold medal, he would dedicate it to Jane. At the beginning of the 500-meter race he committed a false start, something he rarely does. Then, barely 10 seconds into the race, he fell, sliding helplessly across the ice, tripping a Japanese skater before crashing into the foam cushion surrounding the track. Jansen had never fallen during a race. "I think he was thinking about Jane," his dad told *People*. "I knew he'd either fall or he'd skate the race of his life."

Four days later, still upset over his sister's death, Jansen skated in the 1,000-meter sprint. He was skating at a record-setting pace through the first 800 meters when he fell again. "At that time," Jansen remembered in *People* magazine, "I was more concerned about my sister than I was about skating. But now it's time for me to look ahead." He then told *Rolling Stone:* "People tend to see athletes as almost not human. A personal tragedy like my sister's death makes people realize we go through tough times, too." Jansen was given the Olympic Spirit Award in honor of his determination to compete despite the personal tragedy.

ANOTHER CHANCE. After his Olympic disappointment, Jansen was determined to work even harder to prove he was the best speed skater in the world. In 1988 he won the World Sprint Championships (made up of the 500- and 1,000-meter races) and in 1990 he won the overall men's title at the 1990 U.S. International Speedskating Association championships, despite having frostbitten toes. Three weeks before the Olympics, in Davos, Switzerland, Jansen set the world record in the 500-meter race with a time of 36.41 seconds. He was favored to win a gold medal at the 1992 Winter Olympics in Albertville, France, with his main competition expected to come from Germany's Uwe-Jens Mey, the 1988 Olympic champion in the 500-meter competition. In the best shape of his life, Jansen seemed certain to win a medal. "As far as my Olympic chances go," he told *People*. "I'm just thankful to be in a position to win a medal."

Dan Jansen in Albertville talking to reporters a few days before the 1000-meter race.

Changing weather in Albertville left the track either too bumpy or too slushy throughout the Olympics. On the day of his 500-meter race, the track was sloppy and slow, not good for Jansen, who preferred hard ice. One of the first racers on the track, Jansen cleanly completed his race, but knew his time of 37.46 seconds wasn't good enough. Mey won the gold medal with a time of 37.14. Jansen finished fourth. "Maybe his nerves didn't hold out as much as he imagined," Mey told *Time* magazine. "The Olympics don't obey normal rules."

Jansen still had another chance to win a medal, in the 1,000-meter race, but he wasn't confident. He had never been very successful in 1,000-meters and often got tired on the last lap of the race. Feeling that he hadn't been aggressive enough in the 500-meters, perhaps because he was afraid of falling, Jansen started out strong in the 1,000-meter race. But he didn't have the energy to skate strongly at the end of the race and finished a disappointing 26th. "The 1,000 really isn't my race," he told the *Sporting News.*

SUPERSTAR

LAST CHANCE. After his second straight Olympic defeat, many people began to wonder if Jansen had what it took to win an Olympic medal. His worst critics said that he choked, or didn't perform well under pressure. Because the Winter Olympics were moved up two years to 1994, Jansen had one final chance to win his medal. He won the seven-event 1992-93 World Cup championship in the 500-meters. In December 1993 he broke his own world record in the 500-meters on the Olympic track in Lillehammer, Norway. He became the first skater to break the 36-second barrier during that race.

Jansen was the overwhelming favorite in the 500-meter race at the 1994 Winter Olympics. But disaster struck once again. Entering a turn, he slipped, touching his hand to the ice. "Why, God? Why again?," his wife Robin said when she saw him stumble. Though the slip was minor, it cost him time. He finished eighth, and was out of the medal chase. The whispers began again about him choking and the experts said he didn't have the killer instinct necessary to win. "Everyone knows I'm the best, but it just didn't happen—again," Jansen said in *USA Today.* "It's hard right now to figure out."

Jansen stayed up until three o'clock in the morning worrying about his failure. "You want people to pull for you," he explained to *Sports Illustrated.* "And it was good because you like to have support. But it was bad because I didn't want to disappoint people anymore." He found a reporter from his hometown paper, the *Milwaukee Sentinel,* and told him to write, "Sorry, Milwaukee." Unable to deal with his disappointment, Jansen skipped a scheduled press conference.

OLYMPICS AREN'T EVERYTHING

Jansen regrets that the Olympics have been the only event by which his career has been judged. He has won more than 30 races and 50 medals in international World Cup competition and has won 20 medals at world championships in the past decade. He has also held the world record in the 500-meters since 1991. "As far as I'm concerned, he's the best," Jansen's coach, Peter Mueller commented in *Sports Illustrated.* "He always will be in my book. If he skates 100 times, he's going to win 95. This doesn't take away from what he is—the greatest sprinter of all time and a gentleman."

"I LOVE THE 1,000." Jansen's last chance to win an Olympic medal came in the 1,000-meters. (He had already announced that he wouldn't skate in the 1998 Olympics.) "The way I relaxed was not to care," he confided to *Sports Illustrated*. "No matter what happened in the 1,000, my family wasn't going to be gone. And losing the 1,000 wouldn't be as big a shock as not winning the 500. I went in with low expectations because I didn't want to set myself up for disappointment."

Jansen trained hard, both mentally and physically, to skate well in the 1,000-meters. In fact, at the top of a sheet he used to write down his goals, he wrote "I love the 1,000. Igor Zhelezovsky of Belarus was the favorite in the race, but Jansen, who had always tired late in the 1,000-meter, was in the best shape of his life. When he took the ice, however, he didn't feel right, so he worked out on an exercise bike to warm up his legs before the competition.

FINALLY. When it was his turn to skate, Jansen started out fast, but didn't seem to be working too hard. "He was smooth as glass," his wife, Robin, observed in *Sports Illustrated*. The crowd, knowing Jansen's history, held its breath, waiting for disaster. It almost came on the next-to-last turn, as Jansen again slipped and touched his hand down on the ice. This time, however, he kept his cool. "For some reason I was calm about it," he told *Sports Illustrated*. "I told myself that if I tried to get back too fast, I would slip again." When he crossed the finish line he realized he had skated the race of his life. He broke the world record in the 1,000-meters with a time of 1:12.43. Jansen had finally won his gold medal.

The crowd exploded with cheers, and Jansen's wife, overcome with excitement, was rushed to get medical treatment. "The slip, he just skated through it," Mueller told *Sports Illustrated*. "This time the man upstairs took care of him."

"Maybe He did," Jansen told the same magazine. "Or maybe Jane had something to do with it."

Jansen, filled with emotion, had a hard time singing the national anthem after receiving his gold medal. He began to cry, and at the last moment raised his hand in a salute to his sister. After leaving the medal stand he started to skate a victory lap when a security guard handed him his baby daughter, Jane, named for his sister. Father and daughter circled the ice as the crowd went wild. "Finally, I feel I've made other people happy instead of having them feel sorry for me," he told *Sports Illustrated.* In honor of his victory, Jansen's teammates chose him to carry the U.S. flag in the Olympic closing ceremonies.

OFF THE ICE. Jansen lives in Greenfield, Wisconsin, with his wife, Robin, and their daughter, Jane. When he met Robin in 1988, both of them were in long-standing relationships with other people. Jansen split up with his fiancee, Canadian skater Natalie Grenier, and married Robin in 1990. Jansen enjoys golf and played baseball and football in high school. He works for the Miller Brewing Company. In honor of his sister, Jansen helped raise more than $20,000 for the Milwaukee Leukemia Society.

Jansen remains close to his family, and being a father has helped him put things in perspective, as he explained to the *Sporting News.* "It [being a father] changes my outlook on everything.... I can leave training ... knowing that Jane's going to be looking up at me when I get home."

WHERE TO WRITE

U.S. INTERNATIONAL SPEEDSKATING ASSOCIATION,

2005 N. 84TH ST., WAUWATOSA, WI 53226.

EARVIN "MAGIC" JOHNSON

1959—

"Magic" seemed like a natural nickname for Earvin Johnson. Whenever he played basketball, he was a magician, casting his spell over both his opponents and the fans. He had a great scoring touch, superb ball-handling skills, and the ability to always find an open teammate with a bullet pass. When Johnson was at the top of his game, he made his team better, leading Michigan State University to the National Collegiate Athletic Association (NCAA) championship and the Los Angeles Lakers to five National Basketball Association (NBA) championships. He won the NBA Most Valuable Player (MVP) award three times (1986-87, 1988-89, and 1989-90) and was the league's all-time assist leader.

Johnson accomplished all of this with a smile on his face. One of the nicest and most popular players in basketball, Johnson, along with his arch-rivals **Larry Bird** (see entry) of the Boston Celtics and **Michael Jordan** (see entry) of the Chicago Bulls, made NBA basketball the most popular sport in the United States. Unfortunately for basketball fans, at a November 7, 1991, press conference, Johnson announced that he had been infected with the Human Immunodeficiency Virus (HIV)—which leads to the incurable, fatal disease Acquired

Immune Deficiency Syndrome (AIDS)—forcing his retirement. He has dealt with this development the way he used to deal with players trying to guard him: he has worked to figure out a way to win.

GROWING UP

Johnson was born on August 14, 1959, in Lansing, Michigan, the sixth of ten children. His father, Earvin, Sr., worked on an assembly line at General Motors, and his mother, Christine, was a cafeteria worker. Often his father worked two jobs to support his large family. "When I was young, I didn't really think about what [my father] was doing," Johnson recalled in the *Los Angeles Times*, "but now I understand how much he did for me and my brothers and sisters." In his free time, Johnson's dad would watch basketball on television with Johnson and give him tips on how to play the game.

"JUNE BUG." Johnson was interested in basketball from an early age and spent many hours on the court. The neighbors called him "June Bug," because he used to hop from one court to the next. "I just wanted to learn to do everything I could to win," he told the *Washington Post*. "In the schoolyard, the only way you can stay on the court when there are lots of people around is to keep winning.... And I wanted to keep playing. All day and all night long." He added that he was "blessed" with everything he needed to become a top-notch player—size, supportive parents, and good coaching.

BECOMES "MAGIC." As a sophomore at Lansing's Everett High School, Johnson led his team to the Class A state tournament quarterfinals. The next year the team reached the semifinals, and in Johnson's senior year, they won the championship. Johnson was named All-State three times, and, after he scored

"Magic" Johnson

36 points and pulled down 18 rebounds in one game, a local sportswriter nicknamed him "Magic."

NATIONAL CHAMP. After graduating from high school, Johnson decided to stay home in Lansing and attend Michigan State University. He had an immediate impact on the team, leading the Spartans to the 1977-78 Big Ten championship as a freshman. In the NCAA tournament, Michigan State advanced to the Mideast finals, where they lost to the eventual champions, the Kentucky Wildcats, 52-49. Johnson had an off game against Kentucky, scoring only six points. He vowed to return to the tournament the next year.

As a sophomore Johnson shattered a school record with 269 assists, and the Spartans advanced to the 1979 NCAA tournament semifinals. Michigan State, led by Johnson's 29 points, crushed the University of Pennsylvania, 101-67, to earn the right to play for the national championship. In the final game, the Spartans met Indiana State University, led by forward Larry Bird. The Indiana State star had been named College Player of the Year, but Johnson starred in the championship game—outscoring Bird 24 to 19—as the Spartans won 75-64. Johnson was named the tournament's Most Valuable Player.

TURNS PRO. After his sophmore year at Michigan State, Johnson decided to give up his remaining two years of college eligibility and enter the NBA. His decision paid off as the Los Angeles Lakers made him the first pick in the 1979 NBA draft. (Bird was chosen by the Boston Celtics.) Johnson's friendliness immediately charmed his teammates and the local media in Los Angeles. He was always in a good mood and ready for an interview. He felt a bit out of place in the big city, but he was at home on the court. Johnson was an instant success as a rookie, averaging 18 points and 7.3 assists per game. (Larry Bird won the Rookie of the Year award.)

NBA CHAMP. Most importantly, Johnson gave the Lakers the boost they needed to win the 1979-80 NBA championship. During the final playoff series against the Philadelphia 76ers, Johnson shined. In the sixth game, with legendary teammate Kareem Abdul-Jabbar unable to play due to an injury, Johnson started at center. He scored 42 points, grabbed 15 rebounds, had 7 assists, 3 steals, and 1 blocked shot in one of the most remarkable playoff performances of all time. For his efforts he was named the championship series MVP.

SOPHOMORE JINX. While Johnson's rookie season was a dream, his second season was a nightmare. He suffered a serious knee injury and was forced to miss 46 games. When he returned, his teammates called him a show-off and said he was trying to take over the team. The Lakers made the playoffs and were heavily favored to beat the Houston Rockets in the first round, but lost two games to one.

Johnson received most of the blame for the team's defeat. The tension between him and his teammates increased when he signed a $25-million, 25-year contract with the Lakers in June 1981. Johnson's problems exploded when he and head coach Paul Westhead argued over strategy. Johnson blasted Westhead in the media and asked to be traded. Westhead was fired the next day. It seemed to people both inside and outside the Lakers organization that Johnson was calling the shots for the team. He was booed, even in Los Angeles.

Despite the problems, Johnson continued to perform on the court. He averaged 18.6 points and 9.5 assists per game in 1981-82. New coach Pat Riley installed the "Showtime" fast-break style offense, an offense that took full advantage of Johnson's ball-handling and passing abilities. The Lakers won the NBA championship, beating the Philadelphia 76ers four games to two. Johnson again led the way, winning his second championship series Most Valuable Player award. Johnson led the NBA in assists (10.5 per game) in 1982-83 and the Lakers made it back to the finals. There they ran into the improved 76ers, who were completing an awesome season behind All-Star center Moses Malone. Philadelphia swept Los Angeles four games to none.

TEAMWORK

Magic Johnson was known more for his assists (helping his teammates score) than for his own scoring. At six-feet-nine-inches tall, Johnson could see and pass over the shorter guards who tried to guard him. As *Chicago Tribune* columnist David Israel observed, "If you are open, Magic will get you the ball. He may not be looking your way, but that is no problem. He will throw the ball over his shoulder or between his legs— while he is running full speed in the other direction." Johnson retired with the all-time NBA record for assists in the regular season (9,921) and during the playoffs (2,320). By helping to make his teammates better players, Johnson led his team to five NBA championships.

MAGIC VS. BIRD. During the next five seasons (1983-88), either Johnson and the Lakers or Larry Bird and the Boston Celtics would win the NBA championship, marking one of the great rivalries in NBA history. Johnson described his rivalry with Bird to the *Los Angeles Times*: "We feed off one another, that's why we go on. That's why we always want to top each other." In 1983-84 Johnson again led the NBA in assists, with a career-best 13.1 per game, and the Lakers and Celtics met in the NBA finals. In a hard-fought series, in which two games went to overtime, the Celtics won four games to three. The Lakers turned the tables the next year (1984-85), beating the Celtics four games to two. They were prevented from repeating as champions in 1986, when the Houston Rockets defeated them four games to one in the Western Conference finals. The championship was won by the Lakers's arch-rivals, the Celtics.

SUPERSTAR

MVP. When the 1986-87 season opened, it appeared once again that the Celtics and the Lakers would be the teams to beat. Bird, winner of the last three NBA regular season MVP awards, and Johnson, who had yet to win one, were at the peak of their careers. While Bird continued his excellent play, Johnson took his game to a whole new level. He averaged 23.9 points per game, led the NBA in assists with 12.2 per game, and led the Lakers to 65 wins and the NBA's best record. At the end of the regular season he won what many believed was a long-overdue Most Valuable Player award. His near-perfect season was topped off when the Lakers returned to the top of the NBA by beating the Celtics, four games to two, in the finals. Johnson won his second Most Valuable Player award of the season when he was named the outstanding player in the

NBA finals. This would be the last time Johnson and Bird would meet in the NBA playoffs.

REPEAT. Entering the 1987-88 season, no team had repeated as NBA champions since the Boston Celtics in 1969. At the victory celebration following the Lakers's 1987 triumph, Los Angeles coach Pat Riley "guaranteed" that the Lakers would repeat as champions. He counted on Johnson to help him back up his boast, and he wasn't disappointed. While Johnson's statistics (19.6 points and 11.9 assists per game) were not as impressive as in his MVP season, the Lakers won 62 games and once again earned the NBA's best record.

After two tough playoff rounds, beating both the Utah Jazz and Dallas Mavericks four games to three, the Lakers returned to the NBA finals against the Detroit Pistons. The series featured tough play and the first playoff meeting between Johnson and his close friend, Piston guard **Isiah Thomas** (see entry). The two players kissed before the opening tip-off of Game One, but showed on the court that their friendship was not going to prevent them from trying to beat each other. In the end, the Lakers made history, repeating as champions with a four games to three victory over the Pistons.

CELEBRITY. The Lakers had become Hollywood's favorite team, and Johnson was the Lakers's biggest star. Many of Hollywood's most famous names—Jack Nicholson, Michael Douglas, and Michael Jackson—were seen frequently at Lakers games. Johnson traveled with bodyguards, lived in a guarded estate, and was mobbed by fans wherever he went. He explained to the *Detroit Free Press* "people see the glitter and say to themselves, 'If only I could be Magic for a day.' I doubt if they could handle it, even for only a day. The glitter is part of it, but so are the people with schemes, the thieves running scams; so are the people who want to get so close that it becomes scary. There is never a normal day."

"THREEPEAT" DEFEAT. Johnson won his second regular season MVP award in 1988-89, averaging 22.5 points and 12.8 assists per game. The Lakers swept through the playoffs, going undefeated in winning the Western Conference championship and putting themselves in position to "threepeat" (win three championships in a row). Before the final series against the Pistons, Lakers guard Byron Scott was injured. Then, in the second game of the series, disaster struck the Lakers. Coming down court on a fast break, Johnson felt something in his leg pop. He had pulled a hamstring muscle and, though he tried to come back, he was unable to play the rest of the series. The Pistons would win four games to none. Although Johnson was happy for his friend Isiah Thomas, he was disappointed by his injury.

Determined to overcome his disappointment, Johnson won his second straight (and third overall) Most Valuable Player award in 1989-90, as he led the Lakers to 63 wins and the NBA's best record. But in a major upset, the Lakers lost to the Phoenix Suns in the Western Conference semifinals four games to one. The 1990-91 season marked Johnson's last trip to the NBA finals. The Lakers failed to win the Pacific division title for the first time since 1980-81, but they won the Western Conference crown by defeating the Portland Trail Blazers, four games to two, in the Conference Championship series. Unfortunately for Johnson, Los Angeles faced the Chicago Bulls in the finals. Despite a Lakers victory in the first game, it soon became clear that the Bulls were the better team, and Chicago won the first of three straight NBA crowns, four games to one. More importantly, this series would mark the end of Johnson's official NBA career.

RETIREMENT. In September 1991 Johnson married his long-time friend, Earletha "Cookie" Kelly. A few weeks later his life turned upside down: during a routine physical examination for an insurance policy, Johnson tested positive for the HIV virus that leads to AIDS, an incurable and fatal illness. Johnson held a press conference on November 7, 1991, to make his illness public and announce he was retiring from basketball. Before the press conference, Johnson told his teammates. "Breaking the news to my teammates was the most emotional experience of this entire ordeal," Johnson told *People* magazine. "Everyone was crying, including me."

In retirement, Johnson became a spokesman for AIDS awareness and also served as a member of the National AIDS

Commission. On September 25, 1992, Johnson resigned from the commission, frustrated by the government's lack of interest in fighting AIDS. Despite his retirement, Johnson was invited to play in the 1992 NBA All-Star game, an indication of how much the league and it players respected and missed him. He dominated the game, scoring 25 points and winning the game's MVP award.

"DREAM TEAM." Johnson's number "32" Lakers jersey was retired in an emotional ceremony at the Great Western Forum early in 1992. He played with the U.S. Olympic "Dream Team" in the summer of 1992, helping the team win the gold medal in Barcelona, Spain. He also attempted to make a comeback with the Lakers for the 1992-93 season, but quit during training camp after other players expressed their concerns about catching AIDS from him, something experts say is almost impossible. Johnson continues to play in exhibition games and hopes to someday own an NBA team.

Johnson formed and coached his own team, the "Magic Johnson All-Stars," which played exhibition games around the world. He decided to accept the head coaching job with the Lakers with 15 games remaining in the 1993-94 NBA season. The Lakers had become a poor team and were about to miss the playoffs for the second straight year. "Can you believe I'm the coach of the Lakers?" Johnson told *Sports Illustrated.* "What have I gotten myself into?" He won his first game as coach, but decided at the end of the season not to continue as the head man of the Lakers. Johnson planned to continue in his attempt to become an NBA team owner.

THE FUTURE. As of mid-1994, Johnson was free of AIDS symptoms and continues to live his life to its fullest, despite being HIV-positive. "I didn't wake up in the morning and

TRIPLE-DOUBLES

The triple-double—having 10 or more points, rebounds, *and* assists in a game—is considered a good way of determining whether someone is an outstanding all-around player. Not surprisingly, "Magic" Johnson and Larry Bird are first and second on the all-time list. At the beginning of the 1993-94 season, the following were the top five in this statistic, which was first recorded during the 1979-80 season.

Player	Triple-doubles
Magic Johnson	137
Larry Bird	59
Fat Lever	43
Michael Jordan	27
Michael Ray Richardson	21

Earvin "Magic" Johnson

think that I'm going to get AIDS," he told *Sports Illustrated*. I don't dream bad dreams about it.... I've always been this way, thinking positive, with a bright outlook on life. Since this has happened to me, I've met dozens of people who are living with this thing."

WHERE TO WRITE

C/O LOS ANGELES LAKERS, 3900 W. MANCHESTER BLVD., P.O. BOX 10, INGLEWOOD, CA 90306.

LARRY JOHNSON

1969—

Basketball transformed Larry Johnson from high school outcast to hero. It has rewarded him with national college player-of-the-year honors, National Basketball Association (NBA) Rookie of the Year honors, and a 12-year, $84 million contract to play with the Charlotte Hornets. Johnson is a body-banging, rim-rattling, all-star power forward. (A power forward is usually the second tallest player on the team, after the center.) Today he is considered one of the NBA's brightest young talents.

Johnson's story is one of rising from poverty to success. It is also a story of how Johnson made good decisions: to join the Police Athletic League (PAL); to leave the neighborhood for high school; to leave Dallas, Texas, for college; and to stay at the University of Nevada-Las Vegas (UNLV) rather than jump to the NBA before graduating.

GROWING UP

Larry Demetric Johnson was born March 14, 1969, in Tyler, Texas. Basketball helped lift him from the projects of South Dallas, Texas. He grew up in a neighborhood known as Dixon Circle, where he was, he admits, a childhood troublemaker.

"I love to dunk. I love to jump right into somebody's face and jam it so hard that your elbows go flying, your legs kick out and folks just kind of scatter beneath you."— Larry Johnson

He threw rocks at cars, stole, and broke windows. As a ten-year-old he was picked up by the police for fighting so often that he was scheduled to be sent to a detention home. Because the detention center was full, however, officers instead would pick him up each weekend and drop him off at the PAL gym for enforced (guarded) recreation. "It took me off the streets," Johnson told the *Philadelphia Inquirer*. "If the Police Athletic League helped anybody, it helped me. No telling what would have happened to old Larry otherwise."

By the seventh grade, Johnson already stood six-feet-two-inches tall. He began to dominate PAL basketball games, averaging 45 points per contest. Still, despite his athletic interests, Larry continued to get into trouble. His mother, raising him without a father, blamed the neighborhood. "Everything [in the neighborhood] was drugs, fighting and killing," his mother Dortha Johnson told the *Charlotte Observer*. "Larry is a pretty average kid when you consider where he came from."

LEAVES THE 'HOOD. When it came time to go to high school, Johnson's mother and his junior high school coach decided he should leave his home district to go to Skyline High, the city's biggest school. Skyline was known for tough basketball and tough discipline. Johnson rode the bus 45 minutes each way every day. "I was somewhat of an outcast," he told the *Charlotte Observer*, describing his early high school years. "I didn't have any real friends. Everyone knew I was from Dixon, which is like a 'hood [neighborhood]. I was never Larry. I was the kid from Dixon, or the kid from South Dallas."

GAINS ROLE MODEL. The coach at Skyline was J. D. Mayo, a tough coach who made his players lift weights and promise not to smoke, drink, take drugs, or gamble. Johnson, who never met his father, looked to Mayo as a role model and excelled under his coaching. Johnson started for the varsity team as a ninth grader, and during his four years there, the Skyline Raiders never lost a home game. Mayo first nicknamed Johnson "The Baby," but eventually changed it first to "Baby-Man," then to "The Man."

HIGH SCHOOL STAR. By his senior season, Johnson was named the national High School Player of the Year. Chicago Bulls star **Michael Jordan** (see entry), in Dallas for a game, stopped by to see him play, which Johnson still considers the thrill of his life. College recruiters also came by. Dave Bliss, the coach at Southern Methodist University, told the *Charlotte Observer* that the first time he went to see Johnson, "I walked into the weight room and he was doing thrusts [pushing weights over his head]—and the weight machine was coming off the ground. But the first thing that sticks out about him is his character. He has an amazing capacity to make a situation better by his mere presence."

Larry Johnson

Larry had planned to go to Southern Methodist, but he failed to earn the minimum National Collegiate Athletic Association (NCAA) score on his first Scholastic Aptitude Test (SAT). He instead attended Odessa Junior College in Texas for two seasons. "Junior college was good for me," he later told the *Peninsula Times Tribune*. "I had a coach who kept me into things and thinking positive. It was good basketball, but more than that, it prepared me for the academic scene at a university."

JUNIOR COLLEGE. At Odessa, Johnson averaged 22 points per game as a freshman and 30 points per game as a sophomore. He was named national Junior-College Player of the Year after both seasons. He then accepted a scholarship to the University of Nevada-Las Vegas, a school famous both for its excellent basketball program and for its athletic scandals.

Fairly or not, the UNLV Runnin' Rebels were cast as a team of misfits and thugs who would just as soon fight as play basketball. Their coach, Jerry Tarkanian, had spent most of his career fighting off NCAA investigators who accused him of violating the organization's rules. "We were always characterized [called] hoodlums," Johnson later told South Carolina's *Columbia State*. "Both times we played Duke, we'd read in the newspaper how it was a case of evil against good, and I think that made us mentally tough. It was always us against the world. We didn't let what other people said bother us. We just made it our business to do whatever it took to win."

NATIONAL CHAMPIONS. UNLV knew how to win. With Johnson leading the way, the Rebels won the NCAA championship in 1990, beating Duke by 30 points, 103-73, in the title game. Johnson scored 22 points and grabbed 11 rebounds in the championship contest and was named to the all-tournament team. "Larry's strength is astonishing," Duke coach Mike Krzyzewski told the *Washington Post* after that game. "He's got to be the strongest guy in college basketball. Plus, he's got agility and a soft touch. He's a special player now and he will be a special player for 10 years."

Johnson, a power forward, averaged 21 points and 11 rebounds per game during his first season at UNLV and was named to the All-American team. He considered leaving school to enter the NBA draft, where he would have certainly been among the first three players picked. But he decided to stay for his senior year, to improve his game, help UNLV win a second-straight national title, and finish his degree. "I need to stay in school, it's the right thing to do," he told the *San Jose Mercury News*. "I'm having a hard enough time just adjusting to the Division I (big college) level. I don't think I'm ready for the NBA."

UNLV's 1990-91 team was regarded by many as one of the greatest in college basketball history. The team won 34 straight games and was on the verge of winning another title when Duke won a rematch, 79-77, in the semifinals of the NCAA tournament. It was a disappointing finish, but Johnson, again, was an All-American and won several honors, including being named College Basketball Player of the Year. In 35 games, he averaged 23 points and 11 rebounds.

TURNS PRO. On June 26, 1991, the Charlotte Hornets made Johnson the first pick in the NBA draft. "I think I can do for Charlotte what I did for Las Vegas, what I did for Odessa Junior College and what I did in high school," Johnson told the *Charlotte Observer*, "and that is play hard and play the best I can and hopefully bring us some victories."

Johnson's impact was immediate. By mid-season, he was the runaway choice for Rookie of the Year honors. Even as a rookie, Johnson was emerging as the Hornets's best player and on-court leader. But he was uncomfortable in his new role. "As far as being the man, you can't do those things until you earn the confidence of your teammates. When that happens, you feel free to go out and make mistakes. Once you feel they have the confidence in you to take the shot, then you know you can make it."

SUPERSTAR

ROOKIE OF THE YEAR. Johnson finished his first NBA season 11th in the league in rebounding (11 per game) and 24th in scoring (19.7 points per game). Johnson was rewarded with the Rookie of Year award. "Larry's a guy we know we can build our franchise around," Hornets's coach Allan Bristow told the *Columbia State*. "He's our building block, our foundation; he's our untouchable.... A leader is tough to get.... We have a leader, not a loud leader, but a mature leader who leads by example."

GRANDMAMA. Following Johnson's great rookie season, he became a favorite not just of fans and coaches, but also of commercial sponsors. Converse signed Johnson to become its spokesman. "Larry looks like he was chiseled [carved] out of granite. We knew he would be very popular. We just didn't know Grandmama would be nearly this popular."

Grandmama—a slam-dunking senior citizen in a hat, flowered dress, and Converse sneakers—was the character created for Johnson. The ad campaign tried to show that even Johnson's grandmother could beat pro players in basketball if she wore Converse shoes. Johnson's ads were a big hit, and soon his number "2" Charlotte Hornets jersey became the second-leading seller nationwide behind only the number "23" of Michael Jordan.

ALL-STAR. Johnson began the 1992-93 season with two goals: he wanted to play in the NBA All-Star game and he wanted the Hornets to make the playoffs for the first time in team history. (The Hornets joined the NBA in the 1988-89 season.) He accomplished both goals. In February he was voted a starter on the Eastern division All-Star team, the first Hornet ever to achieve that honor. And, in April, the Hornets finished the season with a winning record and made the playoffs. Johnson averaged 22.1 points per game and 10.5 rebounds per game in his second season. The Hornets beat the Boston Celtics, three games to one, in the first round of the playoffs, before losing to the New York Knicks, four games to one. Johnson averaged 19.8 points and 6.9 rebounds per game in the playoffs. Charlotte missed the playoffs during the 1993-94 season, mainly because Johnson was injured and could not play at full strength. He averaged 16.4 points per game and was limited to only 51 games.

THE FUTURE. Johnson's long-term goal is to play his entire career in Charlotte. After the 1992-93 season Charlotte signed Johnson to largest contract in NBA history up until that time, $84 million over 12 years, even though he has had back problems. "I want to play 11, 12 years right here and then retire—and win us some national championships, and be called the Michael Jordan of Charlotte," he told the *Charlotte Observer*.

When he retires, Johnson hopes to go back to South Dallas and Dixon Circle. The housing project he grew up in has been torn down, but the basketball court is still there. Johnson is considering buying the land the court sits on and building a recreation center. "I want to do something helpful," he told the *Observer*. "Ain't no telling how many little Larrys can come out of Dixon."

WHERE TO WRITE

C/O CHARLOTTE HORNETS,

ONE HIVE DR., CHARLOTTE, NC 20217.

MICHAEL JORDAN

1963—

Known for his ability to "fly" through the air, Michael Jordan, the former Chicago Bulls basketball star, was, until his retirement in 1993, the most dominant player in the National Basketball Association (NBA), and possibly the greatest player ever. He could score almost at will and was an outstanding defensive player. Jordan's individual accomplishments are almost beyond belief: three-time NBA Most Valuable Player (1987-88, 1990-91, and 1991-92); three-time NBA finals Most Valuable Player (1991, 1992, and 1993); league leader in scoring seven straight seasons (1986-93); and holder of the highest lifetime regular season (32.3 points per game) and playoff (34.7 points per game) scoring averages.

More important than the individual statistics, however, is the fact that Jordan always led his teams to victory. In 1982 he made a 16-foot jump shot to win the National Collegiate Athletic Association (NCAA) championship for the University of North Carolina. In 1984 and 1992 Jordan starred on U.S. Olympic teams that won the gold medal. In his last three seasons in the NBA, the Bulls won the championship, becoming the third team in NBA history to win three or more consecutive titles and the first to do so since 1966.

"Maybe this guy is God disguised as Michael Jordan."—former Boston Celtics player Larry Bird

GROWING UP

Michael Jordan was born on February 17, 1963, in Brooklyn, New York, to James and Delores Jordan. He was raised in Wilmington, North Carolina, where his father was an equipment supervisor in a General Electric plant and his mother was in charge of a bank's customer service department. "I had great parental guidance," Jordan told the CBS news magazine "Sixty Minutes." "From day one, they taught me right from wrong." Jordan also was close to his brother, Larry. As a matter of fact, Jordan selected jersey number 23 because it was half of the number 45 that Larry wore.

CUT FROM TEAM. Although the Jordans emphasized academics over athletics with their five children, they soon realized Jordan had athletic skills. They encouraged him to practice hard, to set high but realistic goals, and to keep his grades high. Jordan originally preferred baseball and football to basketball, but when he was in ninth grade, he decided to become a professional basketball player. At five-feet-nine-inches tall, he was too short for the varsity squad at Laney High School and was cut. Instead of giving up, Jordan spent hours practicing his jump shot. By the time he was a junior, he had grown another six inches and improved his basketball skills enough to make the team. (He eventually reached six-feet-six-inches tall.)

COLLEGE. Between his junior and senior years in high school, Jordan was invited to spend the summer at the Five-Star Basketball Camp in Pittsburgh, Pennsylvania, a special session for the country's best high school players. At the camp he displayed his outstanding skills. Jordan was suddenly a hot prospect among college teams, and early in his senior year he accepted a basketball scholarship from the University of North Carolina.

BUZZER BEATER. Jordan made the starting team at North Carolina, which was an unusual feat for a freshman under Coach

Dean Smith. He became a national star on March 29, 1982, when he made a 16-feet jump shot, with only two seconds left on the clock, to propel the Tar Heels past the Georgetown University Hoyas, 63-62, to win the NCAA championship. It was North Carolina's first national championship in 25 years, and Jordan was named to the all-tournament team.

Jordan continued to amaze basketball fans throughout his college career. He soared through the air, set a North Carolina scoring record, and was the best defensive guard in the nation. Jordan was named to the All-American team each season, and was voted College Player of the Year in 1983 and 1984. He also helped the U.S. team win gold medals at the 1983 Pan American Games and the 1984 Summer Olympics in Los Angeles, California.

BECOMES A BULL. With college basketball no longer a challenge, Jordan left school the University of North Carolina after his junior year. (He would finish his degree in geography in 1985.) The Chicago Bulls chose Jordan with the third pick in the 1984 NBA draft. (Considering his later accomplishments, it seems hard to believe that two players were drafted ahead of Jordan: **Hakeem Olajuwan** (see entry) of the University of Houston was picked first by the Houston Rockets, and Sam Bowie of the University of Kentucky was chosen second by the Portland Trail Blazers.) The Bulls, who had finished near the bottom of their division for several years, were in desperate need of a superstar to help keep the franchise afloat.

AIR JORDAN. Jordan didn't disappoint the franchise. He put on a one-man show wherever he went. Fans soon began turning out in droves to see "The Michael Jordan Air Show." They were treated to wild, whirling dunks in which Jordan soared above players who were taller than himself, with his tongue hanging out. (While at North Carolina, Coach Smith tried to stop Jordan from sticking out his tongue while playing, a habit

Michael Jordan

Jordan says he learned from his dad. Smith was unsuccessful, but Jordan tells his fans not to copy this part of his basketball style.) Fans were constantly amazed at Jordan's dazzling ball-handling skills, and he was a popular favorite during the league's slam-dunk competition (which he won in 1987 and 1988). Jordan averaged 28.2 points per game in his first season (the only season he did not average at least 30 points per game when not injured) and was elected a starter in the NBA All-Star game. At the end of the season, Jordan was named NBA Rookie of the Year.

Jordan missed most of the next season with a broken foot. Although the Bulls wanted him to sit out the entire season to make sure his foot healed, Jordan insisted on playing in the team's first-round playoff series against the Boston Celtics. He not only played, but Jordan scored an all-time playoff record 63 points in the second game of the series. Boston won in three straight games on the way to the NBA title, but Jordan had proven that he was perhaps the most intense competitor in the game.

SCORING LEADER. Jordan's 1986-87 season was one of the most phenomenal performances of all time. His scoring average, 37.1, was the fifth-highest single season average in NBA history, while his 3,041 total points was the third-highest point total ever recorded in a single season. He also set an NBA record by scoring 18 consecutive points in a game against the New York Knicks. Showing that he also had outstanding defensive ability, Jordan finished second in the NBA in steals. The season ended in disappointment for the Bulls, however, as they once again were eliminated from the playoffs in the first round by losing three straight games to the defending-champion Celtics.

MVP. During the 1987-88 season, Jordan went from being a star to a being a superstar. He averaged 35 points per game and led the league in steals. He won his first Most Valuable Player award, was named the Defensive Player of the Year, and was the Most Valuable Player of the annual All-Star game. The Bulls won 50 games and defeated the Cleveland Cavaliers in the first round of the playoffs. But the season ended in disappointment, with the Bulls losing to the Detroit Pistons in the Eastern Conference semifinals, four games to one.

Several key players, including Jordan, suffered injuries during the 1988-89 season. Jordan again led the league in scoring (32.5 points per game) and was named to the NBA All-Defensive first team. The Bulls advanced to the Eastern Conference semifinals, where they lost to the Pistons, four games to two.

Despite high expectations entering the 1989-90 season, the Bulls once again were disappointed. Jordan continued to score (33.6 points per game), but the team was stopped short again in the playoffs, losing for the third straight season to their arch-rival, the Pistons, in the Eastern Conference finals. At one frustrating point in the series with the Pistons, Jordan uncharacteristically lashed out at his teammates, accusing them of not playing up to their potential and expecting too much of him. A few responded by saying Jordan was a ballhog who never tried to help them improve their games.

SUPERSTAR

TEAMWORK. Perhaps the team just needed to air its "dirty laundry," because the next season seemed to come together. Jordan made an effort to get his teammates more involved and let them do more in important situations. Jordan remarked: "I try to be aware of when my team needs my creativity. If things are going well, I don't have to score too much. I can stay in the background and get everyone else involved. If I sense we need that extra push, I can pick the time to explode."

CHAMPIONS. The Bulls went on to finish first in the NBA's Central division in 1990-91. Individually, Jordan was still outstanding (scoring 31.5 points per game), but the rest of the team, especially **Scottie Pippen** (see entry) and Horace Grant,

Serious hang time for "Air" Jordan.

raised the level of their play. The Bulls roared through the NBA playoffs, losing only two games. They finally defeated the Pistons—in four straight games in the Eastern Conference finals—then defeated **Earvin "Magic" Johnson** (see entry) and the Los Angeles Lakers, four games to one, in the NBA finals. Jordan was a unanimous choice as Most Valuable Player in the finals.

After the Bulls had finally won the championship, Jordan told reporters: "I don't know if I'll ever have this same feeling again.... It's been a seven-year struggle for me and for the city of Chicago. And we did it as a team; all season long we did it as a team."

JORDAN, INC. At a time when basketball popularity was dropping, Jordan, along with **Larry Bird** (see entry) and "Magic" Johnson, renewed interest in the sport. Jordan was the most popular basketball player in the world and is in great demand as a spokesperson for various products. Even before he played his first regular-season game with the Bulls, Jordan signed with Nike to promote a special line of basketball shoes introduced in 1985 under the name "Air Jordan." The line of merchandise eventually expanded to include tote bags, gym shorts, T-shirts, and sweatshirts. Soon other companies appeared at Jordan's doorstep—Wheaties, Coca-Cola, Gatorade, McDonald's, Hanes, and the Illinois State Lottery. By 1991 Jordan was endorsing more products than any athlete in the world.

BE LIKE MIKE. One of the reasons Jordan has become so popular is his "good-guy" image. He is friendly and open, and he is active in various charities through the Michael Jordan Foundation. Jordan regularly visits sick children in hospitals, lectures on drug abuse, holds summer camps for impoverished inner-city youths; he also gave away game tickets to four kids he met in the rough neighborhood around Chicago Stadium. (He also would check their report cards to make sure they kept their grades up.) Jordan appreciates the good things he hears about himself, but he is also worried about having to live up to a certain image. "My biggest concern is that people view me as being some kind of god, but I'm not," he told *Esquire* magazine. "I try to live a positive life, love to live a positive life, but I do have negative things about me and I do make mistakes."

Being as well-known as Jordan is also has its down side. He cannot go out to restaurants, the mall, or the movies without people asking him for autographs. When the Bulls traveled, Jordan used fake names when he signed into hotels. The only time he really felt comfortable in public was when he played. "When I hear that kids wish they were me, I tell them [they ought] to try it not for a day or a year, but for a long time," he told *Sports Illustrated for Kids*. "For a little while, they would probably love it. They'd think it was a vacation. But after a while, they'd see the aggravation and irritation of it."

REPEAT. The 1991-92 season saw two repeats for Jordan: Most Valuable Player and NBA champion. Jordan was once again unstoppable on the offensive end, scoring 30.1 points per game, and the Bulls won an incredible 67 games, threatening the all-time record for wins in a season. (The record of 69 wins was set by the Los Angeles Lakers during the 1970-71 season.) The Bulls beat the New York Knicks in the Eastern Conference finals, four games to three, and defended their title by defeating the Portland Trail Blazers in the finals four games to two. Once again Jordan was named the finals Most Valuable Player. He topped off his year by being a member of the 1992 U.S. Olympic "Dream Team," which overwhelmed the rest of the world in the basketball competition.

THREEPEAT. The two previous NBA champions, the Los Angeles Lakers and the Detroit Pistons, had each repeated. Only two teams, the Minneapolis Lakers (1951-54) and the Boston Celtics (1958-66), had won three or more consecutive NBA titles. Jordan, who always looked for new challenges,

SCORING KING

Michael Jordan holds the NBA records for highest scoring average in both the regular season and the playoffs. Here are the top five in each category:

Regular Season

Player	Average
Michael Jordan	32.3
Wilt Chamberlain	30.1
Elgin Baylor	27.4
Jerry West	27.0
Dominique Wilkens	26.5

Playoffs

Player	Average
Michael Jordan	34.7
Jerry West	29.1
Karl Malone	27.3
Elgin Baylor	27.0
George Gervin	27.0

made the "threepeat"—three titles in a row—his goal in the 1992-93 season. The main challengers to the Bulls were the New York Knicks, led by **Patrick Ewing** (see entry) and the Phoenix Suns, led by **Charles Barkley** (see entry). During the regular season, the Suns earned the NBA's best record, and Barkley ended Jordan's reign as league MVP.

Entering the playoffs, the Bulls were underdogs. Both Jordan and Pippen seemed tired, worn out by their participation on the Olympic "Dream Team." When the playoffs began, however, the team seemed to catch its second wind, sweeping the Atlanta Hawks and Cleveland Cavaliers. By defeating the New York Knicks in the Eastern Conference finals, four games to two, the Bulls earned the right to meet Barkley and the Phoenix Suns for the NBA title. The Bulls, on a clutch three-point shot by John Paxson, won Game Six of the finals and the championship. For the third straight year the Bulls were the best team in the world and Jordan was the MVP of the NBA finals. In the series Jordan averaged 41 points per game, setting a record for highest scoring average in the finals.

TRAGEDY AND RETIREMENT. 1993 was a difficult and tragic year for Jordan. During the playoffs the media publicized instances where he lost large sums of money through gambling. Then, on July 23 his father, James, was found murdered in North Carolina, a victim of a random crime. On October 6 Jordan shocked basketball fans everywhere by announcing his retirement from basketball. "There's nothing left for me to prove," Jordan declared. "I can't step out on the court and know it's for no reason. It's not worth it for me. It's not worth it for my teammates." Jordan claimed that his father's death had nothing to do with his retirement.

Jordan began working out with the Chicago White Sox during the winter following his retirement. He took batting practice with the team and announced that he would try out for the team in spring training in 1994. Jordan did not make the White Sox major league squad, but he impressed the team enough that Chicago decided to give him a chance to play in the minor leagues. He was sent to the Birmingham (Alabama) Barons and led the team in hitting and stolen bases early in the season.

THE FUTURE. Jordan will continue to be a spokesperson for Nike, with whom he has a multiyear, multimillion-dollar contract. (His television commercials for Nike, first with film director Spike Lee and then with Bugs Bunny, are among the most popular of all time.) He has hinted he may join the professional golf tour at some point in his life. Basketball fans think that Jordan will be back with the Bulls. "The word retire means you can do anything you want," Jordan said. "So if I want to decide to play again, that's what I'll do. I'm not going to close that door."

WHERE TO WRITE

C/O CHICAGO BULLS, ONE MAGNIFICENT MILE,

980 N. MICHIGAN AVE., SUITE 1600, CHICAGO, IL 60611.

JACKIE JOYNER-KERSEE

1962—

Jackie Joyner-Kersee has been described as the greatest multi-event track and field athlete of all time. An Olympian to be reckoned with since 1984, Joyner-Kersee is the first American woman ever to win a gold medal in the long jump and the first woman in history to earn more than 7,000 points in the grueling seven-event heptathlon. (The heptathlon consists of the 200- and 800-meter dashes, the 100-meter hurdles, and four field events: the high jump, long jump, shot put, and javelin throw. Points are awarded for an athlete's performance in each event.) Joyner-Kersee has won three Olympic gold medals, one silver, and one bronze, and has held the world record in the heptathlon since 1986. Her achievements have made her one of America's favorite track athletes.

GROWING UP

Born Jacqueline Joyner on March 3, 1962, Joyner-Kersee grew up in East St. Louis, Illinois, a poor city on the Mississippi River. Her parents, Alfred and Mary Joyner, were 14 and 16 respectively, when they were married. They were still in their teens when Joyner-Kersee was born. Both parents worked hard to provide for their growing family. Her father worked in construction and her mother was a nurse's aid. Despite their hard work, Joyner-Kersee's parents barely made enough money to support their family. "Their house was little more than wallpaper and sticks, with four tiny bedrooms," wrote Kenny Moore in *Sports Illustrated.* "During the winters, when the hot-water pipes would freeze, they had to heat water for baths in kettles on the kitchen stove."

The Joyner family wished for a better life, especially Joyner-Kersee. Her grandmother named her Jacqueline, after Jacqueline Kennedy Onassis, the wife of President John F. Kennedy, hoping that the youngster would someday be "first lady" of something. Joyner-Kersee's brother Al, himself an Olympic gold medalist, told *Sports Illustrated,* "I remember Jackie and me crying together in a back room in that house, swearing that someday we were going to make it. Make it out. Make things different."

EARLY TRAINING. Their mother encouraged—even bullied—her children to improve themselves. Having been a teenage parent herself, she did not allow the children to date until they were eighteen. She did encourage them to become involved in many activities. As a child, Joyner-Kersee studied modern dance at the local Mary Brown Community Center. One day she saw a sign advertising the center's new track program and decided to give it a try.

At the age of nine Joyner-Kersee entered her first track meet [competition]. She finished dead last. After this defeat she began training harder and was soon winning her meets. Her best event was the long jump and when she was 12 years old she jumped over 17 feet. Her parents installed a long jump pit at the end of their porch. They hauled sand in potato chip bags from a local playground to make the pit. The first competitor she beat regularly was her older brother, Al. The brother-and-sister team began to spur one another on to greater and greater achievements, and grew very close in the process.

Jackie Joyner-Kersee

MULTI-SPORT STAR. At the age of 14, Joyner-Kersee won the first of four straight National Junior Pentathlon championships (a pentathlon is an athletic contest in which participants compete in five track and field events). Track and field was only one of the sports in which she excelled. In high school she was state champion in both track and basketball. Her Lincoln High School basketball team won games by an average of 52.8 points during her senior year and won 62 of 64 games during her last two years of school. Joyner-Kersee also played volleyball and continued to encourage her brother in his sports career. She was also an excellent student who finished in the top ten of her graduating class. Her parents encouraged her studies by grounding her for any Ds or failing grades.

COLLEGE. A number of colleges were interested in Joyner-Kersee, but she finally chose the University of California, Los Angeles (UCLA). She began classes in 1980 on a basketball scholarship. Joyner-Kersee also qualified for the U.S. Olympic team in the long jump. But instead of competing in the Olympics, she and the rest of the American squad watched from the sidelines, due to the U.S.-led boycott of the 1980 Olympic Games in Moscow, Soviet Union, to protest that country's invasion of Afghanistan. Further heartbreak came when her mother died of meningitis at the age of 38. Stunned by the sudden and unexpected loss, both Jackie and Al Joyner dedicated themselves to athletics with new determination.

Jackie became a starting forward on the UCLA Women's basketball team and worked with the track team as a long jumper. She soon drew the attention of assistant track coach Bob Kersee, who detected untapped possibilities in the young athlete. "I saw this talent walking around the campus that everyone was blind to," he told *Sports Illustrated*. "No one was listening to her mild requests to do more. So I went to the athletic director and made him a proposition [asked to make a deal]."

NEW COACH. Kersee literally put his job on the line, threatening to quit if he was not allowed to coach Jackie in multievents. The university athletic department agreed to his plan. The coach told *Sports Illustrated,* "By 1982, I could see she'd be the world record holder." Joyner-Kersee was already a powerhouse in the long jump and the 200-meter sprint. Al Joyner taught her how to run the hurdles and to throw a javelin—a type of spear—and the shot put—a large heavy metal ball.

By 1983 Joyner-Kersee qualified for the world track and field championships in Helsinki, Finland. Her first chance to be a world champion ended in disaster when she pulled a hamstring muscle and could not complete the heptathlon. Her brother Al was also on the team, and he too was injured. Al Joyner told *Sports Illustrated* that he tried to make his sister feel better by telling her, "It's just not our time yet."

OLYMPIAN. In 1984 both Jackie and Al Joyner qualified for the U.S. Olympic team. Having recovered from her injuries, Jackie was a favorite to win the heptathlon. Al, on the other hand, was not considered likely to win his event, the triple jump. Jackie won the silver medal in the heptathlon, missing the gold by .06 seconds in the final event, the 800-meter, despite reinjuring her hamstring muscle. Meanwhile, Al Joyner became the first American in 80 years to win the Olympic triple jump. The tears Jackie shed at the end of the day were not for her loss, but for joy at her brother's victory. Both of them knew that Jackie would be back to compete again.

COACH BECOMES HUSBAND. The depths of Joyner-Kersee's potential became clear in 1985 when she set a U.S. record with a long jump measuring 23 feet 9 inches. She had quit playing basketball and devoted herself exclusively to track, under the guidance of Bob Kersee. After years spent working together as friends, their relationship became romantic and they were married on January 11, 1986.

SUPERSTAR

WORLD RECORD HOLDER. In 1985 Joyner-Kersee was ranked third in the world heptathlon. She changed that ranking forever in 1986 at the Goodwill Games in Moscow, Soviet Union, where she set a new world record in the event with 7,148 points—more than 200 points higher than her nearest competitor *in history*. Just three weeks later she broke her own record with a score of 7,161 points in Houston, Texas. She won several awards in 1986, including the Sullivan Award for best amateur athlete, the Jesse Owens Award, and the *Track and Field News* Athlete of the Year award.

In 1987 Joyner-Kersee won gold medals in the heptathlon and long jump at the world track and field championships in Rome, Italy. Later that year she received the McDonald's Amateur Sportswoman of the Year award and was named the 1987 Female Athlete of the Year by the Associated Press.

OLYMPIC CHAMPION. At the 1988 Olympics, Joyner-Kersee's performance was spectacular. Not only did she win a gold medal in the heptathlon, she also took the gold medal in the long jump. Her score of 7,291 points was her fourth world record. Joyner-Kersee became the first American woman to win a gold medal in the Olympic long jump and was the first athlete in 64 years to win a gold medal in both a multi-event and a single event. She shared the spotlight with her sister-in-law, Florence Griffith Joyner, who won three gold medals.

HUSBAND AND WIFE. Much attention has been focused over the years on the relationship between Jackie and her coach-husband, Bob. The pair have been spotted quarreling during competition, and Kersee is known to have been tough on Jackie. "We want to make it in terms of the coach-athlete relationship, and we want to stay married for the rest of our lives," Bob Kersee told the *Chicago Tribune*. "So we've got rules in terms of our coach-athlete relationship and our husband-wife relationship. I'm surprised it works as well as it does, and I'm happy it does for both of us. We enjoy sports so much, and we enjoy one another so much, it would be a shame if we let track and field get in the way of our personal life, or our personal life get in the way of track and field."

RETURN TO OLYMPICS. Joyner-Kersee has never broken her 1988 Olympic heptathlon record. Since then she has reinjured her hamstring and had moments when she lacked the desire to continue. In the 1992 Olympics she sought to become the fourth woman in Olympic history to win four gold medals. Her performance in the heptathlon earned her another gold medal. In the long jump, however, a bronze medal was the best she could do. Joyner-Kersee was disappointed, but happy that her close friend, Heike Drechsler, of Germany, won the gold. "With other athletes, even though you're fierce competitors, you get a sense of them as people, whether they're nice," she told the *Los Angeles Times.* "You still want to beat them, but when the competition is over, you realize that there's more to life than athletics."

THE FUTURE. Though she has passed the age of 30, Joyner-Kersee still plans to compete in track and field for as long as she can. After that, she says, she may try her hand at other sports. She plays both tennis and golf when her training schedule allows. "I don't think there is anything I cannot do in athletics if someone showed me how," she told the *Chicago Tribune.* "If they told me what to do, I could easily pick it up."

WHERE TO WRITE

C/O UNITED STATES OLYMPIC COMMITTEE,

ONE OLYMPIC PLAZA, COLORADO SPRINGS, CO 80909.

JIM KELLY

1960—

> *"I've busted my butt ever since I was eight years old to get to where I am now. But I'll never forget where I came from."—Jim Kelly*

The quarterback is the leader of a football team, often called the field general. He must be tough and able to make split-second decisions as the coach of the field. This description fits Jim Kelly, one of the most successful quarterbacks in National Football League (NFL) history. He has led his team, the Buffalo Bills, to five division titles and an NFL record four straight Super Bowl games (1991-94). But despite their regular season and playoff success, the Bills have lost all four Super Bowl games, leaving Kelly's ultimate goal—an NFL championship—just out of reach.

GROWING UP

James Edward Kelly was born February 14, 1960 (Valentine's Day), in East Brady, Pennsylvania, about 70 miles northeast of Pittsburgh. The area in which he grew up is famous for producing star quarterbacks, like Hall-of-Famers Johnny Unitas, George Blanda, Joe Namath (Kelly's idol), and future Hall-of-Famers **Joe Montana** (see entry) of the Kansas City Chiefs and **Dan Marino** (see entry) of the Miami Dolphins. According to Kelly, every boy in that part of the country wants to become a Super Bowl quarterback. "I came from East Brady, a town with 800 people," Kelly told the *Buffalo News*. "There were 23 people on my football team saying 'God, wouldn't it be great to have the feeling of playing in a Super Bowl and coming out in front of a national audience.'"

HARD WORK. Kelly's father, Joe, was a machinist by trade, but the work was not steady, and he often had to work two or three jobs. Kelly was the fourth of six sons. "We went through hell while we were growing up," Kelly told the *St. Louis Post-Dispatch*. "Me and my brothers would be fighting over food at the dinner table. Many times we went to bed without much to eat. Sometimes the only thing we'd eat all day was peanut butter and jelly. But we learned that we had to work for everything we got." Kelly helped his parents financially by giving them the money he earned cutting grass and shoveling snow.

Kelly thinks growing up the way he did made him tough. "When you grow up in a family like I did, where your brothers are bigger than you, you learn not to back down," he told the *Boston Globe*. "If you did, you got your butt kicked." The boys formed their own sports teams, playing baseball, football or basketball every day. Eventually, five of the six brothers played college football and two, Pat and Jim, made it to the NFL. "We were wild when we were growing up," Kelly told the *St. Louis Post-Dispatch*. "We used to strap on the helmets, go into the living room and beat on each other. We'd take turns diving over the top of the sofa, with the other brothers seeing how hard they could body-slam you. We just liked hard contact."

HIGH SCHOOL STAR. At the age of ten, Kelly came close to winning the national Punt, Pass and Kick competition. At East Brady High School he became an all-state basketball player who led his tiny school to the state championship. Kelly was so good in football that East Brady High was undefeated for his last two-and-one-half seasons and won two state championships. "By Jim's senior year we were usually ahead of everybody 30-0 at halftime, so he didn't play much," East Brady

---

SCOREBOARD

LED NFL IN TOUCHDOWN PASSES THROWN (33) IN 1991 AND IN COMPLETION PERCENTAGE (63.3) IN 1990.

HAS BEEN NAMED TO ALL-PRO (ALL-STAR) TEAM FIVE TIMES (1987, 1988, 1990, 1991, AND 1992).

QUARTERBACKED BUFFALO BILLS TO FIVE DIVISION TITLES AND FOUR STRAIGHT SUPER BOWL APPEARANCES (1991-94).

ONE OF THE NFL'S BEST PASSERS AND TEAM LEADERS.

PARENTAL PRESSURE

Kelly's dad, who grew up as an orphan and never had a chance to play sports, pushed his son to be the best football player he could be, ordering him to come home from school during his lunch hour and throw the football through a tire hung in the backyard. "He pushed me so hard it was unbelievable," Kelly told *Sports Illustrated*. "He wouldn't let me eat until I'd worked out. Sometimes there wouldn't be time to eat. Sometimes I wouldn't even come home because I hated it so much. Looking back now, I'm really glad I had a father like mine. I think I'd do the same for my own son."

coach Terry Henry told *Sports Illustrated*. "Normally, the only incompletions he had were drops. His senior year at East Brady he was the all-conference punter, place kicker, safety [defensive back], quarterback and league player of the year." When Kelly graduated, East Brady High retired his jersey.

GOES TO MIAMI. After his high school career, Kelly realized the dream of most Pennsylvania football players when legendary coach Joe Paterno wanted him to come to Penn State. But Paterno wanted the six-feet-three inches, 213-pound Kelly to play linebacker, not quarterback. Kelly's older brother Pat, who had played linebacker in the NFL, told Jim to stick with playing quarterback, telling him that quarterbacks made more money. Kelly passed up Penn State, going instead to the University of Miami, which, in those days, did not have very good teams.

Miami coach Howard Schnellenberger liked Kelly's toughness, comparing him to the great Joe Namath, who Schnellenberger had coached at the University of Alabama. At Miami all the players called him "Country Jim Kelly." Schnellenberger started Kelly in the eighth game of his first season (1979) against Penn State. Kelly responded, throwing for 280 yards and three touchdowns, leading Miami to a 26-10 upset. In 1980 Kelly was the Hurricane's starting quarterback, leading them to a 9-3 record, and in 1981 Miami upset Penn State, Florida State, and Notre Dame en route to a 9-2 record. Going into his senior season, Kelly was a leading contender for the Heisman Trophy, an award given annually to the best college football player. His season was cut short, however, when he separated his shoulder in a game against Virginia Tech. Kelly graduated from Miami with a degree in business management.

PASSES ON BUFFALO. The 1983 NFL draft has become known as the "Quarterback Class" draft. Its first round included superstars **John Elway** (see entry) of the Denver Broncos and **Dan**

Marino (see entry). Future starters Todd Blackledge, Tony Eason, and Ken O'Brien were also drafted. Kelly was selected by the Buffalo Bills with the fourteenth pick in the first round, but was not happy about being drafted by Buffalo. He told the *Washington Post:* "I cried when I was drafted by Buffalo.... You can't be a great quarterback in snow and 30 mile-an-hour wind." Instead of signing with the Bills, Kelly decided to play for the Houston Gamblers of the United States Football League (USFL), a new professional league set up to compete with the NFL.

In Houston Kelly found a league and a system tailor-made for him. Using the run-and-shoot offense, designed to make passing much easier, Kelly became a star. In his two seasons in Houston, Kelly passed for 83 touchdowns and nearly 10,000 yards. In 1984 Kelly was named the USFL Most Valuable Player (MVP). In August 1986, however, the USFL went out of business. For the Bills, who needed a quarterback, it meant a new chance to sign Kelly, who still did not want to play in Buffalo. He asked to be traded to a West Coast team. The Bills, however, talked him into signing with them, promising they would work to build a winning team and awarding Kelly the biggest contract in the NFL. "When Jim didn't come here in 1983, it hurt this city more than just in losing a player," Bills general manager Bill Polian told the *Philadelphia Inquirer.* "It was another chance for people to laugh at Buffalo, to say, 'Here's another guy who won't play there.' In the end, signing Jim ... became a matter of civic pride."

BECOMES A BILL. When he finally did sign, Kelly was given a hero's welcome in Buffalo. He flew to the city in a private jet. Fans cheered and waved as his limousine passed by on its way from the airport to the hotel, where Kelly was officially welcomed by the mayor and New York Governor Mario Cuomo. In Kelly's first season (1986) the Bills's record improved,

Jim Kelly

though not by much—from 2-14 to 4-12. Midway through the season, the Bills fired coach Hank Bullough and hired Marv Levy. Kelly threw for 22 touchdowns and 3,593 yards in his first season, and ranked fourth among NFL quarterbacks.

In his second season (1987), Kelly and the Bills continued to improve. Kelly played only 12 games, due to a players' strike, but threw 19 touchdown passes and was named to his first All-Pro (all-star) team. In 1988 the Bills went 12-4, their best record in a decade, and won the American Football Conference (AFC) East division title. Kelly had his first off season in 1988 (13 touchdowns and 17 interceptions), but his leadership was important to the Bills success. In the playoffs, Buffalo defeated the Houston Oilers, 17-10, before losing, 21-10, to the Cincinnati Bengals in the AFC championship game, with Kelly throwing three interceptions.

HARD TIMES. 1989 was a tough season for Kelly and the Bills. Buffalo slipped to 9-7, their decline caused by injuries to key players, including Kelly, and arguments among teammates. While Kelly was out, backup quarterback Frank Reich led the Bills to three straight victories, causing some fans to say that Reich should be the regular starter. In 13 games Kelly threw for 25 touchdowns and 3,130 yards, but the criticism from fans hurt. "I probably will never live up to the expectations of every fan," Kelly told the *Buffalo News*. "When I throw four touchdowns and we win, it's going to be great. But when I throw two interceptions and we lose, then it's going to be my fault. When you get a big contract like mine, people expect Superman feats out of you. And sometimes, it just doesn't work that way." Buffalo lost in the first round of the NFL playoffs to the Cleveland Browns, 34-30, despite 405 passing yards by Kelly.

SUPERSTAR

SUPER BOWL I. The Bills decided to put their problems of 1989 behind them, and had the best season in the team's history in 1990. Using a new, no-huddle, offense (in a no-huddle offense, the team does not meet between plays, and the quarterback calls the play at the line of scrimmage), Kelly had his best season ever, throwing for 23 touchdowns and only nine interceptions.

The Bills won their third straight AFC East title, with a 13-3 record, and scored 95 points in their first two playoff games, both victories. The two wins earned Buffalo their first ever trip to the Super Bowl, where they faced the New York Giants. Kelly had a great Super Bowl game, completing 18 of 30 passes for 212 yards. The game was one of the best ever, with the Giants winning, 20-19, when Buffalo kicker Scott Norwood missed—by inches—a 47-yard field goal with four seconds left.

REPEAT. Kelly and the Bills once again went 13-3 in 1991 and were again AFC Eastern division champions. Kelly threw for an NFL career best 33 touchdowns and 3,844 yards. Buffalo blew out the Kansas City Chiefs, 37-14, in the first round of the playoffs, then snuck by the Denver Broncos, 10-7, to earn their second straight trip to the Super Bowl where Kelly threw four interceptions. The Bills were outplayed by the Washington Redskins, who won 37-24.

THREE-PEAT DEFEAT. In 1992 the Bills's record fell to 11-5 and they lost the AFC East division title to the Miami Dolphins. Kelly did not have a good season, leading the NFL in interceptions with 19. Entering the playoffs, Buffalo was an underdog, especially since Kelly was injured and back-up Frank Reich would have to start. In their first playoff game, the Bills fell behind the Houston Oilers 35-3 in the third quarter. In one of the most amazing comebacks in sports history, the Bills rallied for a 41-38 victory. Kelly also missed the second playoff game, a 24-7 victory over the Pittsburgh Steelers. Against all odds, the Bills, with Kelly back in charge, defeated the Miami Dolphins, 24-3—a victory that sent them back to the Super Bowl. The Dallas Cowboys handed Buffalo their third straight defeat, 52-17, as Kelly threw two interceptions and had one fumble before being injured in the first half.

RECORD DEFEAT. In 1993 the Bills made history by playing in their fourth straight Super Bowl. Returning to the top of the AFC East, Buffalo finished 12-4, despite another so-so year by Kelly, in which he passed for 18 touchdowns and 18 interceptions. The Bills were once again the best team in the AFC playoffs, defeating the Los Angeles Raiders, 29-23, and the

Kansas City Chiefs, 30-13. In doing so, Buffalo became the first team in NFL history to play in four straight Super Bowls, and the game featured the first ever Super Bowl rematch, with the Bills facing the defending champion Dallas Cowboys. Buffalo again made history when they became the first team in major professional sports (baseball, basketball, football, and hockey) to lose four straight years in the championship final— once again falling to the Cowboys, 30-13.

OFF THE FIELD. Kelly lives with his brother in Orchard Park, New York, where the Bills's Rich Stadium is located. During the season Kelly hosts his own weekly radio and television shows in Buffalo and is a spokesperson for Nuprin, Domino's Pizza, Wheaties, and the *Sporting News*. In 1986 Kelly formed the Kelly for Kids Foundation which raises money for children's charities in the Buffalo area. He is also active in the NFL Gatorade Punt, Pass, and Kick program, and each summer hosts football programs for students. "He does more than just teach a kid how to throw a spiral," said his friend Dan Trevino in the Rochester, New York *Democrat and Chronicle*. "He teaches them about hygiene and manners and nutrition and the importance of staying off drugs and staying in school."

Kelly is close to his family. Even though he has been very successful, Kelly promises to never forget where he came from. "There are times when you stop and say, 'God, I can't believe how far I've come—from a little dinky town like East Brady, Pennsylvania.... I've busted my butt ever since I was eight years old to get to where I am now. But I'll never forget where I came from."

WHERE TO WRITE

C/O BUFFALO BILLS,

ONE BILLS DR., ORCHARD PARK, NY 14127.

JULIE KRONE

1963—

At four-feet-ten-and-one-half-inches tall and 100 pounds, Julie Krone is about the average size for a professional jockey. What is unusual about her is that she is a woman in the male-dominated sport of horse racing. In 1993 Krone made history, becoming the first woman jockey to win one of horse racing's Triple Crown (made up of the Kentucky Derby, the Preakness Stakes, and the Belmont Stakes) when she rode Colonial Affair to victory in the Belmont Stakes. One of the nation's top jockeys, Krone has spent her entire career trying to prove to people who doubted her that women can be successful jockeys.

"You can't fake anything in racing. Every race, you have to prove yourself again."—Julie Krone

GROWING UP

Julieanne Louise Krone was born July 24, 1963, in Benton Harbor, Michigan. She and her older brother, Donnie, grew up on a farm in Eau Claire, Michigan. Their dad, Don, taught art at Benton Harbor High School. The Krone children learned to ride from their mother, Judi, who gave riding lessons and trained horses. When she was two, Krone rode a horse for the first time with her mom, and soon she would ride by herself. "I was a wild kid," she told *Ms.* magazine. "I got bit, I got stepped on, I got kicked in the head. I got dumped [by the horse] five miles from home; the pony ran back and I had to walk."

When she was five, Krone was entering and winning horse shows where she was competing against riders up to 21 years old. After passing up a chance to join a circus, she decided she wanted to be a jockey. Her hero was Steve Cauthen, a teenaged jockey, who in 1978 rode the horse Affirmed to victories in all of the Triple Crown races. Krone also set her goals high. "I'm gonna be the greatest jock in the world," she wrote in her diary at age 15.

STARTS RACING. At 16, during spring vacation, Krone was given a job walking horses at Churchill Downs, the famous race track in Louisville, Kentucky, which is home to the Kentucky Derby. It soon became obvious that she knew how to handle horses, even though they were much bigger than she and were often hard to control. In 1980 Krone became an apprentice (student) jockey at Tampa Bay Downs in Tampa, Florida. On February 12, 1981, Krone won her first race, riding a horse named Lord Farkle.

CUTE. NOT! Within a couple of years, Krone was racing at larger, more famous tracks in Maryland, Delaware, and New Jersey. In both 1982 and 1983 Krone was the leading jockey at Atlantic City in New Jersey. By the mid-1980s, Krone was one of the top five riders on the East Coast of the United States. She earned praise as an intelligent rider, a jockey who made horses "run for her," and showed an ability to communicate with the horse she was riding. She was also considered tough and competitive. "In a lot of people's minds, a girl jockey is cute and delicate," she told *Newsweek*. "With me, what you get is reckless and aggressive."

Krone learned early on that she would have to show she was tough enough and strong enough to be a good jockey. Most horse trainers thought that women tired out during races

and weren't able to control the powerful horses. And to make matters worse, when a female jockey did make a mistake, trainers made a big deal out of it. Krone tried not to let this attitude bother her. "I guess I don't think it's that big a deal that I'm a woman competing against men," she told the *Chicago Tribune*. "Who cares about that? Times have changed." When fans insult her because she's a woman, Krone tries harder to win. "I only hear 'Go home, have babies, and do the dishes' after I've lost," she said. "I know they'll be cheering for me when I come out the next day and win."

PROBLEMS. Despite being able to prove to some trainers that she was strong enough to ride their horses, Krone still had problems, on the track and off. At the age of 17, she was caught with marijuana and received a 60-day riding suspension. "When you're that young and you're caught doing something wrong, it's devastating," Krone told *Ms.* "I was very depressed." In 1980, at Maryland's Pimlico Park, she fell off her horse and broke her back. Krone was out of racing for four months. "When I came back I was probably more reckless and aggressive than ever," she told *People* magazine. Then, in the summer of 1986, Krone faced another crisis. During a race at Monmouth Park, jockey Miguel Rujano hit her with his riding whip. After the race, Krone punched him. Rujano then pushed her into a swimming pool and held her under water. Krone broke free from him and hit him with a lawn chair. Both jockeys were fined $100 and Rujano was also suspended for five days.

RECORD SETTERS. Krone worked hard to put her problems behind her and build what she called an "apple-pie image." "That fight would never happen now," she told *People*. "Every year I get a little more intelligent. At least I hope so." She continued to be successful on the track, becoming one of only three riders, male or female, in the history of Monmouth Park in New Jersey to win six races in one day. In 1987, Krone became the first woman to win four races in one day in New York and the first woman to win a riding title (winning the most races in one year) at a major racetrack when, at Monmouth Park, she led all riders with 130 wins. She repeated as champion in 1988 and 1989 and then won three straight titles at the Meadowlands, also in New Jersey, between 1988 and 1990. In 1988 she passed Patricia Cooksey's career record of 1,203 victories, earning the rank of all-time winningest female jockey. Her fellow jockeys celebrated the event by showering her with champagne.

SUPERSTAR

In 1992 Krone's horses won $9.2 million, ranking her ninth in the nation. Before the 1993 Belmont Stakes, the 125th running of the race, Krone had been criticized because she hadn't won many big races. She had lost all four of the Triple Crown races she had been in (one Kentucky Derby and three Belmont Stakes). Only three other women, Patti Cooksey, Diane Crump, and Andrea Seefeldt, had ever ridden in a Triple Crown race (three Kentucky Derbys and one Preakness Stakes). Krone was riding Colonial Affair, a long-shot, in the Belmont Stakes, and the horse's trainer gave her some encouragement before the race. "They say you can't win the big ones, but this is just another race," Flint (Scotty) Schulhofer told her. "Let him [the horse] relax the first part of it. Be patient. You can do it." Talking to Colonial Affair, Krone leaned over and said: "Let's go out and make some history."

Halfway through the race, Krone started to think she could win. "No horse was running as strong as my horse," she told *Sports Illustrated*. Heading toward the finish line, Krone knew she was going to win. "I am going to win the race I watched on TV when I was a kid," she thought. "It was like a dream come true. Schulhofer told *Sports Illustrated* that after Krone crossed the finish line in first place, he yelled to her, "I told you that you could do it!" After the race, Krone called her mother in Florida and her father in Michigan, to whom she said, according to *Sports Illustrated*, "Hi, Dad. I won the Belmont!" The only down part of her day came when she heard that Prairie Bayou, the winner of the Preakness Stakes only three weeks before, had broken down during the race. The horse suffered multiple fractures to his legs, and had to be destroyed.

Krone was seriously injured in a race at Saratoga Race Track in August 1993. Her horse fell and Krone was trampled by another horse. She suffered a shattered right ankle, a badly cut left elbow, and a bruised heart. Doctors inserted 14 screws and two metal plates to correct Krone's injuries and predicted she would not be able to ride again for at least a year. Krone proved them wrong by returning to the track in May 1994. "Once you've almost lost something you really love, like I almost lost racing, it means even more to you," Krone confessed to the *Detroit Free Press*.

OFF THE TRACK. Currently, Krone is the winningest female jockey in the history of racing. She has won purses (the prize money for winning in horse racing) worth just under $54 mil-

WILLIE SHOEMAKER

Krone is often compared to legendary jockey Willie Shoemaker. In his 41-year career, Shoemaker won more races (8,833) and rode in more races (40,350) than any other jockey in history. He won the Kentucky Derby four times (1955, 1959, 1965, and 1986), the Preakness Stakes two times (1963 and 1967), and the Belmont Stakes five times (1957, 1959, 1962, 1967, and 1975). In 1991 Shoemaker was involved in an automobile accident and is now paralyzed from the neck down.

Krone rides home another winner.

lion, of which she is given 10 percent, and more than 2,700 races. Krone was among the country's top ten jockeys in 1993, ranking third in races won and sixth in total money won. She owns a home in New Jersey and lives with her four cats. When not riding, Krone likes to read, ski, lift weights, and do aerobics. When she has a bad day, as she told *Sports Illustrated for Kids*, she tries to "Have a good cry. Think about what went wrong, and try to fix it. If you can't, just forget it. But show up again tomorrow!"

Describing her love of horses, Krone told *New York Newsday*, "Shakespeare [an English author] says, 'There's no secret so close as between a horse and a rider', and it's true. You just look in their eyes. The horses with a lot of talent always seem like they're looking into the way beyond. They always have the look of eagles in their eyes. It's very romantic."

WHERE TO WRITE

C/O JOCKEY'S GUILD, 250 W. MAIN STREET, SUITE 1820, LEXINGTON, KY 40507

Further Reading

The sources used to compile the entries are included in this list.

ATHLETE

JIM ABBOTT

Gutman, Bill. *Star Pitcher*. Brookfield, Conn.: Millbrook Press, 1992.

Hollander, Zander, ed. *Complete Handbook of Baseball: 1990*. New York: Signet, 1990.

Johnson, Rick L. *Jim Abbott: Beating the Odds*. Minneapolis: Dillon Press, 1991.

Reiser, Howard. *Jim Abbott: All American Pitcher*. Chicago: Children's Press, 1993.

Savage, Jeff. *Sports Great Jim Abbott*. Hillside, N.J.: Enslow Publishers, 1993.

Sporting News, July 19, 1993.

Sports Illustrated, May 25, 1987.

White, Ellen Emerson. *Jim Abbott: Against All Odds*. New York: Scholastic, Inc., 1990.

ANDRE AGASSI

Collins, Bud, and Zander Hollander, eds. *Bud Collins' Modern Encyclopedia of Tennis*. 2nd ed. Detroit: Visible Ink Press, 1994.

New York Times Magazine, October 30, 1988.

Newsweek, September 12, 1988.

Sports Illustrated, March 13, 1989; July 12, 1993.

Tennis, February, 1993.

TROY AIKMAN

Hollander, Zander, ed. *Complete Handbook of Pro Football: 1993.* New York: Signet, 1993.

Sport, January 1991; July 1993.

Sporting News, February 8, 1993.

Sports Illustrated, November 14, 1988; August 21, 1989; February 15, 1993.

ROBERTO ALOMAR

New York Times, October 11, 1993.

Sport, March 1991.

Sports Illustrated, March 28, 1988; June 8, 1992; November 1, 1993.

ARTHUR ASHE

Ashe, Arthur. *Arthur Ashe: Portrait in Motion.* Boston: Houghton Mifflin, 1975.

Ashe, Arthur. *Days of Grace: A Memoir.* New York: Alfred A. Knopf, 1993.

Ashe, Arthur. *A Hard Road to Glory.* 3 vols. New York: Warner Books, 1988.

Ashe, Arthur. *Off the Court.* New York: New American Library, 1981.

Collins, Bud, and Zander Hollander, eds. *Bud Collins' Modern Encyclopedia of Tennis.* 2nd ed. Detroit: Visible Ink Press, 1994.

Chicago Tribune, November 28, 1988.

McPhee, John A. *Levels of the Game.* New York: Farrar, Straus & Giroux, 1969.

Robinson, Louie. *Arthur Ashe: Tennis Champion.* Garden City, N.Y.: Doubleday, 1967.

Sports Illustrated, December 21, 1992.

OKSANA BAIUL

Detroit Free Press, February 24, 1994.

The Olympic Factbook: A Spectator's Guide to the Winter Games. Detroit: Visible Ink Press, 1994.

People, December 6, 1993.

Sporting News, February 14, 1994; March 7, 1994.

Sports Illustrated, March 22, 1993; February 7, 1994.

Sports Illustrated for Kids, February 1994.

CHARLES BARKLEY

Barkley, Charles. *Outrageous!: The Fine Life and Flagrant Good Times of Basketball's Irresistible Force.* New York: Simon and Schuster, 1992.

Barkley, Charles, and Rick Reilly. *Sir Charles: The Wit and Wisdom of Charles Barkley.* New York: Warner Books, 1994.

Chicago Tribune, February 15, 1987; February 1, 1988.

Esquire, March 1992.

Los Angeles Times, May 8, 1985; February 22, 1987; January 10, 1988; January 17, 1988.

Macnow, Glen. *Sports Great Charles Barkley.* Hillside, N.J.: Enslow Publishers, 1992.

New York Times Magazine, March 17, 1991.

People, April 27, 1987.

Philadelphia Daily News, May 13, 1986; May 14, 1986; May 15, 1986; December 22, 1987.

Sporting News, January 18, 1988; February 22, 1988.

Sports Illustrated, March 12, 1984; March 24, 1986; January 11, 1988; August 10, 1992; November 9, 1992; March 8, 1993; April 12, 1993; May 3, 1993; June 7, 1993; June 14, 1993.

Washington Post, April 23, 1984; February 2, 1987.

LARRY BIRD

Bird, Larry. *Bird on Basketball: How-to Strategies From the Great Celtics' Champion.* Reading, Mass.: Addison-Wesley Publishing Co., 1985.

Bird, Larry, and Bob Ryan. *Drive: The Story of My Life.* 1st ed. New York: Bantam, 1990

Burchard, Marshall. *Sports Hero Larry Bird.* New York: G.P. Putnam's Sons, 1982.

Burchard, S. H. *Larry Bird.* San Diego: Harcourt Brace Jovanovich, 1983. Doubleday, 1989.

Italia, Robert. *Larry Bird.* Edina, Minn.: Abdo & Daughters, 1992.

Kavanagh, Jack. *Sports Great Larry Bird.* Hillside, N.J.: Enslow Publishers, 1992.

Krugel, Mitchell. *Magic and the Bird.* New York: St. Martin's Press, 1989.

Levine, Lee Daniel. *Larry Bird: The Making of an American Sports*

Legend. New York: McGraw-Hill, 1988.

New Yorker, March 24, 1986.

Rosenthal, Bert. *Larry Bird: Cool Man on the Court.* Chicago: Children's Press, 1988.

Schron, Bob. *The Bird Era: A History of the Boston Celtics, 1978-1988.* Boston: Quinlan Press, 1988.

Sport, June 1993.

Sports Illustrated, January 23, 1978; February 5, 1979; April 2, 1979; October 15, 1979; November 9, 1981; March 21, 1988; December 11, 1989; March 23, 1992; December 14, 1992; February 15, 1993.

BONNIE BLAIR

Maclean's, February 1988.

The Olympic Factbook: A Spectator's Guide to the Winter Games. Detroit: Visible Ink Press, 1994.

People, February 15, 1988.

Sporting News, March 7, 1994.

Sports Illustrated, January 27, 1988; March 7, 1988; January 15, 1990; February 17, 1992; February 24, 1992.

TYRONE "MUGGSY" BOGUES

Hollander, Zander, ed. *Complete Handbook of Pro Basketball: 1994.* New York: Signet, 1994.

Sporting News, November 8, 1993.

Sports Illustrated, February 16, 1987; April 12, 1993.

BRIAN BOITANO

Newsweek, February 29, 1988.

The Olympic Factbook: A Spectator's Guide to the Winter Games. Detroit: Visible Ink Press, 1994.

Sporting News, February 14, 1994.

Sports Illustrated, February 16, 1987; January 27, 1988.

Sports Illustrated for Kids, February 1994.

Washington Post, February 12, 1988.

BARRY BONDS

San Francisco Examiner, October 8, 1990.

Sports Illustrated, June 25, 1990; October 11, 1993.

RIDDICK BOWE

Los Angeles Times, November 12, 1992; November 15, 1992; November 29, 1992; December 21, 1992.

Sports Illustrated, December 10, 1992; March 11, 1991; August 19, 1991; July 27, 1992; November 23, 1992; November 30, 1992.

MICHAEL CHANG

Collins, Bud, and Zander Hollander, eds. *Bud Collins' Modern Encyclopedia of Tennis.* 2nd ed. Detroit: Visible Ink Press, 1994.

Sports Illustrated, June 19, 1988; October 17, 1988.

Tennis, April 1994.

ROGER CLEMENS

Clemens, Roger. *Rocket Man: The Roger Clemens Story.* Lexington, Mass.: S. Greene Press, 1987.

Clemens, Roger, and Peter Gammons. *Rocket Man.* New York: Penguin Books, 1987.

Devaney, John. *Sports Great Roger Clemens.* Hillside, N.J.: Enslow Publishers, 1990.

Los Angeles Times, October 11, 1990; October 12, 1990.

Newsday, May 22, 1988.

Providence Journal, February 12, 1991.

Sport, May 1993.

Sports Illustrated, June 6, 1988; October 1, 1990; November 26, 1990; February 11, 1991.

JIM COURIER

Collins, Bud, and Zander Hollander, eds. *Bud Collins' Modern Encyclopedia of Tennis.* 2nd ed. Detroit: Visible Ink Press, 1994.

New York Times, February 3, 1992.

Sports Illustrated, June 17, 1991; February 24, 1992.

Tennis Illustrated, September 1991.

Tennis Week, December 24, 1992.

CLYDE DREXLER

Los Angeles Times, June 2, 1992.

Oregonian, May 27, 1992.

Philadelphia Inquirer, June 2, 1992.

Sporting News, May 18, 1992.

Sports Illustrated, June 11, 1990; January 27, 1992; May 11, 1992.

Sports Illustrated for Kids, February 1993.

LENNY DYKSTRA

Philadelphia Daily News, June 21, 1989; June 15, 1991; July 2, 1991.

Philadelphia Inquirer, May 20, 1990; June 15, 1991; September 8, 1991; February 21, 1993.

Philadelphia Inquirer Magazine, October 1, 1989.

Sports Illustrated, June 4, 1990; May 11, 1992.

JOHN ELWAY

Akron Beacon Journal, January 22, 1987.

Boston Globe, January 24, 1987; January 30, 1988; January 25, 1990.

Fox, Larry. *Sports Great John Elway.* Hillside, N.J.: Enslow Publishers, 1990.

Los Angeles Daily News, December 3, 1989.

Orlando Sentinel, January 28, 1990.

Sport, November 1993.

Sporting News, October 20, 1986.

Sports Illustrated, November 10, 1986; January 19, 1987; January 26, 1987; February 8, 1988; November 6, 1989; January 29, 1990; July 27, 1992; August 2, 1993.

JANET EVANS

Chicago Tribune, August 18, 1988; August 28, 1988; September 19, 1988; September 23, 1988.

New York Times Magazine, July 12, 1992.

The Olympics Factbook: A Spectator's Guide to the Winter and Summer Games. Detroit: Visible Ink Press, 1992.

St. Louis Post-Dispatch, August 7, 1988; September 21, 1988; September 23, 1988; October 16, 1988.

PATRICK EWING

Ebony, February 1986.

Kavanagh, Jack. *Sports Great Patrick Ewing.* Hillside, N.J.: Enslow Publishers, 1992.

Newsday, October 9, 1988.

Sports Illustrated, September 19, 1988; October 3, 1988; October 10, 1988.

Time, March 14, 1983; July 8, 1985; July 29, 1985.

NICK FALDO

Golf, June 1990; September 1990; February 1991; September 1992; October 1992.

People, August 17, 1992.

Sports Illustrated, July 10, 1989; April 16, 1990; July 30, 1990; August 20, 1990; April 8, 1991; July 27, 1992; July 26, 1993.

CECIL FIELDER

Boston Globe, April 5, 1991.

Detroit Free Press, May 12, 1990; September 25, 1990; October 4, 1990; October 5, 1990; December 26, 1990.

Philadelphia Daily News, September 18, 1991.

Philadelphia Inquirer, August 31, 1990; July 28, 1991.

EMERSON FITTIPALDI

Fittipaldi, Emerson. *Flying on the Ground*. London, England: W. Kimber, 1973.

Motor Trend, January 1990.

New York Times Magazine, October 15, 1989.

Sports Illustrated, June 5, 1989; May 28, 1990; June 7, 1993.

GEORGE FOREMAN

Boston Globe, March 11, 1987.

Jet, May 6, 1991; April 27, 1992; June 28, 1993.

Sport, May 1991.

Sports Illustrated, October 8, 1984; July 17, 1989; January 29, 1990; June 25, 1990; March 25, 1991; April 20, 1992.

JUAN GONZALEZ

Detroit Free Press, September 17, 1993.

Sport, May 1992; May 1993.

Sporting News, April 5, 1993.

Sports Illustrated, July 23, 1990; April 1, 1991; April 5, 1993; July 26, 1993.

Washington Post, August 23, 1993.

STEFFI GRAF

Collins, Bud, and Zander Hollander, eds. *Bud Collins' Modern Encyclopedia of Tennis.* 2nd ed.

Detroit: Visible Ink Press, 1994.

Sports Illustrated, March 16, 1987; June 15, 1987; July 11, 1988; March 27, 1989; June 19, 1989; July 17, 1989; September 18, 1989; February 5, 1990; April 23, 1990; July 15, 1991; September 16, 1991; June 15, 1992; July 13, 1992; June 14, 1993; July 12, 1993; September 20, 1993.

Tennis, October 1984; July 1986; August 1986; September 1986.

WAYNE GRETZKY

Gretzky, Wayne. *Gretzky: An Autobiography.* 1st ed. New York: HarperCollins Publishers, 1990.

Hanks, Stephen. *Wayne Gretzky.* New York: St. Martin's Press, 1990.

Hollander, Zander, ed. *The Complete Encyclopedia of Hockey.* 4th ed. Detroit: Visible Ink Press, 1993.

Los Angeles Herald Examiner, September 17, 1988.

Maclean's, October 5, 1992.

Raber, Thomas R. *Wayne Gretzky: Hockey Great.* Minneapolis: Lerner Publications Co., 1991.

Sporting News, November 9, 1992; May 24, 1993; November 29, 1993; April 4, 1994.

Sports Illustrated for Kids, November 1993.

KEN GRIFFEY, JR.

Gutman, Bill. *Ken Griffey, Sr., and Ken Griffey, Jr.: Father and Son Teammates.* Brookfield, Conn.: Millbrook Press, 1993.

Jet, April 6, 1992.

People, July 17, 1989.

Sport, March 1991.

Sports Illustrated, May 16, 1988; May 7, 1990; August 9, 1993.

Sports Illustrated for Kids, April 1993.

FLORENCE GRIFFITH JOYNER

Aaseng, Nathan. *Florence Griffith Joyner: Dazzling Olympian.* Minneapolis: Lerner Publications Co., 1989.

Chicago Tribune, July 22, 1988.

New York Times Magazine, July 21, 1993.

Newsday, July 24, 1988; September 7, 1988; September 30, 1988.

Newsweek, August 1, 1988.

The Olympics Factbook: A Spectator's Guide to the Winter and Summer Games. Detroit: Visible Ink Press, 1992.

Sporting News, October 10, 1988; October 17, 1988; February 23, 1989.

EVANDER HOLYFIELD

Boston Globe, December 9, 1988; October 24, 1990.

Chicago Tribune, May 4, 1990; April 18, 1991.

Current Biography, August 1993.

People, November 16, 1992.

Philadelphia Daily News, July 27, 1989.

Philadelphia Inquirer, October 9, 1990.

Sporting News, November 15, 1993.

Sports Illustrated, July 5, 1993.

BRETT HULL

Goldstein, Margaret J. *Brett Hull: Hockey's Top Gun.* Minneapolis: Lerner Publications Co., 1992.

Hollander, Zander, ed. *The Complete Encyclopedia of Hockey.* 4th ed. Detroit: Visible Ink Press, 1993.

Los Angeles Times, November 2, 1989; March 31, 1991.

People, April 9, 1990.

Sporting News, January 21, 1991.

Sports Illustrated, December 23, 1985; December 25, 1990; February 4, 1991; March 18, 1991.

St. Louis Post-Dispatch, March 8, 1988; February 7, 1989; January 20, 1990; June 23, 1990; October 4, 1990; January 20, 1991.

MIGUEL INDURÁIN

Abt, Sam. *Champion: Bicycle Racing in the Age of Induráin.* San Francisco: Bicycle Books, Inc., 1993.

Bicycling, July 1992; September/October 1992; July 1993.

Economist, August 1, 1992.

Sports Illustrated, August 3, 1992; August 2, 1993.

BO JACKSON

Devaney, John. *Bo Jackson: A Star for All Seasons.* New York:

Walker and Co., 1992.

Gutman, Bill. *Bo Jackson: A Biography.* New York: Pocket Books, 1991.

Jackson, Bo. *Bo Knows Bo: The Autobiography of a Ballplayer.* 1st ed. New York: Doubleday, 1990.

Johnson, Rick L. *Bo Jackson: Baseball/Football Superstar.* 1st ed. New York: Maxwell Macmillan International, 1991.

New York Times, December 29, 1984; May 19, 1985; November 4, 1985; December 2, 1985; December 7, 1985; December 8, 1985; June 22, 1986.

Rolfe, John. *Bo Jackson.* New York: Warner Juvenile Books, 1991.

Sports Illustrated, October 3, 1983; September 5, 1984; May 13, 1985; December 2, 1985; March 31, 1986; July 14, 1986; June 12, 1989; March 1, 1993; April 19, 1993.

USA Today, June 24, 1986.

DAN JANSEN

The Olympic Factbook: A Spectator's Guide to the Winter Games. Detroit: Visible Ink Press, 1994.

People, January 14, 1992.

Rolling Stone, February 20, 1992.

Sporting News, March 2, 1992; February 14, 1994; February 28, 1994.

Sports Illustrated, February 24, 1992; December 20, 1993; February 21, 1994; February 28, 1994.

Sports Illustrated for Kids, February 1994.

Time, February 24, 1992.

USA Today, March 1, 1994.

EARVIN "MAGIC" JOHNSON

Chicago Tribune, February 1, 1980.

Detroit Free Press, May 11, 1986.

Greenberg, Keith Elliott. *Magic Johnson: Champion With a Cause.* Minneapolis: Lerner Publications Co., 1992.

Gutman, Bill. *Magic Johnson: Hero On and Off Court.* Brookfield, Conn.: Millbrook Press, 1992.

Haskins, James. *Sports Great Magic Johnson.* Hillside, N.J.: Enslow Publishers, 1992.

Johnson, Earvin. *Magic.* New York: Viking Press, 1983.

Johnson, Earvin. *My Life.* New York: Random House, 1992.

Johnson, Rick L. *Magic Johnson: Basketball's Smiling Superstar.* 1st ed. New York: Dillon Press., 1992.

Krugel, Mitchell. *Magic and the Bird.* 1st ed. New York: St. Martin's Press, 1989.

Levin, Rich. *Magic Johnson: Court Magician.* Chicago: Children's Press, 1981.

Los Angeles Times, May 18, 1987.

Morgan, Bill. *The Magic: Earvin Johnson.* New York: Scholastic, Inc., 1992.

People, November 25, 1991; December 30, 1991.

Sports Illustrated, May 13, 1985; June 29, 1987; November 18,

1991; January 20, 1992; February 17, 1992; October 11, 1993.

Strauss, Larry. *Magic Man.* Los Angeles: Lowell House Juvenile, 1992.

Washington Post, May 31, 1984.

LARRY JOHNSON

Peninsula Times Tribune, January 10, 1990.

Philadelphia Inquirer, March 20, 1991.

San Jose Mercury News, March 22, 1990.

Washington Post, April 5, 1990.

MICHAEL JORDAN

Aaseng, Nathan. *Sports Great Michael Jordan.* Hillside, N.J.: Enslow Publishers, 1992.

Charlotte Observer, January 10, 1990; June 27, 1991; October 31, 1991; October 13, 1992; November 6, 1992; February 20, 1993; February 21, 1993.

Columbia State, June 30, 1991; January 11, 1992.

Ebony, March 1985; June 1987.

Greene, Bob. *Hang Time: Days and Dreams With Michael Jordan.* 1st ed. New York: Doubleday, 1992.

Gutman, Bill. *Michael Jordan: Basketball Champ.* Brookfield, Conn.: Millbrook Press, 1992.

Herbert, Mike. *The Bulls' Air Power.* Chicago: Children's Press, 1987.

Jordan, Michael. *Rare Air: Michael on Michael.* 1st ed. San Francisco: Collins Publishers, 1993.

Krugel, Mitchell. *Jordan.* New York: St. Martin's Press, 1992.

Naughton, Jim. *Taking to the Air: The Rise of Michael Jordan.* New York: Warner Books, 1992.

New York Times Magazine, November 9, 1986.

Newsweek, August 23, 1993; October 18, 1993.

People, March 19, 1984.

Raber, Thomas R. *Skywalker.* Minneapolis: Lerner Publications Co., 1992.

Sakamoto, Bob. *Michael "Air" Jordan.* Lincolnwood, Ill.: Publications International, 1991.

Sporting News, October 18, 1993.

Sports Illustrated, November 28, 1983; April 30, 1984; October 1, 1984; December 10, 1984; January 21, 1985; May 13, 1985; March 24, 1986; November 17, 1986.

JACKIE JOYNER-KERSEE

Chicago Tribune, September 25, 1988.

Cohen, Neil. *Jackie Joyner-Kersee.* 1st ed. Boston: Little, Brown, and Co., 1992.

Los Angeles Times, August 8, 1992.

The Olympics Factbook: A Spectator's Guide to the Winter and Summer Games. Detroit: Visible Ink Press, 1992.

Sports Illustrated, April 27, 1987; September 14, 1987; October 10, 1988.

JIM KELLY

Boston Globe, December 29, 1988; January 23, 1991; January 27, 1991.

Buffalo News, September 7, 1989; December 30, 1989; March 24, 1990; May 10, 1990; May 13, 1990; January 27, 1991.

Detroit Free Press, January 31, 1994.

Kelly, Jim. *Armed and Dangerous.* 1st ed. New York: Doubleday, 1992.

Philadelphia Inquirer, January 5, 1990.

Sports Illustrated, July 21, 1986; September 15, 1986; September 10, 1990; January 28, 1991.

St. Louis Post-Dispatch, January 25, 1991.

Washington Post, November 1, 1987.

JULIE KRONE

Callahan, Dorothy M. *Julie Krone: A Winning Jockey.* Minneapolis: Dillon Press, 1990.

New York Times Magazine, July 25, 1993.

Newsweek, December 28, 1987.

People, May 2, 1988.

Sports Illustrated, June 14, 1993.

Sports Illustrated for Kids, September 1993.

MARIO LEMIEUX

Cox, Ted. *Mario Lemieux (Super Mario).* Chicago: Children's Press, 1993.

Detroit Free Press, June 3, 1984; June 10, 1984; September 24, 1984; October 31, 1984.

Gutman, Bill. *Mario Lemieux: Wizard with a Puck.* Brookfield, Conn.: Millbrook Press, 1992.

Hollander, Zander, ed. *The Complete Encyclopedia of Hockey.* 4th ed. Detroit: Visible Ink Press, 1993.

Maclean's, February 20, 1989; May 1, 1989; April 26, 1993.

Montreal Gazette, November 12, 1983.

Sporting News, May 16, 1988; June 8, 1992; November 22, 1993.

Sports Illustrated, February 6, 1989; November 27, 1989; June 8, 1992; November 16, 1992; April 19, 1993; January 25, 1993.

Sports Illustrated for Kids, December 1993.

CARL LEWIS

Coffey, Wayne R. *Carl Lewis.* 1st ed. Woodbridge, Conn.: Blackbirch Press, 1993.

Inside Sports, August 1984.

Lewis, Carl. *Inside Track: My Professional Life in Amateur Track.* New York: Simon and Schuster, 1990.

New York Times Magazine, June 19, 1992.

The Olympics Factbook: A Spectator's Guide to the Winter and Summer Games. Detroit: Visible Ink Press, 1992.

Philadelphia Daily News, July 26, 1984; August 2, 1984; January 25, 1985; July 23, 1985; June 3, 1988; June 25, 1992; August 7, 1992.

Washington Post, July 22, 1984.

ERIC LINDROS

Boston Globe, March 22, 1991.

Chicago Tribune, June 23, 1991.

Detroit Free Press, September 10, 1991; September 27, 1991.

Hollander, Zander, ed. *The Complete Encyclopedia of Hockey.* 4th ed. Detroit: Visible Ink Press, 1993.

Lindros, Eric, and Randy Starkman. *Fire on Ice.* Toronto, Ontario, Canada: HarperCollins Publishers, 1991.

Philadelphia Inquirer, February 9, 1990; March 3, 1991; June 22, 1991.

San Francisco Examiner, June 23, 1991.

Sporting News, December 27, 1993.

Sports Illustrated, April 1, 1991; September 23, 1991.

St. Paul Pioneer Press, February 10, 1991.

Toronto Globe and Mail, September 10, 1991.

NANCY LOPEZ

Atlanta Journal, December 10, 1992; November 4, 1993.

Golf, May 1990.

New York Times Magazine, July 2, 1978.

Sports Illustrated, August 4, 1986; February 9, 1987; May 29, 1989.

GREG MADDUX

Baseball Digest, March 1994.

Detroit Free Press, April 15, 1994.

New York Times, November 12, 1992; December 10, 1992; November 4, 1993.

Sport, May 1993.

Sports Illustrated, April 5, 1993.

KARL MALONE

Inside Sports, October 1989.

Sporting News, January 16, 1984.

Sports Illustrated, January 14, 1985; November 7, 1988.

Sports Illustrated for Kids, June 1993.

DIEGO MARADONA

New York Times, May 27, 1990.

People, June 18, 1990.

Washington Post, March 6, 1994.

DAN MARINO

Inside Sports, September 1982.

Marino, Dan. *Marino!* Chicago: Contemporary Books, 1986.

New York Times, November 4, 1984.

Rubin, Bob. *Dan Marino: Wonder Boy Quarterback.* Chicago: Children's Press, 1985.

Sports Illustrated, September 1, 1982; December 24, 1984.

MARK MESSIER

Hollander, Zander, ed. *The Com-*

plete Encyclopedia of Hockey. 4th ed. Detroit: Visible Ink Press, 1993.

New York Daily News, November 18, 1991; November 20, 1991.

Newsday, October 3, 1991; October 13, 1991; December 12, 1991; April 12, 1992; May 10, 1992.

St. Louis Pioneer Press, December 29, 1991; April 19, 1992.

Sports Illustrated, May 9, 1988; March 16, 1992.

USA Today, November 30, 1989.

Washington Post, May 9, 1990; May 10, 1990; February 27, 1992.

SHANNON MILLER

Current Health, May 1993.

Dallas Morning News, September 30, 1993.

Sporting News, July 20, 1992.

Sports Illustrated, August 10, 1992; December 14, 1992; August 26, 1993.

Sports Illustrated for Kids, July 1993.

Time, July 27, 1992.

TOMMY MOE

New York Times, February 14, 1994.

The Olympic Factbook: A Spectator's Guide to the Winter Games. Detroit: Visible Ink Press, 1994.

Rolling Stone, February 20, 1992.

Sporting News, February 21, 1994.

Sports Illustrated, February 21,

1994; February 28, 1994.

Time, February 28, 1994.

U.S. News & World Report, February 28, 1994.

JOE MONTANA

Boston Globe, January 20, 1989; January 21, 1989; January 23, 1989.

Kavanagh, Jack. *Sports Great Joe Montana.* Hillside, N.J.: Enslow Publishers, 1992.

Montana, Joe. *Audibles: My Life in Football.* 1st ed. New York: W. Morrow, 1986.

Raber, Thomas R. *Joe Montana, Comeback Quarterback.* Minneapolis: Lerner Publications Co., 1989.

San Jose Mercury News, July 18, 1985; October 13, 1986; November 9, 1986; January 19, 1989; January 23, 1989.

Sporting News, December 20, 1993; January 24, 1994.

Sports Illustrated, December 21, 1981; January 25, 1982; September 4, 1985; November 17, 1986; August 15, 1988.

WARREN MOON

Houston Post, December 25, 1987; March 13, 1988; November 13, 1988; April 8, 1989; July 29, 1989.

Los Angeles Times, November 18, 1989; November 3, 1990.

Rocky Mountain News, November 18, 1990.

Seattle Times, December 2, 1990.

Sports Illustrated, November 5, 1990; December 24, 1990; September 27, 1993.

Sports Illustrated for Kids, December 1993.

St. Louis Post-Dispatch, October 28, 1990.

MARTINA NAVRATILOVA

Collins, Bud, and Zander Hollander, eds. *Bud Collins' Modern Encyclopedia of Tennis.* 2nd ed. Detroit: Visible Ink Press, 1994.

Navratilova, Martina. *Martina.* 1st ed. New York: Knopf, 1985.

New York Times Magazine, June 19, 1977.

Sport, March 1976.

Sports Illustrated, February 24, 1975; September 21, 1987.

HAKEEM OLAJUWON

Chicago Tribune, May 22, 1986.

Ebony, March 1984.

People, December 5, 1983; December 17, 1984.

Sport, April 1988.

Sporting News, May 24, 1993.

Sports Illustrated for Kids, September 1993.

SHAQUILLE O'NEAL

Atlanta Constitution, February 8, 1991; May 30, 1991.

Cox, Ted. *Shaquille O'Neal: Shaq Attack.* Chicago: Children's Press, 1993.

Hollander, Zander, ed. *Complete Handbook of Pro Basketball:*

1993. New York: Visible Ink Press, 1993.

Houston Post, November 5, 1989.

O'Neal, Shaquille, and Jack McCallum. *Shaq Attack.* New York: Hyperion Press, 1993.

Orlando Sentinel, February 24, 1991.

Philadelphia Daily News, February 12, 1991.

Rocky Mountain News, March 2, 1991.

Sporting News, November 29, 1993.

Sports Illustrated, January 21, 1991; May 25, 1992; November 30, 1992.

SCOTTIE PIPPEN

Chicago Tribune, May 24, 1991; June 17, 1991.

Hollander, Zander, ed. *Complete Handbook of Pro Basketball: 1994.* New York: Signet, 1994.

New York Times, October 27, 1991.

Reiser, Howard. *Scottie Pippen: Prince of the Court.* Chicago: Children's Press, 1993.

Sports Illustrated, November 30, 1987; June 14, 1993.

KIRBY PUCKETT

Aaseng, Nathan. *Sports Great Kirby Puckett.* Hillside, N.J.: Enslow Publishers, 1993.

Bauleke, Ann. *Kirby Puckett: Fan Favorite.* Minneapolis: Lerner Publications Co., 1993.

Esquire, April 1992.

Hollander, Zander, ed. *Complete Handbook of Baseball: 1988.* New York: Signet, 1988.

Puckett, Kirby. *Be the Best You Can Be.* Minneapolis: Waldman House, 1993.

Puckett, Kirby. *I Love This Game!: My Life and Baseball.* 1st ed. New York: HarperCollins Publishers, 1993.

Sports Illustrated, July 23, 1984; May 12, 1986; June 15, 1987; April 6, 1992.

JERRY RICE

Dickey, Glenn. *Sports Great Jerry Rice.* Hillside, N.J.: Enslow Publishers, 1993.

Evans, J. Edward. *Jerry Rice: Touchdown Talent.* Minneapolis: Lerner Publications Co., 1993.

Los Angeles Times, December 13, 1987.

Newsday, January 28, 1990.

San Jose Mercury News, September 2, 1988.

Sporting News, February 22, 1990; December 20, 1993.

CAL RIPKEN, JR.

Baseball Digest, June 1983; March 1986.

Macnow, Glen. *Sports Great Cal Ripken, Jr.* Hillside, N.J.: Enslow Publishers, 1993.

Sport, May 1992.

Sporting News, July 22, 1991; April 26, 1993.

Sports Illustrated, September 12, 1983; April 2, 1984; July 23,

1984; June 18, 1990; July 29, 1991; June 28, 1993.

Thornley, Stew. *Cal Ripken, Jr.: Oriole Ironman.* Minneapolis: Lerner Publications Co., 1992.

DAVID ROBINSON

Aaseng, Nathan. *Sports Great David Robinson.* Hillside, N.J.: Enslow Publishers, 1992.

Charlotte Observer, September 28, 1988; December 26, 1989.

Chicago Tribune, June 29, 1987; August 13, 1989; November 19, 1989.

Gentleman's Quarterly, February 1991.

Gutman, Bill. *David Robinson: NBA Super Center.* Brookfield, Conn.: Millbrook Press, 1993.

Los Angeles Times, May 18, 1987; September 24, 1987; December 3, 1987; May 21, 1988; September 30, 1988; August 27, 1989; May 15, 1990.

Miller, Dawn M. *David Robinson: Backboard Admiral.* Minneapolis: Lerner Publications Co., 1991.

Rolfe, John. *David Robinson.* 1st ed. Boston: Little, Brown, and Co., 1991.

Savage, Jim. *The Force: David Robinson, the NBA's Newest Sky high Sensation.* New York: Dell, 1992.

Washington Post, March 20, 1986; October 15, 1986; November 22, 1986; August 19, 1988; October 7, 1988; May 15, 1990; December 7, 1991.

NOLAN RYAN

Lace, William W. *Sports Great Nolan Ryan.* Hillside, N.J.: Enslow Publishers, 1993.

Philadelphia Daily News, June 8, 1989.

Rappoport, Ken. *Nolan Ryan— The Ryan Express.* 1st ed. New York: New York: Maxwell Macmillan International, 1992.

Reiser, Howard. *Nolan Ryan: Strikeout King.* Chicago: Children's Press, 1993.

Rolfe, John. *Nolan Ryan.* 1st ed. Boston: Little, Brown and Co., 1992.

Ryan, Nolan. *Miracle Man: Nolan Ryan, The Autobiography.* Dallas: Word Publishers, 1992.

Sports Illustrated, September 29, 1986; May 1, 1989; May 13, 1991; October 4, 1993.

PETE SAMPRAS

Collins, Bud, and Zander Hollander, eds. *Bud Collins' Modern Encyclopedia of Tennis.* 2nd ed. Detroit: Visible Ink Press, 1994.

New York Times, May 6, 1991.

Sporting News, September 20, 1993.

Sports Illustrated, September 17, 1990; July 15, 1991; September 16, 1991; June 15, 1992; July 13, 1992; June 14, 1993; July 12, 1993; September 20, 1993.

Tennis, September 1993; October 1993.

USA Today, May 6, 1993.

World Tennis, November 1990.

ARANTXA SANCHEZ VICARIO

Collins, Bud, and Zander Hollander, eds. *Bud Collins' Modern Encyclopedia of Tennis.* 2nd ed. Detroit: Visible Ink Press, 1994.

Sports Illustrated, June 19, 1989; July 17, 1989; May 14, 1990; July 22, 1992.

Time, June 26, 1989.

RYNE SANDBERG

Boys' Life, June 1993.

Lundgren, Hal. *Ryne Sandberg: The Triple Threat.* Chicago: Children's Press, 1986.

New York Times, November 14, 1984; October 5, 1989.

Sport, June 1991; June 1993.

Sports Illustrated, March 18, 1991; March 16, 1992; July 27, 1992.

BARRY SANDERS

Chicago Tribune, November 3, 1991.

Detroit Free Press, December 17, 1989.

Gutman, Bill. *Barry Sanders: Football's Rushing Champ.* Brookfield, Conn.: Millbrook Press, 1993.

Kavanagh, Jack. *Rocket Running Back.* Minneapolis: Lerner Publications Co., 1994.

Knapp, Ron. *Sports Great Barry Sanders.* Hillside, N.J.: Enslow Publishers, 1993.

Philadelphia Daily News, August 28, 1991.

Reiser, Howard. *Lion With a Quiet Roar*. Chicago: Children's Press, 1993.

Sporting News, October 24, 1988; December 19, 1988; April 24, 1989; November 20, 1989; January 15, 1990.

Sports Illustrated, December 12, 1988; April 10, 1989; September 10, 1990.

DEION SANDERS

Esquire, June 1992.

Sports Illustrated, June 12, 1989; November 13, 1989; April 27, 1992; August 24, 1992.

Thornley, Stew. *Deion Sanders: Prime Time Player*. Minneapolis: Lerner Publications Co., 1993.

MONICA SELES

Collins, Bud, and Zander Hollander, eds. *Bud Collins' Modern Encyclopedia of Tennis*. 2nd ed. Detroit: Visible Ink Press, 1994.

New York Times, May 27, 1991.

Sports Illustrated, June 19, 1988; August 22, 1988; June 18, 1990; May 27, 1991; July 15, 1991; September 16, 1991; June 15, 1992; July 13, 1992; November 30, 1992; June 14, 1993; September 20, 1993.

Tennis, March 1994.

World Tennis, June 1989; March 1990.

EMMITT SMITH

Sport, August 1993.

Sporting News, September 20, 1993.

Sports Illustrated, November 16, 1987; November 27, 1989; October 21, 1991; September 7, 1992; September 27, 1993.

Sports Illustrated for Kids, September 1993.

LYN ST. JAMES

Sports Illustrated, May 3, 1993.

St. James, Lyn. *Lyn St. James' Car Owner's Manual for Women*. New York: Penguin Books, 1984.

FRANK THOMAS

Sports, April 1992.

Sporting News, September 20, 1993; October 11, 1993; October 18, 1993.

Sports Illustrated, September 16, 1991; September 13, 1993.

Sports Illustrated for Kids, July 1993.

ISIAH THOMAS

Boston Globe, November 1, 1981; April 26, 1985; June 7, 1987.

Chicago Tribune, February 8, 1987.

Hollander, Zander, ed. *Complete Handbook of Pro Basketball: 1991*. New York: Signet, 1991.

Jet, January 31, 1994.

Knapp, Ron. *Sports Great Isiah Thomas*. Hillside, N.J.: Enslow Publishers, 1992.

Los Angeles Times, February 10, 1986; June 7, 1988; June 11, 1988; June 20, 1988.

Myers, Gene, ed. *Bad Boys.* Detroit: *Detroit Free Press,* 1989.

New York Times, January 9, 1994.

Sport, June 1992.

Sports Illustrated, April 6, 1981; January 19, 1987; May 18, 1987; June 20, 1988; June 27, 1988; June 4, 1990; June 11, 1990; June 25, 1990; March 18, 1991; September 30, 1991; January 17, 1994.

Thomas, Isiah, and Matt Dobek. *Bad Boys: An Inside Look at the Detroit Pistons' 1988—89 Championship Season.* Grand Rapids, Mich.: Masters Press, 1989.

THURMAN THOMAS

Houston Post, October 11, 1987; August 5, 1988; August 29, 1989; January 19, 1992.

Newsday, August 4, 1991; January 21, 1992.

St. Paul Pioneer Press, December 15, 1989; January 24, 1992.

Sports Illustrated, January 28, 1991; February 3, 1992; February 1, 1993.

Washington Post, October 10, 1991.

Wichita Eagle-Beacon, August 20, 1987; October 11, 1987.

ALBERTO TOMBA

Chicago Tribune, February 7, 1992.

Detroit Free Press, February 24, 1994.

Los Angeles Times, February 3, 1992; February 19, 1992.

New York Times, December 23, 1990.

The Olympic Factbook: A Spectator's Guide to the Winter Games. Detroit: Visible Ink Press, 1994.

Philadelphia Inquirer, January 14, 1988; February 26, 1988; February 28, 1988; February 6, 1992.

Skiing, September 1988; February 1991; January 1992; February 1993.

Sporting News, February 14, 1994.

Sports Illustrated, January 23, 1988; March 7, 1988; February 3, 1992; March 2, 1992.

Time, March 7, 1988; March 2, 1992.

USA Today, February 28, 1994; March 1, 1994.

Washington Post, February 26, 1988.

REGGIE WHITE

Hill, Terry. *Reggie White: Minister of Defense.* Brentwood, Tenn.: Wolgemuth and Hyatt, 1991.

Philadelphia Daily News, June 7, 1991; April 7, 1993; April 8, 1993.

Sports Illustrated, September 3, 1986; November 27, 1989; March 15, 1993; May 3, 1993; September 20, 1993.

DAVE WINFIELD

Sport, December 1975.

Sports Illustrated, July 9, 1979; January 5, 1981; September 10, 1984; April 11, 1988; May 30, 1988; June 29, 1992; November 2, 1992; December 28, 1992; September 27, 1993.

Winfield, Dave. *Winfield: A Player's Life.* 1st ed. New York: Norton, 1988.

KATARINA WITT

Chicago Tribune, February 17, 1988; February 21, 1988.

Christian Science Monitor, February 4, 1988.

Coffey, Wayne R. *Katarina Witt.* 1st ed. Woodbridge, Conn.: Blackbirch Press, 1992.

Current Biography, 1988 Yearbook.

Maclean's, February 1988; January 14, 1991.

Newsweek, November 29, 1993.

The Olympic Factbook: A Spectator's Guide to the Winter Games. Detroit: Visible Ink Press, 1994.

Sports Illustrated, March 18, 1985; January 20, 1986; March 23, 1987; March 7, 1988.

USA Today, February 10, 1994.

KRISTI YAMAGUCHI

Chicago Tribune, February 15, 1991; February 7, 1992.

Detroit Free Press, February 14, 1991; February 22, 1992.

Los Angeles Times, February 15, 1991; January 26, 1992.

Miami Herald, February 19, 1992.

Newsday, February 2, 1992; February 22, 1992.

The Olympic Factbook: A Spectator's Guide to the Winter Games. Detroit: Visible Ink Press, 1994.

St. Paul Pioneer Press, February 22, 1992.

San Jose Mercury News, February 4, 1990; April 28, 1990; February 10, 1991; February 2, 1992; February 9, 1992.

Sports Illustrated, February 20, 1989; March 25, 1991; January 20, 1992; March 2, 1992.

USA Today, February 6, 1990; January 28, 1992.

STEVE YOUNG

Sport, August 1993.

Sporting News, January 11, 1993.

Sports Illustrated, September 30, 1991; November 23, 1992; May 31, 1993.

Sports Illustrated for Kids, November 1993.

Street and Smith's Pro Football, June 1993.

SPORT

BASEBALL

Baseball Encylopedia: The Complete and Official Record of Major League Baseball. 11th ed. New York: Macmillian Publishing Co., 1993.

Hollander, Zander, ed. *Complete Handbook of Baseball.* New York: Signet, annual.

James, Bill. *The Bill James Historical Baseball Abstract.* New York: Villard Books, 1988.

LaBlanc, Michael L., ed. *Professional Sports Team Histories: Baseball.* Detroit: Gale Research, Inc., 1994.

Neft, Donald S., and Richard M. Cohen, eds. *The Sports Encyclopedia: Baseball.* 14th ed. New York: St. Martin's Press, 1994.

The Series: An Illustrated History of Baseball's Postseason Showcase, 1903—93. St. Louis: *Sporting News* Publishing Co., 1993.

Thorn, John, and Pete Palmer, eds. *Total Baseball: The Ultimate Encyclopedia of Baseball.* 3rd ed. New York: HarperCollins Publishers, 1993.

BASKETBALL

Carter, Craig, and Alex Sachare, eds. *The Sporting News Official NBA Guide.* St. Louis: *The Sporting News* Publishing Co., annual.

Hollander, Zander, ed. *Complete Handbook of Pro Basketball.* New York: Signet, annual.

Hollander, Zander, and Alex Sachare, eds. *The Official NBA Basketball Encyclopedia.* New York: Villard Books, 1989.

LaBlanc, Michael L., ed. *Professional Sports Team Histories: Basketball.* Detroit: Gale Research, Inc., 1994.

Savage, Jim, ed. *The Encyclopedia of the NCAA Basketball Tournament: The Complete Independent Guide to College Basketball's Championship Event.* New York: Dell Publishing, 1990.

FOOTBALL

Dienhart, Tom, and Joe Hoppel, eds. *The Sporting News Complete Super Bowl Book.* St. Louis: *The Sporting News* Publishing Co., annual.

Hollander, Zander, ed. *Complete Handbook of Pro Football.* New York: Signet, annual.

LaBlanc, Michael L., ed. *Professional Sports Team Histories: Football.* Detroit: Gale Research, Inc., 1994.

Neft, David S., Richard M. Cohen, and Rick Korch, eds. *The Sports Encyclopedia: Football.* 11th ed. New York: St. Martin's Press, 1993.

Shimabukuro, Mark, ed. *The Sporting News Pro Football Register.* St. Louis: *The Sporting News* Publishing Co., annual.

GOLF

Golf Magazine's Encyclopedia of Golf: The Complete Reference. 2nd ed. New York: HarperCollins Publishers, 1993.

HOCKEY

Hollander, Zander, ed. *The Complete Encyclopedia of Hockey.* 4th ed. Detroit: Visible Ink Press, 1993.

Hollander, Zander, ed. *Complete Handbook of Hockey.* New York: Signet, annual.

LaBlanc, Michael L., ed. *Professional Sports Team Histories: Hockey.* Detroit: Gale Research, Inc., 1994.

The National Hockey League Official Guide and Record Book, 1992—93. Chicago: Triumph Books, 1992.

OLYMPIC

The Olympics Factbook: A Spectator's Guide to the Winter Games. Detroit: Visible Ink Press, 1994.

The Olympics Factbook: A Spectator's Guide to the Winter and Summer Games. Detroit: Visible Ink Press, 1992.

SOCCER

LaBlanc, Michael L., and Richard Henshaw, eds. *The World Encyclopedia of Soccer.* Detroit: Visible Ink Press, 1994.

TENNIS

Collins, Bud, and Zander Hollander, eds. *Bud Collins' Modern Encyclopedia of Tennis.* 2nd ed. Detroit: Visible Ink Press, 1994.

Index

Z

Zmeskal, Kim 383, 384
Zmievskaya, Galina 38